Best of the Best
from
Hawaiʻi
Cookbook

Selected Recipes from Hawaiʻi's
FAVORITE COOKBOOKS

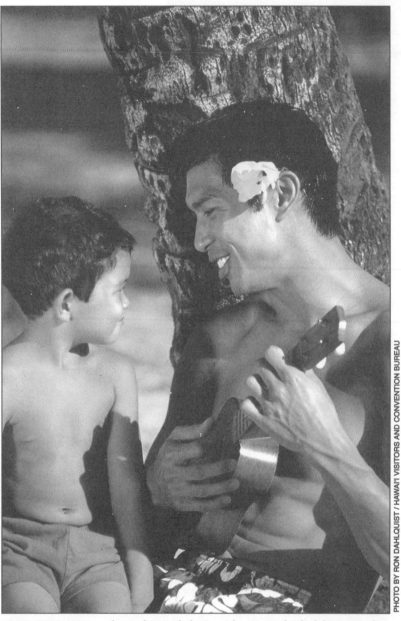

Since 1970, visitors have descended upon the Annual Ukulele Festival at the Kapiolani Park Bandstand in Waikiki for a free concert showcasing the finest ukulele players in the world. The ukulele is Hawai'i's most popular musical instrument.

Best of the Best from

Cookbook

Selected Recipes from Hawai'i's
FAVORITE COOKBOOKS

Edited by
Gwen McKee
and
Barbara Moseley

Illustrated by Tupper England

QUAIL RIDGE PRESS
Preserving America's Food Heritage

Library of Congress Cataloging-in-Publication Data

Best of the best from Hawai'i : selected recipes from Hawai'i's favorite cookbooks /
    edited by Gwen McKee and Barbara Moseley ; illustrations by Tupper England.
    p. cm.
    ISBN-13: 978-1-893062-62-7
    ISBN-10: 1-893062-62-7
    1. Cookery, Hawaiian I. McKee, Gwen. II. Moseley, Barbara.

    TX724.5.H3B47 2004
    941.59969—dc22   2004001125

First printing, May 2004 • Second, October 2004 • Third, January 2005
Fourth, February 2006 • Fifth, March 2007

Front cover: Kalalau Valley, Kaua'i, © Ron Dahlquist, Hawai'i Visitors & Convention Bureau.
Back cover photo by Greg Campbell. • Design by Cynthia Clark.
Printed by Tara TPS in South Korea.

QUAIL RIDGE PRESS
P. O. Box 123 • Brandon, MS 39043 • 1-800-343-1583
email: info@quailridge.com • www.quailridge.com

Contents

Every Wednesday and Saturday at the Hilo Farmers' Market, one can find an amazing variety of isle fruits, vegetables, coffees, herbs and spices, as well as beautiful orchids and other flowers and plants. And there are crafts, too. Editor Gwen McKee enjoyed sampling and learning, and was as much impressed with the friendly people as with the exotic produce.

Preface

Paradise. Hawai'i IS paradise! It is one of the most beautiful places on earth. From the time you are welcomed with a sweet-smelling lei of colorful flowers, your senses become activated to a higher level. No matter which way you look, the landscape is dramatic and awesome and beautiful. You are continually caressed with delightful breezes from the trade winds. There is adventure and discovery everywhere you turn. And as for the food . . . well, it can be all of the above.

I have to admit that traveling to Hawai'i to research this BEST OF THE BEST state cookbook was not a tedious task. The extraordinary setting was matched by the beautiful and friendly people who so generously helped us seek out the best cookbooks and recipes. They showed us the true meaning of aloha.

In Mililani on O'ahu, Steve told us of the wonderful food-related traditions and customs that are unique to Hawai'i. Jeff, whose company is the largest distributor of Hawaiian cookbooks, was a goldmine of information. He and his associate, Bennett, took an entire afternoon off from their busy schedules to provide us with valuable suggestions, recommendations, and directions in our pursuit. They explained that the food in the islands was four things: Pacific Rim (Asian-American); Hawaiian Regional (Pacific Rim with Hawaiian touches); ethnic cooking from five or six nationalities; and local cooking, which is somewhat of a mix of all of that, but not fancy. They spoke with such pride for their state that it was exhilarating, and it set our course enthusiastically for Hawaiian discoveries.

In Hilo on the Big Island, sweet Shirley came out of her tiny coffee shop to have muffins and delicious coffee with us (see photo on following page). Listening to her tell stories (she is a second generation Hawaiian, her father having traveled eight months by boat to get there from Portugal) about food and life in Hawai'i was intriguing . . . almost surreal under the towering banyan trees. We hiked and laughed with Christina, who let us tag along behind her University of Hawai'i students on their volcano study. Saturday the Hilo Farmers' Market was open and gave us the chance to taste and see many of the local fruits, vegetables, seafood, coffees, flowers, plants, clothes, jewelry, and crafts of all kinds. But the best part was chatting with the vendors—so many nationalities with such interesting stories of how they came to Hawai'i.

In Lihue on Kaua'i, when asking lovely Faith (see photo on bottom of next page) if she knew of local Hawaiian cookbooks, she offered to bring

Shirley's little coffee shop in Hilo was a delight. With the banyan trees in the background, we shared coffee, muffins, and wonderful stories.

her own collection for me to see, and did so the next day. Her contagious smile and enthusiasm for simply wanting to help touched me in a way I will never forget. At Waimea Canyon, Joyce recognized me from having seen me on QVC. She raved about specific Hawaiian dishes, including liliko'i ice creams and pies and cheesecakes, and further gave us directions to find cookbooks, restaurants, and points of interest we wouldn't want to miss.

On Maui, we opted for adventure. After a lū'au and show, and only three hours of sleep, we watched a never-to-be-forgotten sunrise at 10,000 feet atop frigid Mt. Haleakala, after which we had the audacity to ride bikes 38 miles all the way down to the beach—a ride that requires only a short distance of peddling and lots of handlebar squeezing. (This adventure was inspired by my daughter's comment that Mom and Dad may not be able to handle this.) That same evening we watched—this time relaxed with champagne—an equally incredible sunset aboard a smooth-sailing catamaran. Because the islands are small, we were able to take in a lot in a short time.

Ever inquisitive, at lū'aus and restaurants and tiny eateries, we shared portions so we could taste as much of the recommended fare as we could. In presentation and taste, it never failed to be quite interesting, and most often delicious—especially the taro-wrapped pork with pineapple sauce, coconut drinks, and oh my, the liliko'i cheesecake (that "Tish, the Dish" near Spouting Horn directed us to) was to die for!

On the North Shore of O'ahu, we thanked Irene for allowing us to share her famous shrimp recipe in this book . . . she wrote it down on a brown paper bag between waiting on customers in her umbrella-tabled yard near her yellow Shrimp Shack truck. The sign says, "Suck, peel, dip, eat." We did. Yum!

We were very impressed with the people we encountered all over the Hawaiian Islands. They were open, friendly, and hospitable. We particularly admired the respect and reverence Hawaiians have for their elders. Hula dancers can be young, old, big, or tiny . . . it doesn't matter. Their commonalities are their grace, and their smiles, and their Hawaiian spirit. They exemplify the true meaning and spirit of aloha. You just want to hug them all.

Cooking Hawaiian is fun and delicious. We realize that *Best of the Best from Hawai'i* has recipes that are more diverse, exotic, and different from other books in the BEST OF THE BEST STATE COOKBOOK SERIES, so we have included a glossary to help define and explain some of the ingredients. Don't hesitate to use your imagination, and to substitute similar ingredients you can find locally—create an island paradise right in your own kitchen.

At the Kaua'i Marriott Resort, when I asked Faith if she knew of local Hawaiian cookbooks, she not only said that she had quite a few at home, but she brought them for me to see at 6:30 the next morning! She is a beautiful example of how friendly and sincerely outreaching Hawaiians are all over the islands.

Beyond these selected recipes collected here, we are pleased to share a few of our favorite photographs and facts about Hawai'i. Did you know that all the islands were formed by volcanoes, some of which are still active? And that aloha means hello and goodbye? And that it's practically impossible to find a license plate that doesn't say Hawai'i?

We are proud to share information on the sixty-three Hawaiian cookbooks that were selected to contribute recipes to this collection. The "Catalog of Contributing Cookbooks" in the back of this book provides a description and ordering information on each of these cookbooks.

We wish to thank all of the wonderful people who contributed to the development of this cookbook: the food editors and bookstore and gift shop managers; the personnel at tourist bureaus and chambers, museums and state offices who helped us with information and photographs; Tupper England for her always delightful illustrations; Keena Grissom and Terresa Ray for countless hours of research; Cyndi Clark for a book design that pulls it all together so beautifully; all the friends we met along the way who helped us find cookbooks and taught us about their food; and especially all the great Hawaiian cooks who created and developed and shared their recipes. *Mahalo nui loa* (thank you very much).

We hope that through our desire to share Hawai'i's rich and diverse food heritage, you will perhaps, through the pages of this book, get a genuine feel and taste for the culinary heritage of America's 50th state. Aloha.

Gwen McKee and Barbara Moseley

Kaua'i

Ni'ihau

O'ahu

Moloka'i

Honolulu

Maui

Lana'i

Kaho'olawe

The Hawaiian Islands

Hawai'i

Contributing Cookbooks

Another Taste of Aloha
Aunty Pua's Keiki Cookbook
The Best of Heart-y Cooking
Burst of Flavor
Classic Cookbook Recipes
Cook 'em Up Kaua'i
Cooking Italian in Hawaii
Dd's Table Talk
Dd's Table Talk II
Eat More, Weigh Less™ Cookbook
Ethnic Foods of Hawai'i
Favorite Island Cookery Book I
Favorite Island Cookery Book II
Favorite Island Cookery Book III
Favorite Island Cookery Book IV
Favorite Island Cookery Book V
Favorite Island Cookery Book VI
Favorite Recipes for Islanders
Fresh Catch of the Day...from the Fishwife
Friends and Celebrities Cookbook II
The Friends of 'Iolani Palace Cookbook
Hawaii–Cooking with Aloha
Hawaii Cooks Throughout the Year
Hawai'i Tropical Rum Drinks & Cuisine
Hawaiian Country Tables
Hawai'i's Best Local Desserts
Hawai'i's Best Local Dishes
Hawai'i's Best Mochi Recipes
Hawaii's Best Tropical Food & Drinks
Hawai'i's Favorite Firehouse Recipes
Hawai'i's Favorite Pineapple Recipes
Hawai'i's Island Cooking
Hawai'i's Spam™ Cookbook
Hawai'i's 2nd Spam™ Cookbook

Contributing Cookbooks

Hilo Woman's Club Cookbook
Honolulu Hawaii Cooking
How to Use Hawaiian Fruit
Incredibly Delicious
Island Flavors
Joys of Hawaiian Cooking
Kailua Cooks
Kau Kau Kitchen
Kona on My Plate
A Lei of Recipes
Paradise Preserves
Pupus–An Island Tradition
Pupus from Paradise
A Race for Life
Sam Choy's Kitchen
Sam Choy's Sampler
Seasoned with Aloha Vol. 2
Shaloha Cookbook
The Shoreline Chef
Sugar and Spice–Cookies Made with Love
Tailgate Party Cookbook
A Taste of Aloha
The Tastes and Tales of Moiliili
Tropical Taste
Unbearably Good! Mochi Lovers' Cookbook
Vegetarian Nights
We, the Women of Hawaii Cookbook
West Kauai's Plantation Heritage
*The When You Live in Hawaii You Get Very Creative During
Passover Cookbook*

Beverages and Appetizers

PHOTO BY RON DAHLQUIST / HAWAI'I VISITORS AND CONVENTION BUREAU

The natural phenomenon Spouting Horn, in Kaua'i, sprays salt water fifty feet into the air. The spray is created when the surf forces water into a lava tube and into the air through a small opening at the surface. At sunset the spray becomes incandescent with the colors of the rainbow.

Café à la Queen of Tonga

Queen Halaevalu Mata'aho, descendant to the throne of Tonga after five hundred years of royalty, was the honored guest for the two-day opening celebration festivities of the Waiākea Village Resort in Hilo, along with her daughter Princess Pilolevu Tuku'aho. In the Queen's honor, Don the Beachcomber concocted the following:

½ cup whipping cream
¼ teaspoon instant coffee
½ teaspoon cocoa
1 drop almond extract

1 light dusting of cinnamon
2 teaspoons coconut syrup*
8 ounces hot Kona coffee
½ ounce gold rum
1 Tahitan vanilla bean

Blend whipping cream, instant coffee, cocoa, almond extract, and cinnamon until granules of coffee dissolve. Whip until stiff peaks form. Into a large cup or glass, add coconut syrup and coffee, and stir until the syrup dissolves. Add rum. Top with a generous dollop of the spiced whipped cream. Add Tahitian vanilla bean and gently stir.

Note: For best results, use Hana Bay Premium Gold Rum.

*A syrup made from coconut milk and sugar. It can be bought in 12-ounce jars.

Hawai'i Tropical Rum Drinks & Cuisine

Donn Beach, best known as Don the Beachcomber, is considered to have single-handedly transformed the hospitality industry in Hawai'i in the 1940s and 1950s through his creation of the International Market Place with its famous Treehouse restaurant, his reformation of the Lahaina Historic District, and his successful Polynesian-theme restaurants, bars, and lū'au. Donn invented more than 90 tropical drinks including the Zombie, Missionary's Downfall, and the Beachcomber's Daiquiri. The Zombie was considered the most lethal tropical drink ever created, and customers in Donn's bar were limited to two. To protect his recipes, Donn wrote them in code, and his bartenders had to follow coded symbols for the ingredients.

Hawaiian Coffee

10 drops almond extract
½ cup crème de cacoa
1 cup sugar
½ cup cocoa
1 teaspoon salt

1 pint whipping cream
3 trays coffee ice cubes made
with Kona coffee (sweetened,
if desired)

Simmer almond extract, crème de cacoa, sugar, cocoa, and salt until well blended. Refrigerate. Whip cream until firm, but not stiff. Fold into coffee mixture. When ready to serve, put ice cubes in punch bowl. Pour in chilled coffee mixture. Makes 30 servings.

Hawaii–Cooking with Aloha

Frosted Hawaiian Coffee

2 cups strong Kona coffee,
chilled
1 cup chilled pineapple juice

1 pint vanilla or coffee ice
cream, softened

Combine all ingredients; beat until smooth and foamy. Pour into tall glasses to serve. Serves 4–5.

The Tastes and Tales of Moiliili

Country Club Iced Tea

Almost every country club in Hawai'i (and some restaurants) make a version of this tea. The trick is to make it with plain ol' black tea, then add fruit juice and lots of fresh mint. Sometimes the juice is pineapple, sometimes it comes from an abundance of lemon trees in the backyard. One kama'āina family made a simple syrup by cooking the sugar first, thereby making it easier to dissolve. There is now a commercial version sold in cans. But fresh is still best.

½ gallon water	12 ounces pineapple juice
12 black tea bags	6 ounces lemon juice
3 sprigs fresh mint	Pineapple spears and fresh
2 cups sugar	mint sprigs for garnish

In a large pot, bring water to a boil. Steep the tea bags and fresh mint in the hot water. Remove the mint after 3 minutes, but continue to steep the tea until it is very dark. Remove tea bags. Add sugar and juices while tea is still warm. Stir to dissolve sugar. Pour into a gallon container and add water to fill. Refrigerate. Serve with ice and garnishes.

Hawaiian Country Tables

Kama'āina is a term that originally meant native-born. It is now used by locals to identify well-to-do haole (foreign) locals who have been in the Hawaiian Islands for several generations.

Banini Shake

Ice cold water
4 bananas, peeled and sliced, frozen
1 tablespoon maple syrup

¼ cup tahini (sesame seed paste)
1 teaspoon vanilla

In a blender, start with one cup of ice cold water. Add the remaining ingredients and blend. If too thick, add more water. Sweeten to taste. Serves 2–3.

Variations: Substitute strawberries, carob, or carob-mint for bananas.

Incredibly Delicious

Orange-Mango Ice Cream Shake

1 medium-size ripe mango, peeled, seeded, and chopped
1 cup orange juice
½ teaspoon vanilla extract

1 cup vanilla ice cream, softened
1 cup ice cubes

In a blender, combine all ingredients until smooth. Serves 2.

Variation: Substitute 1 cup fresh strawberries for mango. Substitute pineapple juice for orange juice, pineapple sherbet for ice cream.

Dd's Table Talk II

Fruit Punch

1 cup grenadine
½ cup lemon juice
1 cup strong tea
1 cup orange juice

1 cup pineapple juice
1 bottle maraschino cherries
Sugar or sugar syrup to taste
Mineral water (optional)

Combine all, sweetening to taste, and add mineral water, if desired. Serve cold.

How to Use Hawaiian Fruit

King Kalākaua's Champagne Punch

6 bottles champagne, divided
2 bottles Sauterne (white Bordeaux wine, not too dry or heavy)
6 lemons, sliced
6 oranges, sliced

6 mint leaves
1 ripe pineapple, peeled and sliced into sticks
1 cup sugar
2 cups brandy
2 quarts fresh strawberries

Chill bottles of champagne and Sauterne 5 hours or overnight.

Into a large punch bowl, add sliced lemons, sliced oranges, mint leaves, pineapple sticks, and sugar. Pour Sauterne and 3 bottles of the champagne into the ingredients in the punch bowl, and stir until sugar dissolves. Add brandy and fresh strawberries; mix gently. Before serving, add remaining 3 bottles of champagne.

Courtesy of Daughters of Hawaii
The Friends of 'Iolani Palace Cookbook

King David Kalākaua was known as the "Merrie Monarch" because he was solely responsible for the resurgence in Hawaiian culture and arts including the hula, which had been banned by missionaries. Each year the Merrie Monarch Festival, considered the world's most prestigious hula contest, is held in his honor.

Tiki Punch

If you are having a small enough party, delight your guests with their own "pineapple glass." When you hollow out the pineapple, take care not to cut through the skin. Use the pineapple for other dishes. It's also a great opportunity to experiment with different garnishes. Recipe serves one.

1 pineapple per guest
  or couple
1 ounce vodka
½ ounce Galliano liqueur

5 ounces orange juice
5 ounces pineapple juice
Champagne

Combine vodka, Galliano, and juices in a pitcher. Pour into pineapple, approximately ⅔ from the top. Fill with champagne and add garnishes.

Hawaii's Best Tropical Food & Drinks

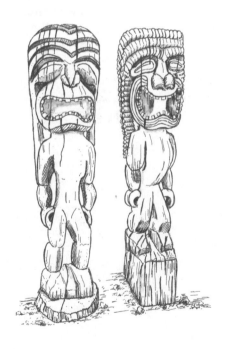

Honolulu Punch

2 (46-ounce) cans pineapple juice
1 (28-ounce) bottle ginger ale
Dash of grenadine
1 pint pineapple sherbet
Mint sprigs for garnish
Maraschino cherries for garnish

Combine pineapple juice with ginger ale; add grenadine to tint to delicate pink. Add sherbet and serve immediately in tall glasses garnished with mint sprigs and maraschino cherries. Serves 20.

The Tastes and Tales of Moiliili

Mai Tai

There is much discussion about the origin of the delightful Mai Tai. Whoever invented it, the Mai Tai has become one of the most popular drinks in the islands.

2 ounces light rum
1 ounce dark rum
1 ounce Triple Sec orange liqueur
½ ounce amaretto
½ ounce lime juice
Crushed ice

Mix the rums, Triple Sec, amaretto, and lime juice in a 7-ounce glass. Add crushed ice and garnish.

Hawaii's Best Tropical Food & Drinks

The origin of the Mai Tai has been debated for decades. Both Donn Beach (Don the Beachcomber) and Victor Bergerson (Trader Vic) claimed to have invented this tropical drink. Even though Trader Vic has been given the most credit, the truth may have gone to the grave with both men.

Almond Pâté

Serve this instead of chopped liver; there's nothing phony-tasting about this meatless substitution. And it freezes well.

1 cup slivered almonds
1 large clove garlic
1 small onion
¾ pound mushrooms
3–4 tablespoons butter or
  margarine

¼ teaspoon thyme
½ teaspoon salt, or to taste
⅛ teaspoon white pepper
1–4 tablespoons oil, as needed

Lightly toast almonds in an ungreased frying pan over medium heat, stirring constantly (about 5–7 minutes or until golden). Put aside. Using the knife blade of a food processor, chop garlic and onion coarsely. Add mushrooms and chop until fine.

Melt butter in frying pan and sauté mushroom and onion mixture, adding thyme, salt, and pepper. Stir occasionally until most of the liquid evaporates.

Reserve 2 tablespoons almonds; process remaining almonds. Add oil until paste consistency; add mushroom and onion mixture. Combine by quickly switching on and off, just until blended; do not overprocess. Chill well before serving. Mold into an attractive shape and decorate with reserved almonds. Makes about 2 cups.

The When You Live in Hawaii You Get Very Creative
During Passover Cookbook

Macadamia Pesto Cheesecake

When you need to serve a crowd, you want this appetizer cheesecake. Serve it with crackers during the holidays or any time of the year.

CRUST:

1 cup dry bread crumbs   ¼ cup butter, melted

Preheat oven to 350°. In a bowl, combine bread crumbs and melted butter. Press mixture onto the bottom of a 9-inch spring-form pan. Bake for 10 minutes.

FILLING:

¼ cup olive oil
2 cups fresh basil leaves
Salt to taste
1 clove garlic, halved
2 (8-ounce) packages cream
   cheese, softened

1 cup part-skim ricotta cheese
3 eggs
½ cup (2 ounces) grated
   Parmesan cheese
½ cup chopped macadamia
   nuts

Place oil, basil, salt, and garlic in a blender. Cover and process on high until smooth. In a large bowl, combine the basil mixture with cream cheese and ricotta cheese. Using an electric mixer at medium speed, blend until well mixed. Add eggs one at a time and mix well. Blend in Parmesan cheese and pour Filling over the warm Crust. Top with macadamia nuts. Bake at 325° for 1 hour and 15 minutes, or until cheesecake is set and lightly browned. Loosen the cake from the rim of the pan; cool before removing the rim. Serve warm or at room temperature with your favorite assorted crackers. Serves 16.

Note: If you don't have macadamia nuts, pine nuts (used in classic pesto) work just as well. If you don't have fresh basil, substitute 1 cup parsley and 1 tablespoon dried basil.

Hawaiian Country Tables

 Astronaut Ellison Onizuka, from Hawai'i, along with the entire crew of the space shuttle Challenger, died on January 28, 1986, when the shuttle exploded one minute thirteen seconds after launch.

Macadamia Cheese Ball

1 pound Cheddar cheese,
  grated
1 (8-ounce) package cream
  cheese, softened
⅓ cup chopped sweet pickles
1 tablespoon Dijon mustard

2 tablespoons mayonnaise
2 tablespoons dry sherry
Dash of cayenne pepper
½ cup chopped macadamia
  nuts

Mix Cheddar cheese with softened cream cheese. Add pickles, mustard, mayonnaise, and sherry. Form into ball, sprinkle with cayenne pepper, and refrigerate. Roll in macadamia nuts before serving. Serve with crackers. May keep refrigerated for up to 2 weeks.

Hilo Woman's Club Cookbook

Spam and Mushroom Rolls

1 pound fresh mushrooms,
  finely chopped
¼ cup butter
1 cup finely chopped Spam
1 (8-ounce) package cream
  cheese, softened

1 tablespoon minced parsley
1 loaf sandwich bread, crusts
  removed
1 stick butter, melted (for
  brushing on rolls)

Sauté mushrooms in butter. Remove from heat and combine with Spam, cream cheese, and parsley. Roll bread slices with a rolling pin, or flatten slices with your hands. Spread bread with cream cheese mixture. Roll each slice like a jellyroll. Cut each roll into 3 pieces and fasten with a toothpick. Place on baking pans. Brush each roll with melted butter and place under broiler until brown. Makes about 60.

Hawai'i's Spam Cookbook

Hot Crab Dip Mary

A winner!

1 (8-ounce) package cream cheese, softened	2 tablespoons minced onion
1 (7½-ounce) can crabmeat	½ teaspoon horseradish
2 tablespoons milk	Pepper to taste
¼ teaspoon salt	1 (3½-ounce) can French fried onion rings

Mix ingredients except onion rings. Place in small oven-proof dish suitable for serving. Sprinkle with onion rings. Bake uncovered at 375° for 15 minutes until bubbly. Serve with crackers.

The Friends of 'Iolani Palace Cookbook

Aloha Dip

1 (8-ounce) package cream cheese, softened	1 cup grated coconut
1 cup crushed pineapple, drained	1½ teaspoons ground ginger
	1 teaspoon lemon juice
	½ cup chopped pecans

Mash cream cheese well. Add remaining ingredients, and stir well. Chill for several hours before serving. Serve with crackers.

Pupus from Paradise

Aloha, pronounced ah-LO-ha, is a Hawaiian greeting but means so much more than hello and goodbye. Aloha is the way people treat each other, a way of life, and a state of mind. Known as the Aloha State, Hawai'i is a string of 137 islands encompassing a land area of 6,422.6 square miles in the Pacific Ocean about 2,400 miles from the west coast of the continental United States. Stretching from northwest to southeast, the major islands are: Ni'ihau (Nee-ee-how), Kaua'i (ka-Wah-ee), O'ahu (Oh-Wa-who), Moloka'i (mo-lo-Kah-ee), Lana'i (la-Nah-ee), Kaho'olawe (kaw-ho-oh-la-vay), Maui (Mow-ee, rhymes with Now-ee), and Hawai'i (ha-Wa-ee or ha-Va-ee).

Baked Fresh Basil Dip

I received this recipe as part of a recipe chain letter. It originally called for a jar of artichoke hearts, chopped. I was making a pūpū (Hawaiian word for appetizer) for a friend's bridal shower and realized I did not have a jar of artichoke hearts. Out to the garden I went, found a large amount of basil, and this recipe has been changed forever. Everyone at the party asked for the recipe, so here it is.

1 cup packed, chopped fresh
  basil (or 1 jar artichoke
  hearts, chopped)
½ cup grated Parmesan
  cheese
¾ cup mayonnaise
2 cloves fresh garlic, chopped

Salt and pepper to taste
Tabasco sauce to taste (don't be
  stingy!)
1 teaspoon Dijon mustard
½ cup slivered almonds
  (optional)

Combine all of the ingredients, except slivered almonds, by hand or by blender or food processor. Spread mixture in bottom of an 8- or 9-inch baking dish. Spread almonds over the top and bake in 350° oven for 20 minutes. Serve immediately with crackers or bagel chips.

Shaloha Cookbook

Avocado-Crab Dip

1 large avocado, diced
1 tablespoon fresh lemon
  juice
2 tablespoons grated onion
1 tablespoon Worcestershire
  sauce

4 ounces cream cheese,
  softened
½ cup sour cream
½ teaspoon salt
1 (7½-ounce) can crabmeat,
  drained and flaked

Use firm avocado to avoid a messy-looking dip and toss, rather than mix, with lemon juice, onion, and Worcestershire sauce. Blend the cream cheese, sour cream, and salt; stir in. Add crabmeat and fold carefully into the seasoned avocado. Serve with tortilla chips or crackers.

Pupus–An Island Tradition

Over-the-Top Spinach Dip

¼ cup bread crumbs
2 tablespoons butter, melted
1 cup grated Parmesan
  cheese, divided
1 (8-ounce) package light
  cream cheese, softened
8 ounces mozzarella cheese,
  shredded
1 (1-ounce) envelope Lipton
  Golden Onion Recipe Soup
  Mix

1 cup light sour cream
2 cloves garlic, minced
3 (6-ounce) jars marinated
  artichoke hearts, drained,
  coarsely chopped
1 (6-ounce) can shrimp,
  drained
2 cups chopped fresh spinach
  leaves

Preheat oven to 350°. In a small bowl, combine bread crumbs, butter, and ½ cup Parmesan cheese; set aside. Combine remaining ingredients; spoon into a 2-quart casserole dish. Cover; bake 25–30 minutes, until bubbly. Remove from oven; sprinkle with bread crumb mixture. Continue baking uncovered 5–7 minutes. Serves 12.

Dd's Table Talk II

After watching the sun rise so spectacularly over the top of Mt. Haleakala, Gwen and Barney didn't meet any other grandparents bike riding the 38 miles all the way down to the beach. (The key word here is "down.") The sheer exhilaration of having achieved this feat was only surpassed by the adventurous thrill of this never-to-be-forgotten ride.

Hot Macadamia Chicken Dip with Toast Points

Crunchy roasted mac nuts top this creamy, flavorful chicken dip.

8 slices homemade-style
  wheat bread
1 (8-ounce) package light
  cream cheese, softened
2 tablespoons milk
1½ cups minced cooked
  chicken or turkey
2 teaspoons prepared
  horseradish

½ cup sour cream
¼ cup finely chopped green
  pepper
1 green onion, chopped
½ teaspoon garlic salt
¼ teaspoon cracked pepper
1 cup chopped macadamia nuts
  or pecans
2 teaspoons butter

Remove crusts from bread and cut each slice into 4 triangles. Toast bread on a baking sheet in preheated 400° oven until browned and very crisp, 5–7 minutes. Meanwhile, in a mixing bowl, beat cream cheese and milk until smooth with electric mixer or by hand. Stir in chicken, horseradish, sour cream, green pepper, onion, garlic salt, and pepper.

Spoon into an ungreased shallow 2-cup baking ramekin or crock. Set aside. In a skillet, sauté the nuts at medium heat in butter for 3–4 minutes, or until lightly browned. Sprinkle over cream cheese mixture. Bake, uncovered, at 350° for 20 minutes. Serve with toast points. Yields 32 or more pūpū servings.

Kona on My Plate

Haleakala, in Maui, is the world's largest dormant volcano with its last eruption thought to be sometime around 1790. The summit of Haleakala is 10,023 feet above sea level and is the highest point of Maui.

Fiery Pupu Wings

2½ pounds chicken wings,
   cut at joints (or drumettes)

Oil for frying

MARINADE:

2 cloves garlic, minced
1 tablespoon sesame seed oil
1 tablespoon brown sugar
1 tablespoon soy sauce
1 tablespoon dry sherry
2 teaspoons sake (rice wine)

2 teaspoons fresh grated ginger
1 teaspoon cayenne pepper
1 teaspoon salt
Pinch freshly ground black
   pepper and red pepper flakes

In a small bowl, combine chicken with Marinade ingredients.
Marinate 2 hours.

BATTER:

½ cup flour
½ cup cornstarch

2 large eggs, beaten
¾ cup water

In a wok or deep fryer, heat oil. In a mixing bowl, combine
Batter ingredients. Dip drained chicken into batter; deep-fry
until golden.

SAUCE:

¼ soy sauce
2 tablespoons brown sugar
2 tablespoons rice wine vinegar
2 tablespoons sesame seed oil
2 cloves garlic, minced

2 teaspoons minced fresh
   ginger
2 stalks green onions, chopped
1 teaspoon Thai chili garlic
   paste

In a mixing bowl, combine Sauce ingredients. Drizzle over
chicken. Serves 8.

Dd's Table Talk II

pūpū [poo-poo] – The Hawaiian term for any hot or cold appetizer, which
can include a wide range of items such as macadamia nuts and won tons.

Coconut Chicken Bites

3½ cups sweetened, shredded
  coconut
2 teaspoons ground cumin
¾ teaspoon ground coriander
½ teaspoon cayenne pepper
Salt and freshly ground
  pepper

2 pounds boneless, skinless
  chicken breasts, cut into
  1-inch pieces
2 eggs, beaten
Dijon mustard for dipping

Preheat oven to 325°. Bake coconut on large, heavy baking sheet until golden brown, stirring frequently, about 15 minutes. Transfer to bowl and cool. Coarsely grind coconut in batches in food processor and place on large plate. Spray 2 large, heavy cookie sheets with cooking spray.

In a large bowl, combine cumin, coriander, cayenne, salt, and pepper. Dredge chicken pieces in seasonings, turning to coat. Dip into beaten eggs. Dredge chicken pieces in coconut, coating completely. Transfer to prepared cookie sheets. Cover and chill for one hour. (Can be prepared one day in advance.)

Preheat oven to 400°. Bake chicken until crisp and golden brown, about 15 minutes, turning pieces over once during baking. Arrange chicken on platter. Serve warm or at room temperature with Dijon mustard for dipping. Serves 6–8.

Kailua Cooks

'Ono Chicken Waikiki

1 pound chicken breasts,
  boned and skinned
¼ cup dry sherry
¼ cup lemon juice
3 tablespoons Worcestershire
  sauce
½ cup flour

1 egg, beaten
2 tablespoons honey
½ cup finely chopped
  macadamia nuts (or pecans)
½ cup dry unseasoned bread
  crumbs

Cut chicken into 1-inch cubes. Place in bowl and pour combined sherry, lemon juice, and Worcestershire sauce over cubes, tossing to coat completely. Marinate in refrigerator for 30 minutes.

Place flour in one bowl, mixed egg and honey in another, and combined nuts and bread crumbs in a third. Dip chicken in bowls in that order. Place chicken in a single layer in a shallow, greased pan. Bake uncovered in preheated 350° oven for 25 minutes. Serve with toothpicks and Chutney Sauce for dipping. Yields about 33 cubes.

CHUTNEY SAUCE:
¾ cup mayonnaise
¼ cup prepared mustard

3 tablespoons chopped chutney

Combine and refrigerate until serving. Makes 1 cup.

Pupus from Paradise

In the Hawaiian language, ono is a term meaning "delicious," sometimes used to create the neologism "onolicious." Ono, without the 'okina accent mark, is "fish"—wahoo or king mackerel.

Macadamia Chicken Strips

2 cups flour
1–2 teaspoons salt
 (depending on saltiness
 of nuts)
12 ounces roasted macadamia
 nuts, finely chopped

1 pound chicken, boned, cut in
 strips ¾x3 inches long
½ cup butter, melted
4 eggs, lightly beaten

Preheat oven to 350°. Pour flour and salt into a plastic bag. Place nuts into another plastic bag. Taking a small handful at a time, dip chicken strips in melted butter to coat, then put in flour-filled bag. Shake to coat; shake off excess flour. Dip in beaten eggs. Shake off excess egg and place in macadamia-nut-filled bag. Shake to coat. Place chicken strips on ungreased, nonstick cookie sheet, and bake 20 minutes. Store in refrigerator in an airtight container, if prepared ahead. Serve at room temperature.

Note: This can also be frozen. Thaw and serve at room temperature, or warm in oven before serving. Chopped pecans can be used in place of the macadamia nuts.

Pupus–An Island Tradition

Chicken Wrapped in Nori

SAUCE:
½ cup shoyu
4 teaspoons sugar

2 teaspoons sake

Combine ingredients.

4 sheets nori
1 pound boneless, skinless
 chicken

1 cup cornstarch

Cut nori in half, then into ½-inch strips. Slice chicken into thin strips. Marinate in Sauce for about ½ hour. Roll soaked chicken in cornstarch and bind with a strip of nori. Fry in deep hot oil until crisp. Serve with additional Sauce.

Favorite Recipes for Islanders

Chicken Roll

2½ cups chopped, cooked
  chicken breasts
½ cup finely chopped celery
2 tablespoons chopped parsley
2 tablespoons chopped
  watercress

½ cup mayonnaise
1 teaspoon horseradish
Dash Tabasco
Macadamia nuts, chopped

Mix all ingredients, except nuts. Roll into 1-inch bar; roll in chopped nuts. Wrap in foil. Chill. Unwrap and slice to serve. Serve on party rye bread or crackers.

Pupus from Paradise

The lei custom was introduced to the Hawaiian Islands by early Polynesian voyagers. These garlands, constructed mainly of flowers, leaves, shells, seeds, or feathers, were worn by ancient Hawaiians to beautify themselves. With the advent of tourism in the islands, the lei quickly became *the* symbol of Hawai'i to millions of visitors worldwide.

Stir-Fried Beef with Lettuce

4 medium shiitake (Japanese black) mushrooms
1¼ pounds ground beef
4 tablespoons peanut oil
2 slices ginger, finely minced
4 ounces bamboo shoots, coarsely minced
2 cloves garlic, finely minced
4 water chestnuts, coarsely minced
1 stalk scallion (green onion), chopped

1 teaspoon salt
¼ teaspoon pepper
1 tablespoon light shoyu
½ tablespoon black bean paste
½ tablespoon hoisin sauce
½ tablespoon sugar
1 tablespoon rice wine or dry sherry
1½ teaspoons sesame oil
2 sprigs parsley to garnish
12 lettuce leaves

Soak mushrooms in hot water for 30 minutes; remove and discard stems. Coarsely mince the caps. Fry beef until browned; drain fat.

In hot oil, stir-fry ginger and mushrooms for 30 seconds before adding bamboo shoots, garlic, and water chestnuts. After 1 minute, add scallions and meat together with the salt and pepper. Cook another 2 minutes, stirring constantly. Add the shoyu, bean paste, hoisin sauce, sugar, and rice wine, and cook another 3 minutes. Add sesame oil and serve garnished with sprigs of parsley. People will help themselves to a couple of spoonfuls of the minced mixture by placing it on a lettuce leaf, wrapping it up carefully, and eating it with their fingers.

Pupus–An Island Tradition

Teriyaki Meatballs

1½ pounds ground beef
2 tablespoons flour
2 eggs
1 teaspoon salt
Dash of pepper
2 tablespoons cornstarch

¼ cup sugar
⅓ cup shoyu
1 (14-ounce) can beef broth
¼ cup sake
2 tablespoons minced ginger
2 teaspoons minced garlic

Combine beef, flour, eggs, salt, and pepper. Mix lightly and shape into small balls. Place in greased baking pan and bake at 400° for 14–17 minutes. Mix cornstarch, sugar, shoyu, beef broth, sake, ginger, and garlic and cook until thick. Add meatballs and simmer. Makes about 50 meatballs.

Note: Mix lean and 25– to 30-percent fat ground beef equally for better flavor. The meatballs can be made ahead and frozen. Thaw and heat in the sauce and serve. Instant pūpū.

Pupus–An Island Tradition

Polynesian Meat Balls

1 egg
½ cup water
1 pound ground chuck or
   ground turkey

1 (8-ounce) can water
   chestnuts, drained, minced
½ cup seasoned bread crumbs

Combine egg and water and beat well. Add remaining ingredients, mixing lightly. Shape into balls and bake on foil-lined cookie sheet for 30 minutes at 350°. Serve in chafing dish with Sauce. Makes about 60–65 meat balls. Meat balls may be prepared in advance and frozen.

SAUCE:
⅔ cup apricot-pineapple
   preserves
1 tablespoon prepared
   horseradish
¼ cup soy sauce

1 clove garlic, minced, and/or
   1 tablespoon minced onion
⅔ cup water
1 tablespoon lemon juice

Bring to a boil, stirring well. Add meat balls and let simmer slowly in Sauce.

Pupus from Paradise

Kailua Crab Cakes

1 pound fresh lump crabmeat
1½ cups panko flakes
2 eggs, well beaten
1 tablespoon Dijon mustard
½ teaspoon Worcestershire
  sauce

2 tablespoons minced parsley
¼ cup chopped scallions
1 teaspoon Old Bay Seasoning
½ cup mayonnaise
Panko flakes to coat
¼ cup cooking oil

Place crabmeat in mixing bowl with 1½ cups panko flakes. Add remaining ingredients, except panko to coat, and cooking oil. Mix gently, leaving the crab lumps as large as possible. Shape mixture into 12–16 equal portions; ball up and flatten into a patty shape about ¾ to 1 inch thick. Coat each crab cake with panko flakes. Chill for at least one hour before cooking.

Heat cooking oil over medium heat. Sauté each cake for 2–2½ minutes per side in the oil. Makes approximately 12–16 petite cakes, or 4–5 dinner-size crab cakes.

TARTAR SAUCE FOR KAILUA CRAB CAKES:

2 tablespoons tarragon
  vinegar
1 teaspoon Dijon mustard
½ teaspoon kosher salt
Pinch cayenne pepper
⅓ cup finely chopped
  cornichons (gherkins)

1 tablespoon finely chopped
  shallots
1 teaspoon finely chopped
  capers
1 tablespoon finely chopped
  leaf parsley
1 cup mayonnaise

Combine ingredients and refrigerate until ready to serve. Makes 1½ cups.

Kailua Cooks

Hawai'i has its own time zone, Hawai'i-Aleutian Standard Time. Hawai'i does not observe Daylight Savings Time. Therefore, in the summer, the islands are three hours behind Pacific Standard Time, four hours behind Mountain Standard Time, etc. In the winter, they are four hours behind Pacific Daylight Savings Time, five hours behind Mountain Standard Time, and so on.

Summer 'Ahi Tartare

When you clean just-caught 'ahi, the bones always have a lot of meat. Get a big spoon, scoop it out, chop that up, and make a fine poke, like tartare—the best.

1 pound very fresh 'ahi (yellowfin tuna)	1 teaspoon olive oil
	1 teaspoon sesame seed oil
¼ cup minced Maui onion	1½ teaspoons grated fresh
Juice of 1 lemon	horseradish
2 tablespoons chopped cilantro	½ teaspoon prepared stone-
1 tablespoon minced fresh ginger	ground mustard
	Pinch red chile pepper flakes
1 tablespoon soy sauce	Salt and white pepper to taste

Cut 'ahi into 1-inch cubes. In a food processor, combine all ingredients and pulse 6 times or until at desired texture. Do not purée mixture. If you don't have a processor, mince 'ahi with a knife into roughly ¼-inch cubes before combining with other ingredients. Serve with toast points, crackers, or field greens. Makes 6 servings.

Note: Summer 'Ahi Tartare is especially delicious with shiso leaves (Japanese basil). This herb, also known as beefsteak plant, can be obtained at Japanese markets. About the size of large basil leaves, they have serrated edges, and come in red or green varieties. They taste like a cross between mint and basil.

Sam Choy's Sampler

Does Hawai'i have seasons? Sure it does! There are two main seasons in Hawai'i. Summer, called Kau, extends from May to October and has an average daytime temperature of 85 degrees F. Winter, called Ho'oilo, runs from November to April with an average daytime temperature of 78 degrees F.

Lomi Salmon

1 pound salted salmon
3 large tomatoes, diced
1 onion, chopped

3 stalks green onions, chopped
3 cubes ice, cracked

Soak salted salmon in cold water for one hour. If salmon is very salty, repeat process. Remove skin and bones, and shred salmon with fingers. Place in a bowl and add tomatoes and onions. Chill; add crushed ice just before serving.

Note: Salted salmon was introduced to Hawaiians by Westerners. Lomi salmon is now known as a "traditional" Hawaiian food, which is always served at a lū'au.

Ethnic Foods of Hawai'i

Shrimp Vegetable Tempura

2 cups flour
¼ cup cornstarch
2 heaping tablespoons sugar
2 tablespoons salt
1 tablespoon baking powder
1½ cups equal parts
   evaporated milk and water

½ pound fresh shrimp,
   peeled and chopped
Carrots, green beans,
   cut in fine julienne strips
Parsley, chopped

Mix flour, cornstarch, sugar, salt, baking powder, and milk mixture slowly, to prevent lumps. Add remaining ingredients and mix well to coat completely. Drop by tablespoons into hot oil and cook until slightly brown.

Note: This recipe can be used to make French fried onion rings also. They're delicious—the kids will love them.

Pupus–An Island Tradition

Shrimp Maunakea

The blend of colors and flavors is reminiscent of Chinatown's Maunakea Street.

20 large shrimp, cooked, peeled and deveined	1 small bunch mint
1 small bunch basil	1 small bunch Chinese parsley
	20 snow peas, blanched

Wrap each shrimp with a basil leaf, mint leaf, a sprig of Chinese parsley, and a snow pea. Then, skewer on a toothpick. Serve at room temperature with Peanut Dip. Serves 8.

PEANUT DIP:

3 tablespoons chunky peanut butter	1 tablespoon sugar
¼ cup soy sauce	2 teaspoons fresh lime juice
3 tablespoons vinegar	1 chile pepper, mashed
	1 clove garlic, finely minced

Combine all ingredients in microwave-safe bowl. Heat on HIGH for 30 seconds and stir to blend.

Note: Dip may be made ahead. Cover and refrigerate. Reheat before serving.

Another Taste of Aloha

Pan Sushi

SUSHI RICE:

3 cups rice, cooked   ½ cup sugar
½ cup Japanese rice vinegar   1 teaspoon salt

Put hot rice in a large bowl. In small bowl, mix together vinegar, sugar, and salt. Sprinkle half of the sauce on hot rice and mix with wooden spoon or rice paddle. Taste; add more sauce to taste.

Wet 9x13-inch pan. Shake off excess water and spread rice in the pan evenly. Place a piece of wax paper over rice and press down gently. Remove wax paper. Top rice with Shoyu Tuna and your choice of Toppings. Cool at least 30 minutes. Cut into squares with a wet knife. Makes 24 squares.

SHOYU TUNA:

1 (6-ounce) can tuna   2 tablespoons shoyu
2 tablespoons sugar

Drain tuna; place it in a small saucepan and add sugar and shoyu. Stir and cook 1–2 minutes. Sprinkle over Sushi Rice.

SUGGESTED TOPPINGS:

Colored shrimp flakes   Thinly sliced veggies such as
Sliced takuwan   carrots and cucumbers
Pickled ginger   Thin slices of nori (seaweed)

Aunty Pua's Keiki Cookbook

Hawai'i is the most isolated population center on Earth. The islands are 2,390 miles from California; 3,850 miles from Japan; 4,900 miles from China; and 5,280 miles from the Philippines.

Poisson Cru

This dish was introduced by Tahitians and can be made with any firm white-meat fish, although 'ahi and ono are favorites. It is prepared in much the same way the Mexicans prepare ceviche. The fish is "cooked" by the lime juice. You can buy frozen unsweetened coconut milk, or use the canned Asian variety. Some versions of this dish do not use coconut milk at all.

1 pound fresh 'ahi or ono
½ quart water with
  2 tablespoons salt added
1 teaspoon salt
1 cup freshly squeezed lime
  juice
1 (12-ounce) can unsweetened
  coconut milk
1 medium tomato, coarsely
  chopped

½ medium onion, coarsely
  chopped
4 small red radishes, coarsely
  chopped
½ cup minced parsley
Salt and pepper to taste
4–5 drops Tabasco

Cut fish into bite-sized pieces and soak in salted water for 30 minutes. Drain well. Sprinkle fish with 1 teaspoon salt and lime juice and marinate in a nonreactive bowl for another 10 minutes, or until "cooked." Mix well and drain most of the liquid from fish. Add coconut milk, tomato, onion, radishes, parsley, salt, pepper, and Tabasco. Marinate for another 30 minutes. Serve with toothpicks as an appetizer or on lettuce as a first course. Serves 10–12.

Hawaiian Country Tables

Oriental Fresh Mushrooms

16 fresh mushrooms, 1–1½
  inches in diameter
Lemon juice
½ pound ground pork
¼ cup minced water
  chestnuts

¼ cup minced green onions
1 egg, slightly beaten
1 teaspoon soy sauce
¼ teaspoon garlic powder
¼ stick butter, melted
¼ cup untoasted sesame seeds

Preheat oven to 350°. Clean mushrooms; remove and reserve stems. If preparing in advance, rub with lemon juice. Chop mushroom stems finely and combine with pork, water chestnuts, green onions, egg, soy sauce, and garlic powder. Stuff caps with mixture and coat cap bottoms with butter. Top with sesame seeds. Put in large baking dish and bake for 30–40 minutes. Serve immediately.

Pupus–An Island Tradition

Stuffed Lychee

1 (8-ounce) package cream
  cheese, softened
2½ ounces crystalized ginger,
  finely chopped

2 (20-ounce) cans whole
  seedless lychee, drained
Chopped macadamia nuts for
  garnish

Combine cream cheese and ginger. Stuff mixture into lychee with small spoon, butter knife, or pastry bag. Chill. Garnish with nuts and serve.

A Taste of Aloha

Winds move from east to west across the islands of Hawai'i, and as a result, the volcanic mountains trap the moist air from the Pacific on the windward sides (east and north). This phenomenon results in a cool, wet windward side, and a warm, dry leeward side (west and south). For example, on the windward side of Maui, the top of the West Maui Mountain receives over 400 inches of rainfall per year, and on the leeward side, the city of Kihei receives less than 10 inches of rain per year.

Sam-Style Poke

Thousands of entries in the Sam Choy/Aloha Festivals Poke Recipe Contest, and thousands of orders for the many kinds of poke we serve at the restaurants, shows me that poke is finally going mainstream.

2 pounds finely diced 'ahi (yellowfin tuna)
4 teaspoons 'inamona
1 cup rinsed and chopped ogo

1 tablespoon sesame oil
1 teaspoon soy sauce
⅔ cup Sam's Secret Sauce

Combine 'ahi with 'inamona, ogo, sesame oil, and soy sauce. Mix thoroughly. Add Sam's Secret Sauce and marinate for 30–60 minutes in the refrigerator. Enjoy. Serves 8.

SAM'S SECRET SAUCE:

2 cups water
2 tablespoons Hawaiian salt

2 Hawaiian chili peppers, finely chopped

Combine ingredients and stir until salt completely dissolves. Makes 2 cups.

Sam Choy's Kitchen

The state tree is the kukui nut tree, sometimes called the candlenut tree. The oil extracted from its seeds was once used to light stone lamps and torches. The shelled nuts were skewered on a coconut frond and lit one by one as they sat in a container of sand or dirt or in the earth itself. Often children were given the responsibility for keeping the "candles" lit. The nuts are now roasted and used in the seasoning 'inamona.

Summer Rolls

1 cup rice sticks, softened by cooking
1 package (20 sheets) rice papers
1 head romaine lettuce, shredded
⅛ cup chopped fresh basil (optional)
1 cup chopped mint leaves
⅛ cup freshly chopped cilantro (optional)
1 cup fresh bean sprouts
1 cup shredded carrots
1 cup firm tofu, cut into strips

Cook rice sticks according to package instructions. Dip rice papers in water and place on paper towels to allow them to soften.

Place lettuce and rice sticks (now soft as noodles) along with other ingredients in a row across the middle of rice papers and roll like a burrito. Place seam-side-down on serving tray. Makes 20 portions. Serve with dipping sauces.

One portion: 131 calories; 1.2g fat; 8% fat; 8% protein; 84% carbohydrates

CLEAR DIP:

2 cloves garlic, crushed
6 tablespoons barley malt, rice syrup, or sugar
1 tablespoon lemon juice
1 tablespoon rice vinegar
4 tablespoons water
Fresh chopped chile to taste

Mix ingredients together and use as a dipping sauce. Makes enough to be used with 20 portions of Summer Rolls.

One portion: 10.4 calories; 0g fat; 0% fat; 1% protein; 99% carbohydrates

AMBER DIP:

1 cup Chinese bean sauce
¼ cup barley malt, rice syrup, or sugar
2 cloves garlic, minced
4 tablespoons water
Cornstarch, as needed for texture

On medium heat, cook bean sauce, sugar, and garlic together for 3–4 minutes, stirring constantly. Add water and stir. Thicken with cornstarch mixed with small amount of water, if necessary. Makes enough to be used with 20 Summer Rolls.

One portion: 19.2 calories; 0.3g fat; 15% fat; 12% protein; 73% carbohydrates

Eat More, Weigh Less Cookbook

Sweet and Sour Broccoli

1 pound broccoli stems	2 tablespoons sesame seed oil
2 tablespoons white vinegar	1 teaspoon salt
2 tablespoons sugar	

Peel broccoli stems and cut into diagonal slices ⅛–⅙ inch thick. Combine vinegar, sugar, oil, and salt in large jar. Add the broccoli and shake to coat well. Cover and refrigerate overnight, shaking occasionally.

Drain and place in serving dish. Serve with toothpicks.

Note: You may use the flowerets in the same manner. They will absorb the marinade faster, so you may want to add them to the marinade later than the stems. I would suggest marinating them in a separate jar. A plastic bag sealed tightly will also work.

Pupus–An Island Tradition

Japanese Party Mix

SAUCE:

⅔ cup sugar	12 drops Tabasco sauce
¼ cup soy sauce plus water to make ⅓ cup	

Combine all ingredients; mix to dissolve sugar.

1 (12-ounce) box rice chex	2 (1.05-ounce) packages nori goma furikake
1 (12-ounce) box corn chex	

Combine rice chex and corn chex; drizzle with Sauce. Mix well. Sprinkle furikake and continue to mix. Bake in 250° oven for 1 hour and 10 minutes; mix every 10 minutes to prevent sticking.

Favorite Island Cookery Book V

Papaya Salsa

This salsa is a refreshing complement to the smoky, salty flavor of grilled seafood.

3 cups diced ripe papaya
1 cup diced tomatoes
1 cup finely diced red bell pepper
1½ cups diced red onion
½ jalapeño pepper, seeded and finely chopped
2 tablespoons extra virgin olive oil
2½ tablespoons red wine vinegar

6 tablespoons freshly squeezed lime juice
2 tablespoons freshly squeezed lemon juice
2 teaspoons ground cumin
1 teaspoon freshly ground black pepper
Dash Tabasco
1 cup coarsely chopped, loosely packed Chinese parsley

Combine all ingredients in a large porcelain or glass bowl. Toss thoroughly. Cover and let stand for 1 or 2 hours. Serve chilled or at room temperature. Makes 1 quart.

Note: Salsa will keep in the refrigerator for up to a week.

Another Taste of Aloha

Parsley and Coconut Sambol

This is a delicious and refreshing sambol that can be served as an appetizer (with crackers) or as an accompaniment to seafood and fish. It should be used within a day or two.

2 cups parsley leaves, washed
½ cup grated fresh coconut
2 green chiles, halved, seeded, and chopped
¼ teaspoon freshly ground black pepper
2 limes, juiced and strained
Salt to taste
½ teaspoon sugar

Place all ingredients in food processor and blend until smooth. Taste; adjust seasoning by adding more lime juice, salt, or sugar. Spoon into a glass bowl. Serve chilled. Makes 4 servings.

Burst of Flavor

Mango Salsa

1 large mango, peeled, pitted, and diced
3 tablespoons chopped onion
3 tablespoons chopped green bell pepper
3 tablespoons chopped red bell pepper
1 teaspoon minced fresh chives
1½ tablespoons white wine vinegar
1 tablespoon minced fresh cilantro
1 tablespoon olive oil
½ avocado, diced
Salt and pepper to taste

Mix all ingredients, except avocado, in large bowl. Right before serving, add avocado along with salt and pepper to taste and stir gently. Great with chips or on grilled chicken. Makes 2 cups.

Kailua Cooks

Hawaiian Fruit Kabobs

1 (14-ounce) can pineapple
  chunks, drained, reserve
  juice
1½ teaspoons finely chopped,
  fresh mint leaves

1 tablespoon lemon juice
1 large banana
1 large papaya
Maraschino cherries (optional)

Combine reserved pineapple juice, mint leaves, and lemon juice.
Cut peeled banana and papaya into 1-inch chunks. Marinate
fruit in juice for 5 or more minutes. Alternate fruit on cocktail
skewers. Serve chilled. Makes 18–24 kabobs.

Pupus from Paradise

Creamy Fruit Dip

1 (8-ounce) package cream
  cheese
1 (7-ounce) jar marshmallow
  crème

Fruit such as apples, bananas,
  strawberries, firm mangoes,
  pears, peaches, and seedless
  grapes

Soften cream cheese by leaving it at room temperature for 30
minutes, or unwrap, place in a bowl, and microwave on MEDIUM
for 3–4 minutes. Put the cream cheese and marshmallow crème
in the mixing bowl and stir until they are blended together.

    Wash fruit; cut into wedges or chunks. Put a toothpick in
each piece of fruit or put several fruits on skewers. Arrange the
fruit on a platter and serve with the dip.

Aunty Pua's Keiki Cookbook

Hawai'i has no snakes other than two reptiles on display in the public
zoo, and those illegally imported by residents who like to have them as
pets. The state imposes fines as high as $25,000 for importing or owning
snakes of any type.

Mixed Fruit Chutney

1½ cups cider vinegar
2 cups light brown sugar
1 teaspoon ground cinnamon
1 teaspoon salt
2 cloves garlic, minced
2 small, hot red peppers,
  seeded and chopped
1 cup chopped seedless prunes

1 cup seedless dark raisins
2 cups cored and chopped tart
  green apples
1 cup peeled and chopped ripe
  tomatoes
1 cup chopped onion
1 tablespoon grated lemon peel

In a saucepan, put vinegar, sugar, cinnamon, salt, garlic, and peppers and bring to a boil; add all other ingredients. Reduce heat, cover, and continue to cook, stirring often until mixture reaches desired consistency, about 30–45 minutes. Pour into hot, sterilized jars and seal. Makes 6–8 jars.

Paradise Preserves

Peanut Dipping Sauce

Use sauce for lumpia, shrimp rolls, etc. Sauce can be prepared one week ahead, covered, and refrigerated.

⅓ cup unsalted dry roasted
  peanuts
½ cup hoisin sauce
⅓–½ cup water

2 tablespoons plum sauce
½–¾ teaspoon ground red
  pepper paste (sambal
  oelek)

Coarsely chop peanuts; place in bowl. Mix in hoisin sauce, ⅓ cup water, plum sauce, and red pepper paste. If sauce is too thick, stir in remaining water.

Favorite Island Cookery Book V

Bread and Breakfast

The Aloha Tower is a prominent feature of the beautiful downtown Honolulu skyline. Standing 10 stories, it was once the tallest building in Hawai'i. Each side has a large clock face and A-L-O-H-A large enough to see for some distance in any direction.

Poi Bread

1 (1-pound) bag poi
¾ cup water
2 cups flour
1 cup sugar
2 teaspoons cinnamon
½ teaspoon nutmeg
2 teaspoons baking powder

1 teaspoon salt
3 eggs, slightly beaten
1 cup vegetable oil
2 teaspoons vanilla
⅓ cup chopped nuts
½ cup shredded coconut
½ cup raisins

Mix poi and water; blend well. In a large bowl, combine flour, sugar, cinnamon, nutmeg, baking powder, and salt. Combine eggs, oil, and vanilla; add to flour mixture. Stir in poi; add nuts, coconut, and raisins. Pour into 2 greased loaf pans, and bake for approximately 45 minutes at 350°. Makes 2 loaves.

Ethnic Foods of Hawai'i

Pineapple Nut Bread

2 cups flour
1 tablespoon baking powder
½ teaspoon salt
¼ teaspoon nutmeg
½ cup vegetable oil
¾ cup sugar

2 eggs
⅔ cup milk
1 teaspoon vanilla
1 (8-ounce) can crushed
   pineapple, drained
½ cup chopped pecans

Preheat oven to 350°; lightly oil and flour one loaf pan. Sift flour, baking powder, salt, and nutmeg onto wax paper. In a large bowl, beat oil with sugar; add eggs, one at a time; mix well. Add dry ingredients alternately with milk. Stir in vanilla; add pineapple and pecans. Bake for 50 minutes. Cool completely before cutting. Makes one loaf.

Dd's Table Talk

Mango Bread

5 cups flour	2¼ cups oil
6 teaspoons baking soda	12 mangoes, peeled and
1 cup wheat germ	mashed
3 cups granulated sugar	3 teaspoons vanilla
4½ teaspoons cinnamon	2 cups raisins
9 eggs	1½ cups chopped nuts

Sift flour and baking soda. Add other dry ingredients and mix thoroughly. Beat eggs with oil, mangoes, and vanilla. Add to dry mixture and mix well. Add raisins and nuts; fold into mixture. Bake in 3 greased loaf pans at 350° until toothpick comes out clean (about 1 hour). Makes 3 loaves.

Tailgate Party Cookbook

Hawaiian Macadamia Nut Bread

¼ cup butter, softened	½ teaspoon salt
¾ cup light brown sugar	¾ cup chopped macadamia
2 eggs, beaten	nuts
1¾ cups flour	1 cup shredded fresh
2 teaspoons baking powder	pineapple, with juice
¼ teaspoon baking soda	

Cream butter and sugar; beat in eggs. Combine flour, baking powder, baking soda, and salt. Stir in nuts. Stir ½ flour mixture into creamed mixture. Gently stir in pineapple and remaining flour mixture. Turn batter into greased 9x5x3-inch pan. Bake one hour in preheated 350° oven, or until it tests done.

Seasoned with Aloha Vol. 2

 Eighteen television series have been filmed in Hawai'i since 1968, some of which include: *Hawaii Five-O, Fantasy Island, Magnum P.I., Tour of Duty, Jake and the Fatman, Raven, The Byrds of Paradise,* and *Baywatch Hawaii.*

Sadie's Purloined Banana Bread

A renowned recipe from my mother, this was "borrowed" 45 years ago by the chef at old Kona Inn. However, her secret ingredient—mace—was missing in his version, and it suffered by comparison.

2 cups raw sugar	2½ cups flour
1 cup butter, softened	1 teaspoon salt
6 ripe bananas, mashed	2 teaspoons baking soda
4 eggs, well beaten	1 teaspoon mace
1 teaspoon vanilla	

Cream sugar and butter together. Stir in mashed bananas, eggs, and vanilla. Sift dry ingredients. Mix dry and wet ingredients together just until combined. Don't overmix. Pour into 2 greased and floured 8x4x3-inch loaf pans. Bake in 350° pre-heated oven for 50 minutes, or until center feels firm to the touch. Yields 2 loaves.

Variation: May include chopped dates, golden raisins, chopped nuts, or other goodies.

Kona on My Plate

Sybil Dean's Banana Bread

It's the mincemeat that makes the subtle difference!

1 cup vegetable oil	2½ cups flour
4 teaspoons baking soda	1 teaspoon salt
2 cups sugar	1 cup mincemeat
4 eggs	1 cup chopped nut meats
2½ cups ripe, mashed bananas	

In large mixing bowl, combine all ingredients. Mix well. Grease and line with wax paper three large or four small loaf pans. Pour batter into pans, filling about ¾ full. Bake large pans in 350° oven for one hour; small pans 45 minutes.

Hawaii Cooks Throughout the Year

Naan Bread

4 cups all-purpose flour	2 eggs
1 tablespoon granulated sugar	¼ cup plain yogurt
1 tablespoon baking powder	¾ cup milk
¼ tablespoon baking soda	2 tablespoons canola oil
1½ teaspoons salt	

In a deep bowl, combine dry ingredients and mix well. Make a well in center and add the remaining ingredients. Mix all ingredients until dough is somewhat sticky; add warm water, if necessary. Knead dough a little on a floured surface until dough is somewhat elastic. Pinch off golf-ball-size pieces of dough, and place on buttered pan to rest. Cover with damp cloth and let rise for about one hour. Dough may also be refrigerated for later use at this point.

To cook, pat dough balls into thin circles, about 6 inches in diameter (they should look like tortillas when ready); place on sheet pan and bake at 450° 2–4 minutes or until dough puffs up and is slightly brown. Serve hot. Makes 8 pieces.

Note: These rolls burn easily, so keep a watchful eye on them while baking.

The Tastes and Tales of Moiliili

Mia's Pineapple Bran Muffins

1 cup bran	⅓ cup butter, softened
1 cup buttermilk	½ cup brown sugar
1 cup flour	1 large egg
1 teaspoon cinnamon	¼ cup molasses
1 teaspoon baking powder	¼ cup crushed pineapple
½ teaspoon baking soda	⅓ cup chopped dates or
½ teaspoon salt	raisins

Combine bran and buttermilk. Mix together flour, cinnamon, baking powder, baking soda, and salt. Add, all at once, to bran mix. Stir just until blended. Cream butter, sugar, egg, and molasses thoroughly. Blend into bran mixture. Stir in pineapple and dates. Put liners in 12 muffin tins. Fill each muffin cup ¾ full. Bake at 400° for 20–25 minutes. Cool slightly. Remove liners.

GLAZE:

1/2 cup honey	1 tablespoon butter
2 tablespoons corn syrup	

Melt honey, corn syrup, and butter in saucepan. Simmer 5 minutes. Dip muffin tops in Glaze, coating thoroughly. Place on a cookie sheet until Glaze is set. Serve warm. Makes 12 muffins.

Hawaii–Cooking with Aloha

The haleakala silversword grows only in the crater and outer slopes of Haleakala Volcano, within Haleakala National Park, Maui, Hawai'i. The silversword matures from seed to its final flowering stage any time from 15 to 50 years. It flowers only once and then dies.

Pineapple Corn Muffins

I have often enjoyed a cup of steaming Kona coffee with a muffin at various outdoor terraces along Waikiki. There always seems to be a wide choice of types of muffins with Hawaiian Island jams. Muffins are a legacy of missionary kitchens, but have been improved with Hawaiian flavors. This combination with pineapple and cornmeal is one of the best.

1 cup flour
¼ cup sugar
3 teaspoons baking powder
1 teaspoon salt
1 cup cornmeal or bran
¼ cup shortening or butter, softened

1 egg, beaten
½ cup milk
1 cup drained, crushed
  pineapple (canned or fresh)

Sift flour, sugar, baking powder, and salt together. Stir in cornmeal or bran. Blend in shortening with a fork or your fingertips to make a crumbly mixture. Add egg, milk, and pineapple, and stir to blend. Place in well-greased muffin pans. Bake at 425° for 15–20 minutes until golden brown. This will make about 2 dozen muffins.

Honolulu Hawaii Cooking

Kona Koffee Kake

1 cup brown or raw sugar	3 teaspoons baking powder
½ cup grated coconut	¾ teaspoon salt
1 (8½-ounce) can crushed	¼ cup shortening
pineapple, drained,	¾ cup juice-milk mix
reserve juice	(reserved pineapple juice)
1½ cups flour	2 eggs

Preheat oven to 375°. Grease a round 9x1½-inch pan or a square 8x8x2-inch pan. Blend the sugar, coconut, and pineapple in a mixing bowl. Reserve ½ cup of this mixture. Add the remaining ingredients to the mix in the bowl and beat vigorously one minute. Pour batter evenly into prepared pan. Bake about 30 minutes or until a toothpick inserted into the center comes out clean. Remove cake from pan and place on serving dish. Spread reserved sugar mix over top of cake. Serve cake warm with butter or margarine and, of course, coffee.

Kau Kau Kitchen

Mea 'Ono Paniolo
(Cowboy Coffeecake)

2⅓ cups sifted enriched flour	½ teaspoon cinnamon
½ teaspoon salt	½ teaspoon nutmeg
2 cups raw brown sugar	1 cup buttermilk
⅔ cup shortening	2 eggs, well beaten
2 teaspoons baking powder	½ cup chopped macadamia
½ teaspoon baking soda	nuts

Combine flour, salt, sugar, and shortening. Mix until crumbly. Reserve ½ cup of the mixture. To remaining crumbs, add baking powder, baking soda, and spices. Mix thoroughly. Add milk and eggs. Mix well. Pour into 2 wax-paper-lined, 8x8x2-inch baking pans. Sprinkle with reserved crumbs. Sprinkle chopped nuts and additional cinnamon on top. Bake at 375° for 25–30 minutes.

The Friends of 'Iolani Palace Cookbook

'Ono (Good) Coffeecake

½ cup sugar
1½ cups sifted flour
1 tablespoon low-sodium
   baking powder

½ cup (1 stick) salt-free
   margarine
1 egg, well beaten
½ cup whole milk

Preheat oven to 375°. Sift dry ingredients together into mixing bowl. Cut margarine into flour mixture until it becomes the size of peas. Add egg and milk, and stir lightly until just blended. Spread batter into well-greased, 8-inch-square cake pan.

FILLING:

½ cup packed brown sugar
2 teaspoons cinnamon
2 tablespoons flour

3 tablespoons salt-free
   margarine
¼ cup chopped pecans

Combine all the ingredients for Filling, except pecans. Spread Filling over the batter. Sprinkle top of Filling with chopped nuts. Bake for 25 minutes or until toothpick inserted in center comes out clean. Cut and serve warm.

Classic Cookbook Recipes

In the mid 1800s, Chinese workers who came to Hawai'i to work in the sugar cane fields brought with them the disease leprosy (today called Hansen's Disease). As more and more Hawaiians contracted the disease, strict isolation was enforced to keep it from spreading further. In 1866, the first sufferers were sent to Kalaupapa, a small peninsula on the north side of Moloka'i surrounded on three sides by the Pacific Ocean and with high sea cliffs on the fourth. In 1873, Father Damien, a Belgian priest, came to minister to the needs of the dying. Through his ministry, order was created in the place of suffering and chaos. After 12 years in service, he contracted the disease and died in 1889. More than 8,000 people died of leprosy in Kalaupapa before sulfone drugs, developed in the early 1940s, put the disease in remission, and rendered the carriers no longer contagious. Today less than 100 residents call Kalaupapa home. The peninsula is now a National Historic Site managed by the U.S. Park Service.

Portuguese Sweet Bread
(Pao Doce)

In the old days, this special bread was reserved for weddings and feast days.

1 teaspoon plus 1 pound sugar, divided
1½ cups lukewarm water, divided
1 yeast cake
2 pounds flour
½ teaspoon salt

1 tablespoon butter plus 2 tablespoons shortening
7 eggs, slightly beaten, divided
5 tablespoons evaporated milk or cream
1 teaspoon vanilla

Dissolve 1 teaspoon sugar in ¼ cup lukewarm water; add yeast, without stirring. Let yeast work until it becomes foamy. Sift flour, 1 pound sugar, and salt together, then cut in butter and shortening. Add 6 slightly beaten eggs, milk, vanilla, and 1¼ cups lukewarm water to risen yeast. Add to flour-shortening mixture. Knead until dough doesn't stick to hand. Let rise until double in bulk. Put dough into 2 greased bread pans. Let rise until even with pan. Brush top of bread with one beaten whole egg, then put in oven. Bake at 325° for 1 hour. Watch carefully, as it browns easily. Makes 2 loaves.

West Kauai's Plantation Heritage

Hiroko's Breakfast Biscuit

4 cups flour
½ cup sugar
1 teaspoon baking powder
1 teaspoon baking soda
1 stick butter

1 stick margarine
1½ cups or less milk
1 teaspoon vanilla
¼ cup sugar mixed with ½–1 teaspoon cinnamon

Combine dry ingredients in large bowl. Add butter and margarine and cut in till pea-size. Add milk and vanilla to form dough. Roll out and cut into long thin strips; spiral from one end (like a snail) to form biscuit. Sprinkle with cinnamon sugar. Bake 25–30 minutes at 375°. Serve when golden brown.

A Lei of Recipes

Steve G's Fabulous Pancakes

Steve's wife, Sharon, says these are "to die for!" They're small and thin, and a Sunday morning treat.

1 tablespoon butter, melted	1 egg, beaten
1 tablespoon matzo meal	1½ tablespoons milk
1 tablespoon sugar	

Whisk all ingredients together thoroughly. Let stand 5 minutes. Grease a griddle or skillet. For each pancake, scoop a tablespoonful of batter from the bottom of mix and drop onto skillet. Batter should be thin, so cakes will spread out. Fry on medium heat until lightly golden. Serve as is, sprinkled with powdered sugar, or put a dollop of jam in the center and roll up like crêpes. Sliced fresh strawberries with a bit of cinnamon and brown sugar, or sliced bananas also make wonderful stuffings. Serves 1. To serve more, just multiply ingredients by the number of people.

The When You Live in Hawaii You Get Very Creative During Passover Cookbook

With Diamond Head as a backdrop, an early morning buffet breakfast right on the Waikiki Beach before it livens up for the day could not be any more delightful. We sampled all the fruits, some of which we had to ask the waiter to identify. I ate the center of the prickly red rambutan before I was told you don't eat the seed—wasn't too bad, but the white part surrounding it was much tastier!

Sheraton Moana's Eggs Volga

A turn-of-the-century dish from the Moana Hotel kitchens.

CHAMPAGNE SAUCE:

1 soup spoon finely chopped
  shallots
1 soup spoon white wine
  vinegar
4 egg yolks
8 ounces (1 cup) clarified
  butter, melted

⅓ cup fine champagne
1 soup spoon chopped fresh
  tarragon leaves
Salt and pepper to taste

Bring shallots and vinegar to boil in small saucepan; reduce slowly to almost dry; cool to lukewarm. Add egg yolks, beating with whisk gently until light yellow. Little by little, add butter, then champagne. Strain through a fine strainer. Keep warm.

4 eggs
4 thinly cut slices of
  fine-cured ham
1 ounce butter

4 light rye bread slices
4 artichoke bottoms, braised
1 ounce Beluga caviar

Poach eggs for 3 minutes and set aside. Fry ham lightly on both sides in skillet with butter; cut rye bread to 4-inch squares and toast; heat artichoke bottoms in skillet.

  Place rye toast croutons on four plates. In order, top it with artichoke bottom, nicely folded ham, and poached egg. Add finely chopped tarragon leaves to Champagne Sauce, and salt and pepper to taste; cover poached egg with small amount of sauce. Top with dab of caviar. Garnish with fresh herb of your choice.

Island Flavors

Coffee Jelly

½ package unflavored gelatin   3 cups black coffee
½ cup cold water   ¾ cup sugar

Soak gelatin in cold water and dissolve in the hot coffee. Add sugar and stir until it dissolves. Strain and turn into a mold. Serve with whipped cream.

How to Use Hawaiian Fruit

Papaya Jelly

½ package unflavored gelatin   1 cup boiling water
½ cup cold water   1 cup papaya pulp
½ cup sugar   Juice of 1 lemon

Soak gelatin in cold water 5 minutes. Dissolve sugar in boiling water; add gelatin and strain. When cool, add papaya and lemon juice. Place on ice (refrigerate) to harden.

How to Use Hawaiian Fruit

Nutty Garlic Loaf

1 (1-pound) package frozen
  bread dough
2 tablespoons butter, melted
2 tablespoons chopped salted
  peanuts or macadamia nuts

3 garlic cloves, minced
1 tablespoon freeze-dried
  chives
1 tablespoon Parmesan cheese

Let bread dough thaw at room temperature until it can be cut with a knife. Slice into 10 equal slices.

Mix butter, nuts, garlic, and chives. Dip bread slices into this mixture. Put slices upright in an 8½x4½x2½-inch lightly greased bread pan. Drizzle any remaining butter mixture over top of loaf. Sprinkle with Parmesan cheese. Let dough rise in warm place until loaf reaches top of pan. Bake at 375° for 25–30 minutes or until loaf is golden brown. Makes 10 slices.

Hilo Woman's Club Cookbook

Garlic Bread Plus

You won't know what hit you when you bite into this delectable garlic bread—it tastes at once buttery, cheesy, and indescribably rich—and it is.

1 baguette (long French bread)
1½ tablespoons butter,
  softened
2 large cloves garlic, pressed
½ cup of your favorite
  mayonnaise

¼ cup grated mozzarella
  cheese
⅓ cup Parmesan cheese
1 tablespoon minced fresh
  herbs (optional)
¼ teaspoon salt (optional)

Preheat broiler, and set baking rack about 4 inches beneath heat source.

Split bread in half lengthwise. Combine remaining ingredients and mix them well. Slather the cut surfaces of bread with mayonnaise mixture, and place on baking tray or cookie sheet in broiler. Broil until bubbly and lightly browned. Cut into pieces and serve immediately. Yields about 10 pieces.

Vegetarian Nights

Pickled Vegetable Sandwich

1½ cups rice vinegar
1¼ cups sugar
¼ cup mirin (sweet rice wine)
1½ tablespoons salt
1 large carrot and equal
   amount of daikon

Mayonnaise
French baguette
Slices of chicken or turkey
Watercress or lettuce to
   garnish

Combine vinegar, sugar, mirin, and salt, and heat until sugar and salt dissolve. Cool. Grate carrot and cut daikon in long strips. Soak in cold water for about 15 minutes. Drain and squeeze before adding to vinegar mixture. May be prepared in advance and kept in refrigerator several days, covered.

Lightly pat mayonnaise on both sides of a French roll; add pickled vegetables, chicken or turkey slices; garnish with watercress or shredded lettuce.

Variation: Fried strips of tofu may be substituted for turkey or chicken.

Favorite Island Cookery Book VI

At 4,038 square miles, the island of Hawai'i is the state's largest single island, and is still growing. Located over a geologic hot spot, lava escapes to the surface and hardens, constantly expanding the island's size. Referred to as the Big Island, it is twice the size of all the other Hawaiian Islands combined.

Taro Fritters

1 cup mashed, boiled taro
¼ cup all-purpose flour
1 egg yolk (save white and
    beat stiff)

1 teaspoon baking powder
¼ cup milk
Salt to taste
Oil for cooking

Combine all of the ingredients except egg white. Fold in the stiffly beaten egg white. Drop in deep, hot fat or oil by the table-spoon, and cook until golden brown. Drain on paper towels. Serves 4.

Variation: You may add chopped, cooked meat, fresh herbs, carrots, or other vegetables. Add a teaspoon of vinegar to batter, and the fritters will not absorb as much oil when frying.

Tropical Taste

Skillet Corn Fritters

These are a delicious accompaniment to fish, meat, or poultry dishes, or can be eaten as a snack.

¼ cup skim milk
½ cup unbleached flour
1 (10-ounce) package frozen
    corn kernels, thawed
3 tablespoons chopped fresh
    parsley

Dash salt
Dash black pepper
2 egg whites

In a large bowl stir skim milk into flour until blended well. Stir in corn, parsley, salt, and pepper. In another bowl beat egg whites until stiff peaks form. Fold the beaten egg whites gently into corn mixture, making sure to mix thoroughly. Spray skillet with cooking spray and heat on medium heat. Drop mixture by tablespoonfuls onto pan, leaving space between them. Cook for about 2 minutes, or until browned slightly; turn and cook other side for about 2 minutes more. Makes about 8 fritters.

Note: To reheat, place on a paper towel, and put in the microwave for about 10 seconds each.

Nutritional analysis per serving: Cal 66; Fat .59mg; Chol 0mg; Sod 50mg

The Best of Heart-y Cooking

Soups and Stews

The world-famous Polynesian Cultural Center in O'ahu showcases seven South Pacific island cultures in each of their villages. Events include a lū'au, Pageant of the Long Canoes, IMAX™ Theater, and "Horizons" evening show.

Hanalei Plantation Hotel's Taro Soup

2 pounds taro, diced small
1 quart chicken broth or bouillon
6 ounces salt pork, ground
6 ounces (1 small) onion, diced small
6 ounces (2 medium) carrots, grated
6 ounces (1 large) leek, diced small

1¼ cups flour
3 cups shredded, cooked chicken
1 pint heavy cream
1 pint milk
1 bay leaf
Tabasco, Worcestershire, salt, and white pepper to taste

Cook washed taro in broth until tender. Drain and set aside, holding broth and taro separately. Sauté salt pork; add onion, carrots, and leek, and sauté. Add flour and cook until it smells like walnuts. Add chicken and most of broth, and bring to a boil in stages; cool.

Combine cream and milk. Add to soup and bring to a boil. Add bay leaf, taro, and remaining taro broth as necessary for thickness. Adjust seasoning with Tabasco, Worcestershire, salt, and white pepper.

Cook 'em Up Kaua'i

Kim Chee Soup with Meat and Tofu

This is a spicy soup, often eaten when one feels like he is coming down with a cold.

1 pound sliced pork, bite-sized, or 1–2 cans Spam, cubed
⅛ cup sesame oil, divided
3–4 cups kim chee, with liquid
1 bag soy bean sprouts
Water
1 wooden spoonful of ko choo jung
¼ cup soy sauce, or to taste
Salt and pepper to taste
1 (12-ounce) block firm tofu, cubed

Brown meat in a little sesame oil on medium-high heat. Drain fat; add kim chee, soy bean sprouts, just enough water to cover, ko choo jung, remaining sesame oil, soy sauce, and salt and pepper to taste. Heat to boiling, then reduce to simmer for about 15 minutes, stirring occasionally. Add tofu and simmer for 15–30 more minutes until kim chee is cooked.

West Kauai's Plantation Heritage

Oxtail Soup

2 oxtails, cut in pieces
6 slices ginger
1 clove garlic
2 stalks green onions (whole)
1 cup shelled raw peanuts
10 pieces dried mushrooms
Salt and shoyu to taste
¼ cup wine
Ajinomoto (MSG)
Squash, any type, cut into big cubes
Chinese parsley for garnish

Wash oxtails thoroughly. Bring to a boil and drain. Wash oxtail of all scum. Add clean water (as much as you desire) to the oxtails, ginger, garlic, and green onions, then cook. Add raw peanuts, dried mushrooms (soaked in water and halved), and cook until oxtails are tender. Add salt, shoyu, wine, and ajinomoto. Finally add squash. Garnish with Chinese parsley before serving.

Favorite Island Cookery Book I

Portuguese Bean Soup

1 pound pinto beans	2 teaspoons chopped garlic
2½ quarts water	½ teaspoon ground pepper
1 ham bone	2 teaspoons seasoning salt
½ pound bacon	½ cup sherry
2 stalks celery, chopped	2 Portuguese sausages, chopped
2 medium onions, chopped	½ cup cubed ham
2 tablespoons flour	½ head cabbage, chopped
Small bunch parsley, chopped	3 potatoes, precooked and
2 bay leaves	cubed
1 pound precooked carrots, chopped	Dash cinnamon

Wash beans and soak overnight in cold water. Drain and rinse. Place in stockpot with 2½ quarts water and ham bone. Cover and simmer. While beans simmer, cook bacon, remove, and cut into small pieces. To the bacon grease, add celery and onions, and sauté until onion is translucent. Add flour and stir one minute. Add this mixture to stockpot with remaining ingredients. Mix thoroughly. Simmer over low heat for at least 4 hours.

Tailgate Party Cookbook

Portuguese Bean Soup

There must be as many versions of this popular Honolulu soup as there are varieties of hibiscus on the city's streets. Local politicians, musicians, and schoolteachers swear by their family recipes, and often cook and sell bean soup for charity fund raisers. Basically it is a bean soup, brought from Portugal by the first Portuguese immigrants. It combines beans, ham hocks, and cabbage in a thick tasty soup. One might call it a "minestrone" of the Hawaiian Islands, meaning that this and that can be added to a basic recipe.

1 pound dried small red or
   kidney beans (or
   combination)
2 quarts water
1 medium onion, sliced
2 ham hocks
Salt and pepper to taste
1 (8-ounce) can tomato sauce
2 medium-sized potatoes,
   peeled and diced

2 stalks celery, diced
1 small cabbage, chopped or
   thinly sliced
½ cup uncooked, small elbow
   macaroni
½ pound Portuguese or any
   hot-style sausage, thinly
   sliced

Cover beans with water and soak overnight. Drain and place beans in a soup pot. Cover with 2 quarts of water. Add onion, ham hocks, salt and pepper. Cover and simmer for one hour, stirring now and then.

Remove cover and take out the ham hocks. Add tomato sauce, potatoes, and celery. Remove ham from bones and dice. Return to the pot and simmer, uncovered, for 20 minutes. Add remaining ingredients and continue to cook for an additional 30 minutes. If the soup is too thick for your taste, thin with water or white wine. Garnish with minced parsley or watercress. Serves 6–8.

Honolulu Hawaii Cooking

The origin of the ukulele can be traced to immigrant Manual Nunes who arrived in Hawai'i from Madeira in 1879 to work in the sugar cane fields. He is responsible for transforming the Portuguese braguinha into the Hawaiian ukulele. Nunes established one of the first ukulele manufacturing companies and remained in business for over 40 years. The ukulele remains Hawai'i's most popular musical instrument.

Nine Bean Soup

2 cups Bean Soup Mix
2 quarts warm water
1 pound lean ham, diced
1 large onion, chopped
1 clove garlic, minced

½ teaspoon salt (optional)
1 (28-ounce) can tomatoes,
   undrained and chopped
1 (4-ounce) can diced chiles

Sort and wash bean mix. Place in Dutch oven. Cover beans with water level 2 inches above beans. Soak overnight.

Drain beans. Add 2 quarts water and next 4 ingredients. Cover and bring to a boil, reduce heat, and simmer 1½ hours or until beans are tender. Add remaining ingredients and simmer for 30 minutes, stirring occasionally. Yields 8 cups.

Variation: Use Portuguese sausage, ham hock, or a mix of sausage, bacon, and ham.

BEAN SOUP MIX:

1 pound barley pearls
1 pound dried pink beans
1 pound dried red beans
1 pound dried pinto beans
1 pound dried navy beans
   or small white beans

1 pound dried Great Northern
   beans
1 pound dried lentils
1 pound dried split peas
   (yellow or green)
1 pound dried black-eyed peas

Combine all beans. Divide into 10 (2-cup) packages for gift giving. Enclose the above Nine Bean Soup recipe.

Variations: Any combination of beans or use kidney, black, or lima beans.

Favorite Recipes for Islanders

Ronit's Chicken Soup

This isn't a consommé, but rather an authentic, hearty chicken soup, guaranteed to cure whatever hurts.

1 fryer chicken
1 stalk celery with leaves
1 onion with skin, cut in half
1 celery root, peeled and
   cut in half
1 tomato
1 potato, peeled, if desired,
   and cut in half

2 carrots, peeled
1 zucchini, cut in half
   lengthwise
½ bunch dill
1 large clump parsley
Salt and pepper to taste
Chicken bouillon to taste, if
   necessary

Clean chicken. Remove liver; reserve for another dish. Place chicken in large pot, cover with water and bring to a boil. Skim fat off top, reduce heat to simmer and add celery stalk, onion, celery root, and whole tomato. Cook for 1½ hours. Add potato, whole carrots, and zucchini, and cook for an additional hour, or until chicken is tender. Add dill and parsley the last 15 minutes. When soup is ready, remove vegetables; strain and season to taste. Add chicken bouillon for more intense flavor, but only if necessary.

Serve each bowl of soup with pieces of shredded chicken, potato, and carrot. Serve with knaidlach (matzo ball) for extra compliments.

Note: This soup freezes well (if you are lucky enough to have leftovers). Use cooked chicken to make chicken salad.

The When You Live in Hawaii You Get Very Creative
During Passover Cookbook

Curried Cream of Chicken Soup

2 tablespoons butter
3 tablespoons flour
Dash of pepper
3 cups chicken broth
1 cup 2% milk
1½ cups chopped, cooked
chicken

½ cup shredded cheese (or
more)
Poultry seasoning
Curry powder
Salt and pepper to taste

In a large saucepan, melt butter, then stir in flour and a dash of pepper. Add chicken broth and milk. Cook and stir until bubbly. Cook and stir one minute more. Stir in the chicken; heat through. Add cheese until soup is at your desired consistency and flavor, then add poultry seasoning, curry powder, salt and pepper to taste. Yields 3 main-dish servings.

Seasoned with Aloha Vol. 2

Velvet Corn Soup with Crab

¼ pound ground pork
1 teaspoon minced fresh
ginger
1 tablespoon vegetable oil
10 cups chicken stock
2 tablespoons sherry
12 ounces creamed corn
3 tablespoons cornstarch
dissolved in 4 tablespoons
water

3 egg whites, slightly beaten
10 ounces fresh or frozen crab,
flaked
Salt and pepper to taste
4 green onions, thinly sliced for
garnish

In a large saucepan, sauté ground pork and ginger in oil. Add stock, sherry, and corn, and bring to a boil. Thicken with cornstarch-water mixture. Slowly stir in egg whites. Add crab and season. Remove from heat. Garnish and serve. Serves 10.

A Taste of Aloha

Chilled Avocado Cream Soup

1 large ripe avocado
1½ cups chicken broth
1½ tablespoons fresh lime
  juice
1 teaspoon salt
¼ teaspoon pepper
½ teaspoon chile pepper
  water or dash of Tabasco
½ cup whipping cream

Peel, stone, and dice the avocado. Put all ingredients except cream into a blender in order given, and blend until smooth. Check seasoning. Add more to taste. Chill covered, and before serving, stir in cream.

Joys of Hawaiian Cooking

Red Bell Pepper and Potato Cream Soup

4 red bell peppers, seeded
  and cut into thin strips
1 potato, peeled and cut into
  very thin strips
1 large onion, cut into thin
  strips
3–4 fresh garlic cloves,
  peeled and cut thinly
2 tablespoons butter
Sweet Hungarian paprika
Freshly ground black pepper
Oregano
Chicken broth (about 2 cups)

Sauté peppers, potato, onion, and garlic in butter, until soft and translucent. Add seasonings to taste. Pour into food processor and process until smooth. Heat and thin to desired consistency with chicken broth.

Tropical Taste

Imitation Bird Nest Soup

3 dried mushrooms
Hot water
2 (1¼-ounce) bundles
   long rice
½ cup ground pork
6 (13¾-ounce) cans chicken
   broth
¼ cup diced ham
4 water chestnuts
⅛ teaspoon MSG
2 egg whites, well beaten
   (optional)
Chinese parsley or green onion,
   chopped

Soak mushrooms in hot water. Drain and chop fine. Soak long rice in hot water. Drain and cut into ½-inch lengths. Brown pork and add chicken broth, mushrooms, ham, water chestnuts, and MSG, and simmer for about 30 minutes. Add long rice and egg whites just before turning heat off. Stir. Serve with Chinese parsley or green onion.

Favorite Island Cookery Book III

Mahi Chowder

4 slices bacon, diced
1 cup diced onion
6 cups water, divided
1 bay leaf, wrinkled
3 potatoes, diced
2 pounds mahi, cubed
2 cups powdered milk, dry
Salt
White pepper

Fry bacon and onion in the bottom of your soup pot until the onion is browned. Add 4 cups water, the bay leaf, and potatoes. Bring water up to boiling and let it simmer until the potatoes are tender. Add mahi. Mix dry milk with remaining water and add it to the pot. When the mahi is tender, add salt and white pepper to taste, and serve. You may want to serve this with a crispy green salad and crusty brown bread.

Kau Kau Kitchen

Potato and Corn Chowder

2 teaspoons dry cooking sherry
Olive oil cooking spray
1¼ cups finely chopped
   sweet yellow onions
2 cloves garlic, crushed
Water
2 cups cubed red potatoes
1 bay leaf
¼ teaspoon paprika

¼ teaspoon thyme
1 teaspoon basil
1 (14¼-ounce) can vegetable
   stock
1 cup corn kernels, fresh or
   frozen
1 cup soy milk
Salt to taste
Pepper to taste

Add sherry to a large, oil-sprayed skillet and heat. Add onions and garlic, and sauté for 5 minutes, stirring frequently to prevent browning (add water if needed). Add potatoes, bay leaf, herbs, and stock to sautéed onions and garlic. Cover pan, bring to a boil, and cook over medium heat for 10–15 minutes. When potatoes are tender, add the corn and milk. Simmer until corn is tender, about 3 minutes. Discard the bay leaf.

Use your hand blender to partially purée the mixture, or remove a cup of soup and purée in blender or food processor, then return it to the pot. This will give your soup a creamy texture. Season with salt and/or pepper to taste. Makes 6–8 portions.

One portion: 113.4 calories; 1g fat, 7% fat; 15% protein, 78% carbohydrates

Eat More, Weigh Less Cookbook

When measured from the ocean floor, the dormant volcano Mauna Kea on the Big Island of Hawaiʻi is the tallest mountain in the world at 33,476 feet. Mauna Kea hosts the world's largest astronomical observatory.

Ellen's Favorite Cioppino
(Fish Stew)

¼ cup olive oil
2 large onions, chopped
2 green peppers, seeded and
  chopped
6 celery stalks, chopped
5 cloves garlic, pressed or
  minced
1 cup minced parsley, divided
1 (48-ounce) can V-8 juice
1½ cups dry red wine
1½ cups dry white wine
1 (8-ounce) bottle clam juice
1 (6-ounce) can tomato paste

3 teaspoons dried oregano
3 teaspoons dried basil
4 bay leaves
1 teaspoon crushed red pepper
  flakes
2 teaspoons sugar
Salt and pepper to taste
3 pounds fish fillets, cut into
  1-inch chunks
1 pound shrimp, peeled and
  deveined
2 pounds other seafood (crabs,
  scallops, clams)

Heat olive oil in a heavy pot over medium-high heat. Add onions, peppers, celery, garlic, and ¾ of the parsley, and sauté until vegetables are soft (do not overcook). Add all other ingredients except the seafood; stir until well blended and bring to just below the boiling point. Reduce heat and simmer stock for ½ hour. Stir frequently.

Add the seafood in order given: fish, shrimp, crabs, scallops, and clams last. Cook only until seafood is done, approximately 10–15 minutes. Serve in bowls topped with remaining parsley. Serves 6.

Note: The stock can be made ahead of time and frozen with only the seafood to be added at a later date.

Fresh Catch of the Day...from the Fishwife

Salads

Water tumbles 420 feet into a stream-eroded gorge at Akaka Falls located in Akaka Falls State Park outside Honomu on the Big Island of Hawai'i.

Seared Sesame 'Ahi Salad

SAUCE:

8 ounces shiitake mushrooms, julienned
¼ cup sliced garlic
1 cup cubed tomatoes
½ cup sesame seed oil, divided

¼ cup lemon juice
¼ cup chopped cilantro
½ cup soy sauce
½ cup olive oil

Sauté shiitake mushrooms with garlic and tomatoes in ¼ cup sesame seed oil. In a bowl, add lemon juice, cilantro, soy sauce, and remaining oils. Combine mushrooms, garlic, and tomatoes with lemon juice-cilantro-soy sauce mixture.

4 (4-ounce) pieces (1-pound) 'ahi
1 cup sesame seeds
½ cup olive oil
¼ cup balsamic vinegar
½ pound baby mixed greens

12 Belgian endive leaves
Salt and pepper to taste
Sauce
2 whole Roma tomatoes
½ cup chopped macadamia nuts

Roll the 'ahi in sesame seeds and sear it very quickly (in hot oiled skillet). Mix olive oil and balsamic vinegar together for vinaigrette. Mix baby salad greens with vinaigrette. Place Belgian endive on plate. Place baby mixed greens on endive. Slice the 'ahi and arrange on top of the greens. Top 'ahi with Sauce and garnish with tomato fans and macadamia nuts. Makes 4 servings.

Friends and Celebrities Cookbook II

Chinese-Style Chicken Salad

Chicken salad is everyone's favorite. It is adaptable and can be served on dozens of occasions. It can be dressed down and taken on a picnic or dressed up and served at a dinner party.

1 medium head lettuce, shredded
½ cup minced green onions
1 bunch Chinese parsley (cilantro), chopped
¼ cup thinly sliced celery (optional)
1 (3-ounce) package fried won ton strips
¼ cup chopped, roasted peanuts
1 pound cooked, boneless chicken breasts, shredded
½ cup char siu (roast barbecued pork), julienned

Combine lettuce, onions, Chinese parsley, and celery in a large salad bowl; toss to mix well. Sprinkle with won ton strips, peanuts, chicken, and char siu.

SESAME VINEGAR DRESSING:
2 tablespoons toasted sesame seeds
1 teaspoon salt
½ teaspoon pepper
¼ cup sugar
⅓ cup rice vinegar
¼ cup salad oil

Combine ingredients; mix well, and pour over salad just before serving. Serves 6–10.

Variation: For Chinese Crab Salad, substitute 1 cup cooked crabmeat for chicken.

The Tastes and Tales of Moiliili

Curried Chicken Salad in Tomato Petals

2 cups cooked and diced
  chicken
1 apple, pared and diced
½ cup diced celery
2 teaspoons grated onion
½ cup halved seedless grapes
⅓ cup toasted, slivered
  almonds

2 teaspoons curry powder
1 cup mayonnaise
1 teaspoon salt
Dash of pepper
6 tomatoes

Combine chicken, apple, celery, onion, grapes, and almonds. Blend curry powder with mayonnaise and seasonings; stir into chicken mixture. Chill. Cut tomatoes in sixths, almost but not all the way through, to form petals. Fill with chicken salad. Yields 6 servings.

Favorite Island Cookery Book II

Chinese Salad

½ pound chicken strips,
  cooked (or ham strips)
1 head lettuce, sliced thin
½ cup chopped green onions
½ cup thinly sliced celery

1 cup oil for frying
⅓ cup or 2 ounces mai fun
  (rice sticks)
12 won ton wrappers

Combine cooked chicken, lettuce, green onions, and celery in a bowl. Heat oil and deep-fry a handful of mai fun at a time until it rises to top of oil. Drain. Cut won ton wrappers into ¼-inch strips and deep-fry until brown; drain. Add mai fun and won ton strips to vegetables. Yields 6–8 servings.

SALAD DRESSING:

2 tablespoons oil
1 teaspoon salt
½ teaspoon pepper

6 tablespoons sugar
6 tablespoons vinegar
2 teaspoons oyster sauce

Combine all ingredients. Just before serving salad, toss with vegetables and chicken.

A Lei of Recipes

Turkey Salad

3 cups diced, cooked turkey
1 can water chestnuts,
  drained
½ cup chopped celery
¾ cup macadamia nuts
2 tablespoons vinegar

2 tablespoons crystallized
  ginger
¾ cup mayonnaise
1 teaspoon curry powder
1 tablespoon soy sauce
1½ cups diced pineapple

Combine turkey, water chestnuts, celery, and nuts. Add vinegar. Mix well. Add ginger. Combine mayonnaise, curry powder, soy sauce, and pineapple. Add to turkey mixture. Mix thoroughly. Chill several hours. Serve on lettuce or in hollowed out pineapple shell. Makes 8 servings.

Hawaii–Cooking with Aloha

Spam Pasta Salad

1 (12-ounce) bag pasta
  (veggie spirals are nice)
¼ medium onion, minced
1 cup diced Spam
1 (6-ounce) jar artichoke
  hearts, including juice
1 cup chopped cucumber or
  zucchini

⅓ cup Italian dressing
  (such as zesty Italian)
½ teaspoon salt
¼ teaspoon pepper
¼ teaspoon oregano
Sliced tomatoes, sliced hard-
  boiled eggs, olives, etc., for
  garnish

Cook pasta according to package directions. Do not overcook. Rinse with cold water and drain well.

Place all other ingredients in a bowl and mix together. Add drained pasta and toss together. Chill. Decorate top with sliced tomatoes, sliced hard-boiled eggs, olives, etc.

Hawai'i's Spam Cookbook

Soba Salad

1 (14.8-ounce) package soba
½ head lettuce, shredded
1 Maui onion, finely sliced
2 cups ogo, blanched,
   drained, and chopped
2 chicken breasts, baked
   and shredded
1 cup shredded imitation crab

Cook soba as instructed. Drain and mound soba on a large platter. Layer soba with lettuce, onion, ogo, and top with chicken and imitation crab. Other toppings may be used as desired. Yields 6–8 servings.

DRESSING:
⅔ cup plus 1 tablespoon
   sugar
1½ cups soy sauce
½ cup oil
Juice of 1 lemon
1½ tablespoons vinegar

Shake well before using.

Favorite Island Cookery Book VI

Somennese Salad

1 (8-ounce) package somen
   noodles, cooked according
   to package directions
1 cup shredded cabbage
1 cucumber, seeded and thinly
   sliced
1 carrot, grated
3 stalks green onions, sliced
   diagonally
½ bunch cilantro, chopped
½ cup chopped, roasted
   peanuts
¼ cup sesame seeds, roasted

DRESSING:
2 cloves garlic, finely minced
1 tablespoon grated fresh
   ginger
3 tablespoons sugar
3 tablespoons vegetable oil
3 tablespoons sesame seed oil
2 tablespoons soy sauce
Pinch red pepper flakes

Combine salad ingredients in a large bowl. In a mixing bowl, whisk together Dressing ingredients and pour over salad mixture. Refrigerate at least 2 hours before serving. Serves 6.

Dd's Table Talk

Honolulu Symphony Sweet Potato Salad

Great potluck offering for picnics, as flavors develop at air temperature.

CILANTRO LIME DRESSING:

1 teaspoon Dijon mustard	3 tablespoons oil
2 tablespoons fresh lime juice	½ teaspoon salt
3 tablespoons chopped fresh cilantro	¼ teaspoon ground black pepper
1 clove garlic, minced	

In a large bowl, whisk together mustard, lime juice, cilantro, and garlic. Slowly stream oil into bowl, whisking constantly. Stir in salt and black pepper.

2 large sweet potatoes, cooked, peeled, and cubed	1 cup corn kernels
1 cucumber, peeled, halved lengthwise, and sliced	½ red onion, thinly sliced
	¼ cup finely chopped peanuts

Add cool cubed sweet potatoes to dressing along with cucumber, corn, and red onion. Toss well. Serve at room temperature or chilled. Stir in the peanuts just before serving. Serves 6.

Kona on My Plate

Honolulu variously translates as "fair haven," "quiet harbor," or "sheltered harbor." "Hono" means valley with a bay in front of it and "lulu" means sheltered.

Sweet Potato Salad

This is a colorful dish.

SALAD:

3–4 Okinawan sweet potatoes, cooked and cubed

½ can Spam luncheon meat, cubed

1 cucumber, sliced

½ Maui onion, thinly sliced

1 cup broccoli florets

Place all ingredients in large bowl. Just before serving, add Dressing and toss. Serves 4.

DRESSING:

¼ cup vegetable oil

3 tablespoons sesame oil

½ cup soy sauce

1 tablespoon sugar

Juice of ½ lemon

Combine all ingredients; mix well.

Note: Cooked taro or yellow sweet potatoes may be substituted for Okinawan sweet potatoes, or a combination of potatoes may be used.

Hawai'i's 2nd Spam Cookbook

Macadamia Nut Pea Salad

DRESSING:

1½ teaspoons lemon juice
½ cup red wine vinegar
1 teaspoon salt
½ teaspoon freshly ground pepper
1½ teaspoons Worcestershire sauce
½ teaspoon Dijon mustard
1 clove garlic, crushed
2 tablespoons sugar
1½ teaspoons grated onion and juice
1½ cups corn oil

Blend all ingredients except the oil. Add oil and beat thoroughly. Store in the refrigerator if not used immediately.

1 (16-ounce) package frozen peas
1 cup chopped celery
¼ cup chopped green onions, including 3–4 inches of green tops
1 cup chopped macadamia nuts or cashews
¼ cup fried crisp and crumbled bacon
1 cup sour cream
½ teaspoon salt
¼ cup Dressing
Boston or Mānoa lettuce leaves

Turn frozen peas into a colander and rinse until thawed. Drain. Combine peas, celery, onions, nuts, and bacon. Mix sour cream, salt, and ¼ cup Dressing and pour over salad, mixing lightly. Cover and chill, preferably overnight. Serve on a bed of lettuce. Remaining Dressing may be refrigerated for later use.

Note: Onion juice is obtained by grating a large white onion on the fine side of a grater, or processing it in an electric blender and straining the purée. Serves 6.

Another Taste of Aloha

Hawaiian Horseradish Salad

Delicious and easy to prepare, this Waldorf-like salad is a nice blend of Hawaiian and traditional Passover flavors.

3 celery stalks
2 large apples, peeled
1 (8-ounce) can crushed
   pineapple in its own juice,
   drained
1 cup walnuts

½ cup mayonnaise
2 tablespoons lemon juice
2 tablespoons sugar
2 tablespoons white
   horseradish

Dice celery and grate apples. Mix all ingredients. Chill and serve in a glass bowl or on lettuce leaves. Serves 6.

The When You Live in Hawaii You Get Very Creative During Passover Cookbook

Chayote Namasu

2 medium chayote squash

1 teaspoon roasted sesame
   seeds

Lay chayote flat on a work surface and cut in half horizontally. Discard the small, flat pit. Slice squash lengthwise into strips, then cut crosswise into small sticks. Blanch the chayote sticks in boiling water about 40 seconds. Drain and run under cold water; set aside.

DRESSING:
2 teaspoons slivered, fresh
   gingerroot
3 tablespoons soy sauce
2 tablespoons lime juice

2 teaspoons sugar
½ teaspoon salt
¼ teaspoon black pepper

In a small bowl, combine Dressing ingredients; stir until sugar dissolves. Pour Dressing over the chayote, toss lightly and sprinkle with sesame seeds. Chill. Serves 4–6.

Note: Lightly salt your hands before peeling squash. Residue will wash off easily.

Favorite Island Cookery Book VI

Mandarin Spinach Salad

This wonderful light spinach salad with oranges mixes up fast for a quick lunch or light supper. The Tarragon Dressing is completely nonfat, and can be made ahead and stored in a jar in the refrigerator.

4 cups fresh spinach, washed, dried, and torn
1 cup sliced fresh mushrooms
1 large tomato, cut into bite-size pieces
1 cup bean sprouts
1 (11-ounce) can Mandarin oranges (drain and reserve liquid)
1 tablespoon imitation bacon bits
Croutons (optional)

Combine all ingredients except oranges and bacon bits, and toss. Add oranges and bacon bits. Just before serving, pour dressing over salad and toss to coat well. Makes 4 servings. Add croutons, if desired.

TARRAGON DRESSING:
Reserved orange liquid
1 tablespoon raspberry wine vinegar
1 tablespoon white wine vinegar
2 teaspoons sugar
½ teaspoon ground white pepper
¼ teaspoon crushed tarragon leaves

Combine orange liquid, vinegars, sugar, pepper, and tarragon leaves. Shake well to combine.

Nutritional analysis per serving: Cal 150; Fat 1g; Chol 0mg; Sod 50mg

The Best of Heart-y Cooking

What's the weather like in Hawai'i? Sunny and warm, of course! Hawai'i is known for its perfect weather conditions—sunny and highs in the mid-80s with cool trade winds. Afternoon rain showers are not uncommon in the mountains and valleys on the northeastern side of the islands.

Christmas Salad Supreme

This beautiful salad draws rave reviews.

JAM VINAIGRETTE:

2 tablespoons raspberry or apple cider vinegar

⅓ cup vegetable oil

2 tablespoons raspberry or other fruit jam

Whisk all ingredients together. Place in small jar and refrigerate. Shake well before using.

SALAD:

¾ pound fresh spinach, torn

1 cup fresh or frozen raspberries, divided

10 fresh strawberries, halved

3 large kiwi, peeled and sliced thin, divided

¾ cup halved chopped pecans (or macadamia nuts)

Combine spinach, about ¾ of the berries, and two kiwi about one hour before serving. Drizzle with Jam Vinaigrette. Toss salad. Place in container with a tight lid. Chill, turning once. (If you use frozen berries, add them just before serving, or they will be too limp).

Just before serving, toss again with rest of berries and pecans, and garnish with last sliced kiwi.

Friends and Celebrities Cookbook II

Avocado and Pomegranate Salad

This recipe is a good way to use the abundant local Kona avocados.

2 ripe avocados
Lemon juice and water

1 pomegranate
4 ounces black grapes

Peel the avocados, remove pits, and slice into thick half rings. Drop the rings into a bowl containing lemon juice and water; this will prevent them from turning black. Cut the pomegranate in half and crush it over a bowl to remove and collect the seeds. Wash grapes and mix with pomegranate seeds. Drain avocado pieces and add to the fruit.

DRESSING:

1 teaspoon sugar
4 tablespoons white wine
  vinegar
2 tablespoons canola oil

1 tablespoon groundnut oil
  (peanut oil)
4 tablespoons chopped mint
Salt and pepper

Put all the ingredients into a glass jar, screw the lid on firmly, and shake vigorously for 2 minutes. Pour over the avocado and fruit. Toss well before serving. Serves 4–6.

Shaloha Cookbook

Geologically, Kaua'i is the oldest of Hawai'i's major islands and is the site where Captain James Cook, the first westerner to set foot in Hawai'i, landed in 1778.

Papaya Seed Dressing

1 cup cider vinegar
¼ cup honey
1 small onion, minced

1 cup oil
1 tablespoon dry mustard
2 tablespoons papaya seeds

In a blender or food processor, mix vinegar, honey, and onion on low speed. Gradually add oil. Increase speed to high and add mustard and papaya seeds. Continue one minute.

Tailgate Party Cookbook

Papaya Seed Salad Dressing

1 cup sugar
1 teaspoon salt
½ teaspoon dry mustard
1 cup vinegar

½ cup oil
1 small onion, chopped
3 tablespoons papaya seeds

Combine ingredients and put in blender until papaya seeds are ground fine. Serve on fresh greens.

A Lei of Recipes

Special Salad Dressing

1 clove garlic, mashed
1 cup oil
½ cup sugar
½ cup rice vinegar

2 teaspoons salt
½ teaspoon pepper
¼ cup mayonnaise
1 teaspoon dry mustard

Mix ingredients in blender and chill. This dressing is delicious with fresh or cooked vegetables.

Variation: It may be used as marinade for fresh shrimp. Wash shrimp, remove legs, and soak with shell on in dressing overnight. Grill over coals.

Favorite Island Cookery Book VI

Fiesta Papaya Boats

2 papayas
2 cups shredded, cooked
  chicken
1 green onion, sliced
1 teaspoon sugar

¼ cup mayonnaise
1 cup grated, raw carrot
1 tablespoon wine vinegar
Salt and pepper to taste

Cut papayas in half and scoop out seeds. Combine all remaining ingredients, then spoon into cavaties of papaya. Chill. Serves 4.

Hilo Woman's Club Cookbook

Herbed Carrot Slices

4 pounds carrots, peeled
  and thinly sliced
1 teaspoon salt
2⅔ cups white vinegar
2⅔ cups water
3 teaspoons dill seed
1 teaspoon mustard seed

1 teaspoon caraway seeds
1 teaspoon celery seeds
2 cups white sugar
2 teaspoons rock salt
1 teaspoon crushed and seeded
  Hawaiian chili pepper

Cook carrot slices with 1 teaspoon salt in very small amount of water until almost tender. Drain and pack the slices into hot sterilized jars and pour over them the hot syrup made by combining all the remaining ingredients in a pan, bringing to a full rolling boil, and boiling for 2 minutes. When syrup has covered carrots in the jars, seal them and let ripen for several weeks before serving.

Paradise Preserves

Polynesian Salad

1½ cups mayonnaise
1 cup mango chutney
2 pounds cooked, diced
  chicken
1 cup salted peanuts
  or macadamia nuts
1 cup golden raisins
1 cup flaked coconut

2 cups diagonally sliced
  bananas
Shredded lettuce
Avocado slices for garnish
Additional sliced banana for
  garnish
Lemon juice

Mix together mayonnaise and chutney; toss with chicken, nuts, and raisins. Gently combine with coconut and sliced bananas. Mound in a large bowl lined with shredded lettuce. Garnish with slices of avocado and banana dipped in lemon juice. Serves 10–12.

Hilo Woman's Club Cookbook

Dell Neely's Pineapple Pickles

6 cups fresh pineapple chunks
2 cups white sugar
1 cup cider vinegar

12 whole cloves
6 (2-inch) pieces cinnamon
  sticks

Put all ingredients into saucepan, bring to a boil, turn heat to medium, and continue cooking until pineapple turns a clear golden yellow. Pour fruit and syrup into hot, sterilized glass jars and seal. Let jars "ripen" about 2 weeks so fruit will absorb spices.

Paradise Preserves

Vegetables

Created by pounding taro root, poi is a staple in the Hawaiian diet and a traditional lū'au food. Poi, usually eaten with your fingers, is named based on the number of fingers needed to eat it: three-finger, two-finger, or the thickest, one-finger poi.

Tropical Sweet Potato Crunch

TOPPING:

⅓ cup firmly packed brown
  sugar
⅓ cup chopped macadamia
  nuts

⅓ cup shredded coconut
½ cup dried cranberries
2 tablespoons butter, melted

Preheat oven to 350°; lightly grease a 6-quart baking dish. In a small bowl; combine Topping ingredients; set aside.

4 pounds sweet potatoes,
  steamed, sliced
¼ cup brown sugar
½ cup pineapple juice
½ cup crushed pineapple
1 large egg, beaten
2 tablespoons butter, melted

½ teaspoon salt
½ teaspoon cinnamon
½ teaspoon ground cumin
1½ teaspoons vanilla extract
1 (16-ounce) can whole
  cranberry sauce

In a mixing bowl; combine potatoes with remaining ingredients, except cranberry sauce. Spoon half of potatoes into prepared dish. Spoon cranberry sauce over potatoes. Top with remaining potatoes and Topping mixture. Bake 30–35 minutes. Serves 10–12.

Variation: Optional to mash potatoes.

Dd's Table Talk II

On the waterfront in historical Kailua-Kona, Hulihe'e Palace was built in 1838 as a home for High Chief Kuakini, governor of the island of Hawai'i. Hulihe'e Palace was a vacation spa for Hawaiian royalty until 1916. Today it serves as a museum, and has been restored and furnished to reflect the lifestyle of the Hawaiian royalty in the late 1800s.

Maple-Glazed Sweet Potatoes and Apples

3 pounds orange-fleshed
  sweet potatoes, peeled, cut
  crosswise into ¼-inch
  rounds
1¾ pounds tart green apples,
  peeled, halved, cored, and
  cut into ¼-inch-thick slices

¾ cup pure maple syrup
¼ cup apple cider
¼ cup (½ stick) unsalted
  butter, cut into pieces
½ teaspoon salt

Preheat oven to 375°. In 9x13-inch glass baking dish, alternate potato and apple slices in rows, packing tightly. (Stand the slices on end.)

Combine remaining ingredients in heavy medium saucepan and bring to boil over high heat. Pour hot syrup over potatoes and apples. Cover dish tightly with foil and bake 35 minutes. Uncover casserole. (Can do this up to 3 hours ahead. Let stand at room temperature, basting occasionally with pan juices.) Reduce temperature to 350°. Bake for 30 minutes until potatoes and apples are very tender. Baste occasionally. Syrup will be reduced to thick glaze. Let stand 10 minutes before serving. Serves 8.

Kailua Cooks

Perfect Baked Sweet Potatoes

4 medium sweet potatoes   Safflower oil

Preheat oven to 400°. Wash and scrub potatoes; dry thoroughly. Coat potatoes lightly with oil. Prick surface with fork. Bake until tender, about 40–60 minutes.

Note: Rubbing potatoes with oil before baking makes them so creamy, they do not need additional butter. Makes 4 servings.

Favorite Island Cookery Book V

'Ono Sweet Potatoes

An old favorite with a tropical taste.

1 (24-ounce) can sweet
   potatoes or yams, drained
3 ripe bananas
1 teaspoon cinnamon
½ teaspoon salt

Brown sugar
¼ cup macadamia nuts bits
¼ cup crushed cornflakes
¼ cup butter, melted

Preheat oven to 350°. Mash sweet potatoes and bananas with cinnamon and salt. Place in a baking dish. Top with a thin layer of brown sugar. Mix nuts and cornflakes. Spread over brown sugar. Pour melted butter over top. Bake for 45–50 minutes. Serves 4–6.

A Taste of Aloha

Sweet Potato Tempura

Sweet potatoes
1 box mochiko (about 2 cups)
1 cup flour
½ teaspoon salt

1 cup brown sugar
2½ cups water
Oil for frying

Cut sweet potatoes in shoe-string pieces. Rinse and drain in colander. Stir together mochiko, flour, salt, and brown sugar. Add water. Toss shoe-string potatoes in batter and deep-fry in hot oil. Drain on paper towels.

Favorite Recipes for Islanders

Kahoʻolawe, an uninhabited island less than 11 miles long, was taken over by the United States Navy at the beginning of World War II for use in bombing target practice. In the 1970s native Hawaiians began campaigning to regain the island from the U.S. Navy, and in 1994 the island was turned back over to the state of Hawaii. The state banned commercial activities, and efforts are underway to replant native vegetation and restore important historic sites.

Stuffed Baked Potatoes

This is an easy gourmet treat!

10 pounds large potatoes
4 cloves garlic
6 tablespoons oil, divided
3 tablespoons tamari or
  substitute, to taste, divided
4 cups sliced mushrooms
1–2 large onions, diced

4–5 tablespoons nutritional
  yeast, divided
4 cups tofu, rinsed, drained
  and mashed, divided
1 teaspoon sea salt
Paprika, for sprinkling

Bake potatoes in oven. When soft, make a slit in the top of each potato, and another crossing it. (Don't slit all the way to edges.) Push both ends towards the middle, opening the potato and loosening it from its skin. (Use a towel to protect your fingers from burning.) Allow them to cool.

In a blender or processor, blend garlic in 3 tablespoons oil and 1 tablespoon tamari. Pour into a large frying pan. Add mushrooms and sauté. When finished, drain liquid from mushrooms and put it in the food processor. Set the mushrooms aside in a large mixing bowl. In the frying pan, sauté the onions with a dash of tamari, water (enough to dissolve yeast), and 2–3 tablespoons yeast.

Using a food processor, purée half of the onion sauté with 2 cups mashed tofu, 2–3 tablespoons oil, 2 tablespoons tamari, and 2 tablespoons yeast. Add to the mushrooms in the large mixing bowl. Repeat this step. Mix in sea salt.

Scoop the potatoes out very carefully (don't hurt the shape of the skins, for stuffing purposes). Mash potatoes together with the tofu-mushroom mixture. Stuff each potato skin with this mixture. Sprinkle with paprika and bake again at 325° for 25–30 minutes. Yields 15–17 potatoes.

Incredibly Delicious

Baked Stuffed Eggplant Parmigiano

Salt
1 large eggplant, peeled and
sliced lengthwise ¼ inch
thick (put 2 slices aside)
Egg wash (one beaten egg)
½ cup flavored bread crumbs
⅛ cup garlic-flavored extra
virgin olive oil

4 tablespoons ricotta cheese
8 teaspoons Parmesan cheese
4 tablespoons mozzarella
cheese
1 cup marinara sauce

Sprinkle salt on each slice of eggplant. Place on plate and cover with another plate for 25 minutes. Squeeze and drain eggplant; pat dry. Dip slices in egg wash and bread crumbs. Sauté in oil. Set aside.

Dice remaining 2 slices eggplant and sauté in oil until well done, about 15 minutes. Set aside to cool. On each eggplant slice, place 1 tablespoon ricotta, diced eggplant, and 1 teaspoon Parmesan. Top with another slice of eggplant matched in size, and place in saucepan. Repeat process with remaining slices. Cover with marinara sauce, and to each portion add 1 teaspoon mozzarella and remainder of Parmesan cheese. Place in 350° oven until cheese melts and sauce starts to bubble.

Note: Salting and squeezing eggplant helps remove that slightly bitter taste. Always begin with this important step. Save the larger slices of eggplant for serving and the smaller end slices for the filling.

Cooking Italian in Hawaii

With 312 endangered plants and animals listed by the U.S. Fish and Wildlife Service, Hawai'i is home to the highest number of endangered species in the United States. California is second with 288.

Tomato and Eggplant

These two vegetables seem to be made for each other. Use purple eggplant and ripe tomatoes for the dish. I use a blend of spices in this recipe. In balanced portions they give a subtle spicy flavor to the vegetables. This dish goes well with lamb.

1 pound eggplant, peeled and cut into ½-inch cubes
2 teaspoons salt
2 tablespoons olive oil
1 yellow onion, peeled and thinly sliced
1 teaspoon grated ginger
1 teaspoon grated garlic

½ teaspoon cayenne pepper
¼ teaspoon turmeric
½ teaspoon ground cumin
½ teaspoon ground coriander
¾ pound tomatoes, peeled, seeded, and cut into ½-inch cubes
Salt to taste

Place eggplant in a bowl, sprinkle with salt, and set aside for 10 minutes. Wash and wipe dry. Heat olive oil in a skillet, add onion and eggplant, and sauté on high heat until eggplant is soft, about 8 minutes. Add ginger, garlic, and remaining spices. Stir to combine.

Add tomatoes; season with salt to taste. Cook for 6 minutes on low heat, shaking the skillet to keep vegetables from sticking to the bottom of the pan. Serves 4.

Burst of Flavor

Spicy Szechuan Eggplant

GARLIC SAUCE:

¼ cup soy sauce
1 tablespoon honey
1 tablespoon distilled white
  vinegar

1 tablespoon cornstarch
2 red chile peppers, minced
2 slices ginger, minced
2 cloves garlic, minced

Mix all ingredients and set aside.

Canola oil cooking spray
1½ pounds eggplant, peeled
  and cut into 3-inch strips

1 cup Chinese wood ear
  mushrooms (or shiitake
  straw, or other variety),
  soaked and sliced into strips

Spray pan with oil. Sauté eggplant over medium flame until golden brown, about 5 minutes. Combine sauce for one minute with eggplant and mushrooms. Makes 4 portions.

One portion: 148 calories; 1g fat; 5% fat; 15% protein; 79% carbohydrates; 5% fat

Eat More, Weigh Less Cookbook

Editor Gwen McKee is dwarfed by a huge banyan tree in Hawai'i.

Maui Baked Beans

2 cloves garlic
⅛ cup oil
½ tablespoon tamari or substitute
1 cup plus 1 tablespoon water, divided
4 cups seitan, sliced and cubed
4 tablespoons nutritional yeast, divided
½ cup tomato paste

¼ cup molasses
¼ cup oil
1 tablespoon vegetable bouillon
1 teaspoon garlic powder
6 cups beans, cooked (Great Northern/pinto)
½ onion, diced
⅓ cup molasses
⅓ cup tomato paste
1 tablespoon tamari
¼ tablespoon onion powder

In a blender, blend garlic with 1/8 cup oil, tamari, and 1 tablespoon water. Pour this garlic oil into a skillet and sauté cubed seitan for 5–10 minutes, adding 2 tablespoons nutritional yeast. Blend one cup water, ½ cup tomato paste, ¼ cup molasses, ¼ cup oil, remaining 2 tablespoons nutritional yeast, bouillon, and garlic powder. Add this blended mixture to a casserole dish with the beans, onion, and seitan.

Bake covered at 350° for approximately 35 minutes, or until onions are soft. Remove from oven. Blend ⅓ cup molasses, ⅓ cup tomato paste, tamari, and onion powder. Mix into casserole, leaving a lot of sauce on top. Bake for another 30–45 minutes, uncovered. Yields 1 large casserole.

Incredibly Delicious

Banyan trees *(Ficus benghalensis)* prefer areas of high humidity and moist soils. These trees put down multiple root systems. They have a main trunk, but as the branches grow, they too put down roots, and when they touch the ground, they grow deep roots themselves, supporting the branch and nourishing the main trunk. Older, mature banyan trees in Hawai'i can completely fill an acre or two of land, creating natural parks beneath their branches and between their vertical root systems.

Vegetarian Stir-Fry

1 bundle long rice
5 dried shiitake mushrooms
1 small head cauliflower,
  broken into florets
10–12 ounces tofu
3–4 tablespoons oil
1 stalk lemon grass, bulbous
  part only, minced
1 leek, white part only, sliced
1 carrot, thinly sliced

½ cup thinly sliced bamboo
  shoots
1 cup thinly sliced string beans
¼ cup water or vegetable
  broth
2 teaspoons sugar
3 tablespoons soy sauce
1 teaspoon nuoc mam (fish
  sauce)

Soak long rice in warm water for 30 minutes. Soak mushrooms in water. Blanch the cauliflower in boiling water; drain and set aside. Slice tofu into 4 pieces; heat some oil in a skillet and fry the tofu until brown. Drain on paper towels and when cool, slice into thin strips.

In the same skillet, heat some oil and stir-fry the lemon grass and leek for about 30 seconds. Add cauliflower and carrot; cook one minute. Add bamboo shoots and string beans, and stir-fry one minute. Drain long rice and cut into 3-inch lengths; drain mushrooms and slice thinly. Add the mushrooms, tofu, and long rice and stir in the water (or vegetable broth), sugar, soy sauce, and nuoc mam. Cook 1–2 minutes. Serves 4–6.

Ethnic Foods of Hawai'i

Vegetarian Loaf

1 cup finely chopped onion
1 cup finely chopped celery
1 cup finely chopped walnuts
1 cup shredded carrots
1 cup fine, dry, whole-wheat
  bread crumbs

½ teaspoon salt
½ teaspoon lemon pepper
¼ teaspoon celery seeds
2 eggs, slightly beaten
½ cup mayonnaise

Line a 8½x2½-inch loaf pan with foil; if using glass pan, grease pan instead of using foil. In a large bowl, stir together all ingredients except eggs and mayonnaise. In a small bowl, stir eggs and mayonnaise until well mixed, then fold into other ingredients. Pour into prepared pan. Bake at 350° for 50 minutes.

Note: Loaf will keep. Good to slice cold for sandwiches.

We, the Women of Hawaii Cookbook

Spam with Veggies

This recipe is for folks who like a little gravy with their stir-fried food.

1 can Spam
1 bunch broccoli
1 package bean sprouts
2 beef bouillon cubes

⅓–½ cup water
2 tablespoons cornstarch
Pepper to taste

Slice Spam and fry. Add sliced broccoli and bean sprouts and stir-fry. Dissolve beef bouillon cubes in water. Add cornstarch. Add liquid to Spam and veggies. Sprinkle with pepper. Do not overcook.

Hawai'i's Spam Cookbook

Tofu Steak with Three Colored Bell Peppers

½ cup soy sauce
½ cup mirin
1 medium-size onion, peeled and cut
½ ounce ginger, peeled and sliced
1 block firm tofu, sliced in thirds

Flour for dusting
Vegetable oil for frying
Unsalted butter for sautéing
1 pack enoki mushrooms, cleaned
1 each: red, yellow, and orange bell peppers, julienned
1 scallion, finely chopped

In an electric blender, combine soy sauce, mirin, onion, and ginger. Blend for 30 seconds until smooth, and set aside. Dust tofu with flour. In a large frying pan, heat vegetable oil and fry tofu until light brown on both sides. Remove from heat.

In frying pan, melt butter; add mushrooms and bell peppers and sauté until mushrooms wilt; set aside and keep warm. Place tofu slices on medium serving plate. Pour sauce over tofu and top with bell pepper mixture. Sprinkle with scallions. Serve immediately. Serves 2–4.

Kailua Cooks

Carved wooden idols are part of the landscape at the Pu'uhonua o Honaunau National Historical Park. The park preserves the site where, until the early 19th century, Hawaiians who broke a kapu or one of the ancient laws against the gods could avoid certain death by fleeing to this place of refuge or "pu'uhonua." After being absolved by a priest, the offender was free to leave.

Baked Tofu Loaf

This meatless loaf is some delicious!

2 (21-ounce) blocks firm tofu
  (mashed and squeezed
  to remove most of water)
1 bunch green onions, finely
  chopped
2 carrots, grated
2 (8-ounce) cans water
  chestnuts, chopped

2 ounces dried shiitake
  mushrooms (soaked and
  finely chopped)
6 eggs, beaten
1½ cups mayonnaise
Salt and pepper to taste
2 (10¾-ounce) cans cream of
  mushroom soup

Preheat oven to 350°. Combine all ingredients except the mushroom soup. Mix well. Pour into a 9x13-inch pan and bake on middle rack for 1 hour and 20 minutes or until golden brown on top.

Warm mushroom soup on stove (do not dilute) and spread evenly over the top of the loaf. Cut into pieces and enjoy.

Recipe by Fire Fighter 3 Geoff Shon
Hawai'i's Favorite Firehouse Recipes

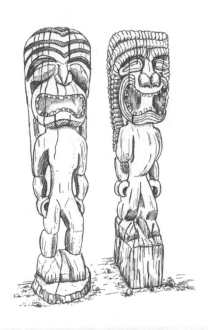

Kirk's Feta Compli

What we had to go through to get this recipe—you shouldn't know from it. So, enjoy.

CRUST:

1 stick margarine	1 egg
1¼ cups matzo meal	¾ cup finely chopped almonds
1 tablespoon sugar	or walnuts

Cut margarine into matzo meal until it is in pieces the size of peas. Add sugar. Beat egg and blend into mixture with a fork; add nuts. Form into a ball. Flatten into greased, 10-inch deep-dish pie pan, building up sides. Prick with a fork. Bake in preheated 400° oven for 7 minutes. Cool thoroughly before filling.

FILLING:

2 large bunches of spinach	½ teaspoon salt
3 tablespoons oil	¼ teaspoon pepper
1 onion, chopped	⅛ teaspoon nutmeg
1 cup grated Swiss cheese	¼ cup soft cream cheese
2 eggs	6 ounces feta cheese, grated or
1¼ cups light cream	crumbled

Wash and stem spinach; steam until wilted. Squeeze out excess water; chop. Heat oil; sauté onion until golden. Remove from heat, mix with spinach and add Swiss cheese.

In a blender or with a whisk, mix eggs, cream, and seasonings with cream cheese.

Spread spinach and onion mixture in Crust. Top with feta cheese. Pour cream cheese mixture on top, making sure it soaks through to the Crust. Bake in preheated 350° oven for 40–45 minutes. If Crust edges begin to burn, cover them with foil. Good hot or at room temperature. Serves 8.

The When You Live in Hawaii You Get Very Creative
During Passover Cookbook

Sukiyaki

6–8 shiitake mushrooms (half-dollar size), slivered

2 cups water, divided

1 medium round onion or green onions, slivered

1 teaspoon sesame oil

Pinch sea salt

¼ cup low-sodium soy sauce

2–4 tablespoons maple syrup

1½ cups bamboo shoots

1 (3-ounce) package cellophane noodles, soaked in 2 cups boiling water

2–3 carrots, sliced into matchsticks

4 cups watercress

2–3 cups mung bean sprouts

4 cups won bok cabbage

½ block tofu (about 6 ounces)

Rinse the shiitake mushrooms and soak in 1 cup of water. Save the water for sukiyaki stock.

Sauté slivered onions and slivered mushrooms in remaining 1 cup water and sesame oil. Sprinkle some sea salt to prevent sticking. Add mushroom water and season to taste with low-sodium soy sauce and maple syrup. Add bamboo shoots to mixture, bring to a boil, and simmer at a low boil. Add soaked and drained cellophane noodles to mixture. Sprinkle julienned carrots. Layer watercress, bean sprouts, won bok, and tofu. Cover and allow layers of vegetables to be steamed. Makes 6–8 portions.

One portion: 173.2 calories; 3.1g fat; 15% fat; 18% protein; 67% carbohydrates

Eat More, Weigh Less Cookbook

Holiday Stuffed Butternut Squash

2 butternut squash
2 cups cooked brown rice
1 cup chopped onions
½ cup chopped celery
½ cup chopped bell pepper
½ teaspoon dried basil
1 teaspoon dried oregano
½ teaspoon herb seasoning
½ teaspoon cumin powder

2 tablespoons tamari or
  substitute
½ teaspoon garlic powder
½ teaspoon onion powder
1 cup chopped walnuts
½ cup chopped pecans
3 tablespoons tahini
3 slices toast

Slice butternuts in half and scoop out the seeds. Bake in a pre-heated oven at 350° for 20–30 minutes, until tender. Remove from oven and let cool. Carefully scoop out insides without breaking shells. Mix squash with rice. Save shells.

Sauté vegetables, then add them to squash-rice mixture. Add seasonings, nuts, and tahini. Slice the toast into small squares like croutons and add to mix. Stuff mixture into hollowed squash shells. Bake for another 20 minutes and serve with gravy. Serves 4.

Incredibly Delicious

Zucchini Lover's Casserole

6 medium zucchini, sliced
1 medium brown onion,
  chopped
3 medium carrots, grated
2 sticks butter (or less),
  divided

1 pint sour cream
2 (10¾-ounce) cans cream of
  mushroom soup, undiluted
8 ounces herbed croutons,
  crumbled, divided

Preheat oven to 375°. Steam zucchini until tender and drain. Sauté onion and carrots in one stick of butter until soft. Mix sour cream with undiluted soup, and add zucchini, carrots, and onions. Stir in ½ of the croutons. Put into a buttered 9x13-inch baking dish. Cover with remaining croutons and dot with butter. Bake 45 minutes or until golden on top.

Shaloha Cookbook

Baked Broccoli

1–2 pounds broccoli
2 (10¾-ounce) cans cream of
  mushroom soup, divided
1 package imitation crabmeat

½ cup grated Cheddar cheese
½ cup grated Monterey Jack
  cheese
½ cup mozzarella cheese

Cut broccoli into bite-size pieces. Parboil slightly until crunchy. Layer into 9x13-inch pan the broccoli, 1 can soup, crabmeat, other can soup, then top with mixed cheeses. Bake in 325° oven until cheese melts.

Favorite Island Cookery Book IV

Gingered Carrots

2 pounds carrots
¾ stick butter
2 tablespoons finely grated,
  fresh ginger

2 tablespoons honey
Salt and pepper to taste

Peel carrots, cut in thin slices, and steam till tender. In large frying pan, melt butter, add grated ginger, and fry briefly. Stir in honey, salt and pepper to taste, then toss in the carrots just to glaze them—about 2 minutes. Serve hot. Serves 8.

Hawaii Cooks Throughout the Year

Having produced a lava flow since January 1983, Kilauea, on the island of Hawai'i, is the longest continuously erupting volcano in recorded history. The Hawaiian name "Kilauea" means "spewing" or "much spreading."

Snow Peas Kahala Style

12–14 water chestnuts, sliced
 ¼-inch thick
1 cup thinly sliced, fresh
 mushrooms
1 cup diced onion
2 tablespoons peanut oil
¾ pound fresh snow peas, or
 3 (6-ounce) packages frozen
 Chinese snow peas

1 teaspoon salt
1 tablespoon soy sauce
1 tablespoon water
½ teaspoon garlic salt

In a wok or large skillet with a tight fitting cover, sauté water chestnuts, mushrooms, and onion in peanut oil for 5 minutes or until onion is tender. Add snow peas, salt, soy sauce, and water. Mix well. Sprinkle with garlic salt. Cover tightly and simmer 5 minutes or until snow peas are tender but still crisp. Serves 4–6.

A Taste of Aloha

Pineapple Glazed Breadfruit

*Breadfruit is a nice starchy fruit that does well in most yams and sweet pota-
to recipes. I like it baked until tender and buttered, but it can be dressed fancy
for company, too.*

2 pounds breadfruit
¾ cup packed brown sugar
½ stick butter or margarine

1 (8-ounce) can pineapple
 chunks

Bake the breadfruit at 320° for about 20 minutes or until it is tender and the skin comes off easily. Remove the skin and seed. Cut it into 1-inch chunks. Mix all other ingredients in a medium to large skillet over medium heat. Stir constantly until sugar and butter have melted, and mixture is smooth and coats pineapple chunks well. Add breadfruit chunks, folding them in gently until they are hot all the way through. Serve hot.

Kau Kau Kitchen

Rice, Pasta, Etc.

PHOTO BY JIM STEINHART / WWW.PLANETWARE.COM

Years of the sea eroding away at lava rock created the unique Holei Sea Arch in Volcanoes National Park on the big island of Hawai'i.

Vietnamese-Style Fried Rice

1 large egg plus 1 large
  egg white, beaten
1 tablespoon vegetable oil,
  divided
3 cloves garlic, chopped
½ cup chopped green
  onions, white parts only
1 medium onion, chopped
½ large, red bell pepper,
  seeded, finely chopped
1 large carrot, peeled, grated
1 Thai bird chile pepper,
  sliced

Pinch red pepper flakes
2 tablespoons soy sauce
1 tablespoon patis (fish sauce)
1 tablespoon rice wine vinegar
1 tablespoon Thai chili garlic
  paste
4 cups cooked jasmine rice (air
  dried or refrigerated)
1½ cups bean sprouts
¼ cup chopped green onions,
  green parts only
¼ cup chopped cilantro
¼ cup chopped peanuts

In a wok over medium heat, scramble eggs in a teaspoon of oil. Remove from wok; reserve. Into wok, stir-fry garlic, onions, bell pepper, carrot, and chile pepper in remaining oil. Add pepper flakes, soy sauce, patis, vinegar, and chili garlic paste. Add rice and eggs; heat through. Remove from heat. Stir in bean sprouts, green onions, cilantro, and peanuts. Serves 3.

Variation: Add ground pork or fishcake (used as substitute for crab, scallops, etc.). Substitute scrambled soft tofu for eggs.

Dd's Table Talk II

Rice Ramen Curry

1 pot cooked brown rice
1 package low-fat ramen
 noodles
1 tablespoon curry powder

1 cup chopped Chinese
 parsley
½ cup raisins

While rice is cooking, break up the ramen noodles while still in package with the heel of the hand until there are no large chunks. Open package, remove spice package, and mix crushed noodles with the cooked brown rice. (The heat of the rice cooks the noodles.) Add the spice packet, curry powder, parsley, and raisins. Ready to serve hot or cold.

A Race for Life

Spicy Fried Rice

This is not a recipe to be forgotten; taste it once and you'll make it again and again. Cook the rice for this dish in advance; it fries best when it's had a chance to cool.

3 tablespoons mild oil, such
 as canola
2 cups finely chopped onions
¾ teaspoon salt
1 tablespoon ume plum
 vinegar
1 tablespoon soy sauce
1–2 teaspoons Tabasco sauce

6 tablespoons tomato paste
Scant ½ cup chopped scallions
¾ cup finely chopped Chinese
 parsley, divided
4 cups cooked rice
1 ripe tomato, cut in wedges,
 for garnish

Heat oil in a wok or large frying pan. When it's hot, add onions and cook until transparent. Combine salt, vinegar, soy sauce, Tabasco, tomato paste, scallions, and ½ cup of the Chinese parsley; set aside.

Add rice to wok; stir-fry 3 minutes. Add tomato paste mixture and stir-fry 5 minutes on high heat. Turn the rice onto a serving platter. Garnish with the remaining Chinese parsley and tomato wedges. Serve immediately. Yields 4–5 servings.

Vegetarian Nights

Yaeko's Fried Rice

SEASONING SAUCE:

3 tablespoons lite soy sauce
2 tablespoons aji-mirin
  (sweet cooking rice wine—
  Kikkoman)
1 clove garlic, minced
½ teaspoon grated fresh
  gingerroot
1 tablespoon sesame oil
2 tablespoons water

Mix all ingredients in bowl ahead of time. It can be left out until all other food preparation is done and it is ready to be added to the Rice.

RICE:

4 cups cooked Japanese rice
  (Calrose or Hinode brand
  works well)
2 tablespoons vegetable oil
¼ cup uncooked, finely diced
  zucchini
½ cup frozen peas and
  carrots mix, thawed
2 eggs, scrambled and broken
  into smaller pieces
1 cup diced, cooked, leftover
  meat (chicken, pork, ham,
  Spam)
1 teaspoon garlic salt
Salt and pepper to taste
1 tablespoon toasted sesame
  seeds
¼ cup finely chopped green
  onions

Heat wok or very large cooking pot with oil, over medium-high heat; when pot is hot, turn heat down to medium. (Don't wait until oil is smoking, as the pot will be too hot, and the rice will stick and burn.) With greased hands, break up the rice before adding to the pot. This will allow for easier stirring and distribution of other ingredients. Stir rice until evenly coated in oil and warmed through. Add zucchini, peas, and carrots. Stir throughout. Add cooked eggs, and stir, scraping bottom of pot to make sure rice is not sticking too much; if so, add a little more oil and turn heat down slightly. Stir for about 2 minutes, then add cooked meat; stir until distributed. Flavor with garlic salt, salt and pepper. Sprinkle sesame seeds in, then slowly pour the Seasoning Sauce throughout the rice (the rice should only be tan in color; if it is turning brown there is too much sauce). Throw in the green onions last and toss for about 2–3 minutes; take off the burner, and serve.

Seasoned with Aloha Vol. 2

Fried Rice

3 strips bacon, chopped
1½ cups diced ham, leftover
  beef, hot dogs or other meat
3 cups cooked rice (leftover
  cold rice is fine)

1 egg
1 tablespoon shoyu
3 stalks green onions, minced

Cook bacon in skillet until it is crisp. Drain most of the fat. Add diced meat of your choice to the pan and cook for 2 minutes. Turn heat to low and add rice. Place egg and shoyu in a small bowl or cup and mix with a fork. Add it to the meat and rice. Add minced onions last. Continue to cook for 2–3 minutes or until slightly set. Serves 4.

Aunty Pua's Keiki Cookbook

Spam Fried Rice

Good with fried eggs.

1½ cups diced Spam
Leftover rice, about 4 cups
  (cooked)

1 egg
1 tablespoon shoyu
3 stalks green onions, chopped

Fry Spam in a bit of oil in a skillet. Turn heat to low and add rice. Mix egg with shoyu and add to the rice and Spam. Add chopped green onions just before serving.

Hawai'i's Spam Cookbook

Hawaiians consume some 4.3 million cans of Spam a year. Spam was introduced to the islands during World War II when military personnel brought it with them from the mainland.

Cheese and Rice Soufflé

1½ cups white sauce
Salt and paprika to taste
1¼ cups grated Cheddar
  cheese

1½ cups cooked rice
2 eggs, separated
⅛ teaspoon baking powder

Season white sauce highly with salt and paprika. Add cheese and heat slowly until cheese is melted. Add rice and beaten egg yolks. Cool slightly. Fold in stiffly beaten egg whites. Add baking powder. Pour into well-buttered soufflé pan set in pan of hot water. Bake in preheated 350° oven for 30 minutes.

We, the Women of Hawaii Cookbook

Citrus-Flavored Herbed Rice

This lemony rice does well with fish or poultry dishes. The only spice used is turmeric, and just enough of it to give a yellow blush to the rice. The herbs add a refreshing note to this citrus-flavored rice.

1½ cups long-grain white
rice
2 tablespoons unsalted butter
⅛ teaspoon turmeric
2 cups water
Coarse zest and juice of
  ½ lemon

Coarse zest and juice of ½
  orange
Salt to taste
¼ cup chopped green onions
½ cup chopped Chinese
  parsley
¼ cup chopped garden mint

Wash and drain rice. Heat butter in a saucepan on low heat, stir in turmeric, and add rice, 2 cups water, lemon and orange zest and juice with salt to taste. Bring to a fast boil. Stir once, cover with tight-fitting lid, turn down heat to very low, and cook for 25 minutes. Add the chopped green onions, Chinese parsley, and mint. Turn off heat and leave unopened for 10 minutes.

Remove and discard lemon and orange zest. Fluff with a fork and serve hot. Makes 6–8 servings.

Burst of Flavor

Macadamia-Pineapple Rice Pilaf

1 tablespoon unsalted butter
1½ cups long-grain white rice
2 teaspoons minced garlic
1 medium white onion, diced
¼ red bell pepper, seeded
  and diced
¼ yellow bell pepper, seeded
  and diced
3 cups strong chicken stock

½ cup golden raisins
½ cup chopped macadamia
  nuts
1 fresh sage leaf
Salt to taste
⅓ cup chopped fresh cilantro
1 cup diced pineapple, reserve
  juice

Preheat oven to 375°. In a flame-proof casserole, melt butter on medium-high heat and add rice. Stir for a few seconds until rice is coated, but not long enough to let rice change color. Add garlic, onion, and red and yellow bell peppers, and cook for a few more seconds. Add chicken stock and bring mixture to a gentle boil. Add raisins, nuts, sage, and salt. Cover and place in oven and bake for 30 minutes. Remove dish from oven and let it rest (without uncovering) for another 10 minutes. Add the cilantro and pineapple bits. Season if necessary and serve at once.

Note: May mix chicken stock and syrup from pineapple to make up the 3 cups of liquid needed. If using salted macadamia nuts, remember to adjust seasonings.

Tropical Taste

Green Rice

1 cup cooked rice
1½ cups grated sharp cheese
1 cup milk
1 egg, slightly beaten
½ medium onion, chopped

½ teaspoon salt
1 (10-ounce) box frozen
  spinach, thawed and
  well drained
¼ cup butter, melted

Preheat oven to 350°. Combine ingredients and pour into greased 1½-quart casserole dish. Cover. Bake 40 minutes. Serves 4.

Kailua Cooks

Pasta Perfecta

Right now, this is my favorite recipe in the (Vegetarian Nights) book. I just ate it for lunch. As you scan the ingredients, you'll notice some expensive ones—dried tomatoes, pine nuts, basil, fresh Parmesan cheese. But the amounts are small, and the flavor rewards are immense. I'd be completely satisfied to receive this dish in the finest Italian restaurant—in fact, I'd go especially for it! Compared to restaurant prices, making this at home is a real bargain. And it's ready in 20 minutes.

2 teaspoons salt
½ pound linguine
3 tablespoons extra virgin
olive oil, divided
5 cloves garlic, pressed
½ cup boiling water
7 dried tomato halves

2 tablespoons Chinese black
beans
½ cup chopped basil leaves
1 tablespoon water
3 tablespoons pine nuts
2–4 tablespoons freshly grated
Parmesan cheese

Bring a large pot of water to a boil and add salt; add linguine. While you're waiting for water to boil, heat 2 tablespoons oil in skillet. Add garlic and cook over very low heat. When linguine water returns to a boil, set timer for 12 minutes.

Pour ½ cup boiling water over tomato halves in small bowl. Rinse and mince Chinese black beans, and add them to garlic in skillet. Let simmer while you chop basil.

When tomatoes have softened, add their soaking water to skillet. Chop tomatoes, and add them when water in skillet boils. Increase heat to medium and simmer 5 minutes. Add basil, and 1 tablespoon each water and oil. When it boils, reduce heat and add pine nuts.

By now, the pasta should be done. Drain thoroughly, shaking the colander until all water is gone. Place pasta on individual plates and top with the sauce and Parmesan cheese. (It won't look like enough sauce, but it is. The flavor is strong.) Yields 2 lunch servings, or 4 first-course servings.

Vegetarian Nights

Peking Pasta

1 onion, chopped
4 cloves garlic, chopped
1 tablespoon butter
3 tablespoons peanut oil
¾ pound ground pork
1 teaspoon sugar
1½ tablespoons soy sauce
1 tablespoon hoisin sauce
1 tablespoon red miso paste
2 tablespoons dry sherry
2 tablespoons water
1 pound spaghetti, cooked
    according to package
    directions
Julienne cucumbers, green
    onions, and bean sprouts for
    garnish

In a large skillet over medium-high heat, sauté onion and garlic in butter and oil. Add pork and stir-fry for 3 minutes. Add remaining ingredients except spaghetti; simmer for 5 minutes. Serve over spaghetti with garnishes. Serves 6–8.

Dd's Table Talk

Quick and Simple Spaghetti with Clam Sauce

1 clove garlic, minced
1 medium onion, chopped
Olive oil
2 (8-ounce) cans diced
    tomatoes
2 small cans chopped clams
    (reserve juice of one can)
1 (8-ounce) can tomato sauce
1 (6-ounce) can tomato paste
1 level teaspoon parsley flakes
⅛ teaspoon oregano
1 teaspoon basil
1 teaspoon sugar
Salt and pepper to taste
1 cup red wine
Pasta of your choice, cooked

Sauté garlic and onion in olive oil. Add diced tomatoes and bring to a boil. Add clams with liquid from one can only. Add tomato sauce and stir in tomato paste to thicken. Add seasonings and wine; bring to a boil and simmer for 20 minutes. Pour over pasta and serve with French bread and wine.

Recipe by HFD Chief Attilio K. Leonardi
Hawai'i's Favorite Firehouse Recipes

Thai Chicken Angel Hair

2 boneless, skinless chicken
  breasts, cut in strips
Salt and freshly ground
  black pepper
Flour for dredging
1 tablespoon plus ¼ cup
  peanut oil, divided
¼ cup sesame seed oil
3 tablespoons Thai fried garlic,
  or 3 cloves garlic, chopped
1 small Hawaiian chili pepper,
  seeded and chopped

2 tablespoons mirin sake
8 ounces angel hair pasta,
  cooked according to package
  directions
1 tablespoon fish sauce
1 tablespoon pickled ginger
3 tablespoons each: chopped
  fresh basil, mint leaves, and
  cilantro
3 tablespoons chopped, toasted
  peanuts
Juice and zest of 1 grated lime

Lightly season chicken with salt and pepper; dredge in flour. In a small skillet over medium-high heat, brown chicken in one tablespoon of peanut oil. Drain on paper towels and set aside.

In a small saucepan, heat remaining oils, garlic, chili pepper, and mirin sake. Combine cooked pasta, chicken, oil mixture, and remaining ingredients. Season to taste. Serves 4.

Dd's Table Talk

Chicken Linguine

1 pound fresh chicken,
  julienned
4 tablespoons garlic-flavored,
  extra virgin olive oil
1 carrot, peeled and julienned
1 each: red and green bell
  pepper, seeded and julienned
½ pound sliced mushrooms

½ zucchin, julienned
  (leave skin on)
Kosher salt
Freshly ground black pepper
1 tablespoon dried basil
1 pound linguine
2 teaspoons Romano cheese

Sauté chicken 5–10 minutes in olive oil. Add carrot and sauté 4–5 minutes. Add bell peppers, mushrooms, and zucchini. Sprinkle with salt, pepper, and basil. Cook linguine in 2 quarts boiling water. Toss cooked linguine in pan with chicken and vegetables. Sprinkle with Romano cheese and serve immediately.

Cooking Italian in Hawaii

Salmon-Spinach Ravioli with Lemon Cream Sauce

2 cups chopped fresh spinach
1 (6-ounce) can salmon,
  cleaned and drained
4 ounces cream cheese,
  softened
32 won ton wrappers
½ cup whipping cream

⅓ cup sour cream
1 teaspoon lemon juice
⅛ teaspoon salt
⅛ teaspoon white pepper
1 tablespoon snipped fresh
  basil, or 1 teaspoon dried
Spinach leaves for serving

Mix spinach, salmon, and cream cheese. On 16 of the won ton wrappers, spread 1 tablespoon filling. Wet edges, top with second wrapper and press firmly.

In small saucepan, heat whipping cream over medium heat. Simmer uncovered for 5–6 minutes, until liquid is reduced by ½, stirring occasionally. Add sour cream. Heat thoroughly, but do not boil. Remove from heat and stir in lemon juice, salt, and white pepper.

Simmer ravioli in sauce 2–3 minutes. Do not boil or simmer too long, or they will fall apart. Put on individual plates lined with spinach leaves. Put sauce on top. Garnish with basil. Serves 6 (makes 16 ravioli).

Seasoned with Aloha Vol. 2

Seafood Pesto Pasta

1 pound shrimp
1½ pounds salmon
1 bunch fresh Thai basil
   (1 cup smashed down)
1 bulb fresh garlic
¾ cup olive oil
1 teaspoon Hawaiian salt
8 ounces shredded Parmesan
   cheese, divided

4 carrots (peeled and sliced)
2 big crown broccoli heads (cut
   into little heads)
1 onion, sliced
16 ounces dry pasta (your
   choice)
Garlic and ground black
   pepper to taste

Peel and devein shrimp. Take skin off salmon and cut into 1-inch cubes; set both aside.

In blender, coarsely chop basil, garlic, olive oil, and salt. Quickly mix in 6 ounces of cheese (reserve rest for garnish). Set pesto aside in a jar with room to spare.

Boil water in large pot. Blanche carrots and broccoli for 3 minutes; take veggies out and set aside in large bowl. Add pasta and cook al dente. Save ½ coffee cup of pasta/veggie water. Drain pasta and add into bowl with veggies. In sauté pan, lightly sauté onion, shrimp, and salmon in olive oil with a little garlic and pepper.

Add seafood mixture to pasta and veggie bowl. Add the saved hot water to pesto and mix. Then toss pesto with everything.

Serve pasta with side salad and garlic bread. Garnish with Parmesan cheese. Serves about 6–8 firefighters.

Recipe by Fire Fighter 3 Ricci Naone
Hawai'i's Favorite Firehouse Recipes

Honolulu International Airport is home to the first runway built completely offshore. The "reef runway," a runway built on an artificial island created on the fringing reef of O'ahu's southern (Kona) coast, was completed in October 1977. It is also used as an alternate landing sight for space shuttles.

Green Chile Pesto

I first tasted Green Chile Pesto on a fabulous veggie burger at Maui Coffee Roasters in Kahului. Owner Nick Matichyn uses macadamia nuts in his pesto; I've substituted pine nuts because they're more widely available. The concept of chiles in pesto was totally foreign to me until the moment it kissed my lips. What a taste!

7 ounces (about 1 cup) canned green chiles, chopped
2 cloves garlic
½ cup pine nuts (or chopped macadamia nuts)
1 cup Chinese parsley or basil leaves, packed into measuring cup
¼ cup extra virgin olive oil
1 teaspoon salt

Blenderize everything using the pulse feature on the blender. Don't aim for a totally smooth paste; it's good to retain some of the texture of the nuts.

This pesto is great on sandwiches and as a topping for pasta, steamed vegetables, grains, and baked potatoes. Yields 3–4 servings (more than 1½ cups, or enough to top 8 ounces of pasta).

Vegetarian Nights

Broccoli Pesto

We use this as a dressing for pasta salad; it is also great tossed with hot pasta!

4 cups broccoli
1 cup chicken stock, divided
4 cloves garlic
1 cup tightly packed basil
¼ cup almonds
¼ cup Parmesan cheese
⅛ teaspoon salt

Steam broccoli. Add 6 tablespoons stock to broccoli. In food processor, add garlic, basil, and almonds, and process until finely chopped. Add 2 tablespoons stock, then add broccoli, Parmesan, salt, and remaining liquid. Process until very smooth, scraping the sides frequently. Makes 2½ cups.

Friends and Celebrities Cookbook II

Super Macaroni and Cheese

Little kids love this dish.

1 (7-ounce) box macaroni and cheese dinner
3 tablespoons butter
2 cloves garlic, minced
1 cup sliced mushrooms

½ can Spam luncheon meat, cubed
Grated Cheddar cheese (optional)

Prepare macaroni and cheese according to directions on box. Melt butter in skillet. Add garlic, mushrooms, and cubed Spam, and cook until mushrooms are soft (if using fresh ones). Add mushrooms and Spam to prepared macaroni and cheese. Place in casserole dish and sprinkle top with additional grated cheese, if desired. Bake for 25–30 minutes in 350° oven. Serves 3–4.

Hawai'i's 2nd Spam Cookbook

A tsunami is a series of waves traveling across the ocean with extremely long wavelengths of up to hundreds of miles between wave crests. Often a tsunami is incorrectly referred to as a tidal wave. Tidal waves are associated with the rise and fall of the tides produced by the gravitational attraction of the sun and moon. Tsunamis are usually the result of a sudden rise or fall of a section of the earth's crust under or near the ocean.

This century, thirteen significant tsunamis have impacted Hawai'i. The most destructive took place on April 1, 1946, resulting in 159 deaths. That morning an earthquake with a reported magnitude of 7.1 occurred in the Aleutian Islands off of Alaska. Almost five hours later, the largest and most destructive tsunami waves in reported history struck the Hawaiian Islands. Maximum runups were reported to be 54 feet in Moloka'i, and 55 feet in Pololu Valley on the Big Island. Waves in some areas penetrated more than half a mile inland. Between wave crests, the drawdown is reported to have exposed some areas of the seafloor 500 feet in the seaward direction.

Meats

PHOTO BY GWEN McKEE

Within hours during the attack on Pearl Harbor, 2,390 service men and women lost their lives; 1,177 of these casualties were from the battleship U.S.S. Arizona. Completed in 1961, the 184-foot-long U.S.S. Arizona Memorial was built over the remains of the sunken battleship.

Okinawan Pot Roast Pork

1 (4- to 5-pound) lean pork butt

SAUCE:

2 cups soy sauce ½ cup mirin
½ cup water 1 (1-inch) piece ginger, crushed
2½ cups sugar 1–2 cloves garlic, crushed

Combine Sauce ingredients in a large saucepan; mix well and
marinate pork overnight in the refrigerator.

Cover and cook over high heat until Sauce comes to a boil.
Lower heat and continue cooking, turning meat over occasion-
ally for 3–4 hours, or until meat is tender. Make and add more
Sauce, if necessary. Serves 6–8.

West Kauai's Plantation Heritage

Oven Kalua Pig

2 tablespoons Hawaiian salt 1 (½-inch) slice ginger,
¼ cup soy sauce   crushed
1 teaspoon Worcestershire 1 tablespoon liquid smoke
   sauce 1 (4- to 5-pound) pork butt
2 cloves garlic, crushed Ti or banana leaves

Mix together salt, soy sauce, Worcestershire sauce, garlic, ginger, and liquid smoke. Place pork on several ti or banana leaves.
Rub with seasonings and let stand one hour. Fold leaves over to
wrap the pork. Wrap the leaf-enclosed pork in foil. Place in a
baking pan and bake in a 325° oven for 4–5 hours. Unwrap
pork, cool, and shred meat. Serves 8–10.

Ethnic Foods of Hawai'i

Kalua pig is a popular dish in Hawai'i, often served at lū'aus. "Kalua"
means "the pit" in Hawaiian and refers to the method the pig is cooked—
in an underground earthen oven called an imu.

Four Peppercorn Pork Roast

1 (4½-pound) boneless pork
  loin, tied
Salt to taste
3 tablespoons unsalted butter,
  softened
¼ cup plus 2 tablespoons
  flour, divided

¼ cup mixed peppercorns,
  very coarsely crushed
1¾ cups chicken broth
1 cup water
2 tablespoons red wine vinegar
Fresh rosemary for garnish

Preheat oven to 475°. Season roast with salt. Combine butter
and 2 tablespoons of flour to make a paste. Spread the top of
the roast with the paste. Lightly press peppercorns into butter
paste. Place pork on a rack in a roasting pan. Roast at 475° for
30 minutes. Reduce heat to 325° and continue roasting for
1½–1⅔ hours, or until meat thermometer registers 155°.

Transfer roast to cutting board and let stand for 10 minutes.
Prepare sauce while roast is standing. Pour all but ¼ cup of fat
from roasting pan. Whisk in ¼ cup flour and cook over mod-
erate heat for 3 minutes, stirring constantly. Slowly stir in the
chicken broth and water. Bring to a boil. Stir in red wine vinegar and salt to taste. Simmer sauce until thickened to desired
consistency. Remove string from the roast and cut into ½-inch
slices. Arrange on platter with sauce and garnish with fresh
rosemary. Serves 8–10.

Another Taste of Aloha

Char Siu

2 pork butts, sliced in 1- or
 1½-inch thick pieces
½ cup shoyu
1 cup sugar (½ white and
 ½ brown)

2 tablespoons hoisin sauce
1 teaspoon red food coloring
 (Chinese type)
1½ teaspoons salt
¼ teaspoon ajinomoto

Boil pork butt pieces until tender or until cooked. Mix remaining ingredients and soak pork in sauce overnight.

Bake for one hour at 300°. Put pan of water in oven while baking; this keeps the pork juicy and moist.

Favorite Island Cookery Book I

Spicy Garlic Eggplant and Pork

1 teaspoon minced gingerroot
1 tablespoon minced garlic
3 tablespoons soy sauce
2 teaspoons sugar
2 teaspoons white vinegar
1 teaspoon minced fresh
 red chile pepper, or ¼
 teaspoon dried flakes

2 teaspoons cornstarch
1 (1-pound) eggplant, peeled
1 cup oil
1 cup thin strips of pork

Mix together ginger, garlic, soy sauce, sugar, vinegar, chile pepper, and cornstarch. Set aside. Slice eggplant into 1-inch strips. Heat oil and fry eggplant until brown, but not burned. Remove from pan and lightly press between paper towels to extract excess oil. Fry pork about 1 or 2 minutes, until cooked. Remove from pan and discard oil. Heat sauce until near boiling. Add pork and eggplant. Mix together until heated. Serves 4.

West Kauai's Plantation Heritage

The largest contiguous ranch in the United States is the 480,000-acre Parker Ranch on the island of Hawai'i.

Sweet and Pungent Pork

1 pound spareribs (in long pieces)	½ cup sugar
	1 teaspoon flour
Bean or wheat flour	Wine glass of sherry
1 tablespoon vinegar	Wine glass of shoyu
Pinch of ginger	1 cup water

Wash spareribs and dry them with a cloth; dip into bean or wheat flour. Fry in deep fat; drain. Place in shallow baking pan and add remaining ingredients. Bake at 350° with lid off until they candy, 45 minutes to one hour.

We, the Women of Hawaii Cookbook

Easy Local Ribs

Oven braise is a local favorite—sweet and sour spareribs packed with pineapple.

3 pounds meaty, country-style, pork spareribs, cut in pieces	Dash pepper
	Pineapple chunks
3 tablespoons soy sauce	Green onions, chopped
1 teaspoon salt	

Rub spareribs all over with soy sauce, salt, and pepper. Place ribs, meat-side-up in a foil-lined shallow baking or roasting pan, and cover with foil or baking-pan lid. Bake 20–25 minutes at 450°. Drain off fat. Makes 4 servings.

SAUCE:

1 cup syrup-packed pineapple chunks, drained	⅓ cup vinegar
	2 tablespoons soy sauce
½ cup packed brown sugar	2 teaspoons grated fresh ginger
⅓ cup ketchup	2 cloves garlic, minced

Combine Sauce ingredients; pour over ribs. Bake at 350° for 1 hour or until tender, basting occasionally. Garnish with pineapple chunks and green onions.

Sam Choy's Sampler

Korean Ribs

¾ cup shoyu
2 tablespoons water
4 tablespoons sherry
½ teaspoon sesame oil
3 tablespoons brown sugar
2 teaspoons minced garlic

¼ teaspoon ginger
2 tablespoons minced green
  onion
1 tablespoon sesame seeds
3 pounds short ribs

Combine all ingredients except short ribs, mixing well. Add ribs to marinade and allow to marinate for several hours. Broil ribs, basting frequently.

Tailgate Party Cookbook

Barbecued Shortribs

5 pounds meaty shortribs,
  cut in 2-inch pieces
Salt and pepper to taste
Flour
2 medium onions, sliced
2 teaspoons vinegar
2 tablespoons Worcestershire
  sauce

1 tablespoon salt
1 teaspoon paprika
1 teaspoon chili powder
¾ cup tomato catsup
½ teaspoon cayenne pepper
½ teaspoon black pepper
  (optional)
¾ cup water

Sprinkle shortribs with salt and pepper to taste; dredge in flour. Place in a roaster and cover with onions. Combine remaining ingredients; mix well and pour over shortribs. Cover and bake at 350° for 3 hours, basting occasionally, and turning meat over once or twice during baking. Remove cover during last 15 minutes of baking. Serves 6–8.

Note: This can be cooked a day or two ahead and refrigerated. Remove and discard solidified grease before reheating to serve.

The Tastes and Tales of Moiliili

Laulau

2 pounds stew meat (pork,
  beef, chicken, or
  combination)
2 pounds pork belly
½ cup Hawaiian salt (or
  rock salt)

Several large ti leaves
1 bunch taro leaves, or fresh
  leaf spinach
String for tying bundles

Cut meat and pork belly into chunks, then mix in salt. Clean ti leaves and trim off back ribs so they'll be flexible. Wrap a piece of pork belly and a piece of meat (or chicken) in 3 or 4 taro or spinach leaves. Cross 2 ti leaves at right angles. Roll up meat and taro leaves one way in first ti leaf, then crossways with the other, and tie bundle tightly. Put in steamer and steam 4–5 hours.

Note: Heavy aluminum foil may be substituted for ti leaves, but the flavor won't be quite the same.

West Kauai's Plantation Heritage

In Volcanoes National Park on the Big Island, hiking trails take you where molten lava has destroyed most everything in its path. In time, little specks of green began to spring forth, beginning life's cycle once again. Though walking through this barren area is desolate and a little eerie, it has a special beauty all its own.

Polynesian Style Brisket

Polynesian flavors seem to blend perfectly in this brisket recipe. This is a wonderful dinner for company, as it cooks without any fuss in the oven. It may even be made a day ahead. This method of cooking with a foil cover keeps all the flavorful juices captured inside the pan. Just be sure to carefully tuck the foil around the pan so you retain a sealed cover without any breaks. You might want to double the recipe and have an extra brisket for a picnic. It is also marvelous cold.

1 (4- to 5-pound) beef brisket
1 cup soy sauce
½ cup dry sherry
½ cup brown sugar
1 cup orange, lemon, or
  pineapple juice
2 cloves garlic, peeled and
  minced

Salt and pepper to taste
2 tablespoons freshly grated
  ginger (or 1 tablespoon
  dried)
1 cup fresh or canned
  pineapple, diced (for garnish)

Place brisket in a bowl or shallow pan. Mix together remaining ingredients, except garnish, and pour over the brisket. Make sure all parts of the meat are covered. Refrigerate at least 4 hours, or preferably overnight.

Place brisket in a baking pan with marinade. Cover tightly with a double layer of foil. Bake at 325° for 3½ hours. Check during baking to make sure there is enough liquid; if not, add extra soy sauce or fruit juice, being sure to replace the foil tightly.

To serve, remove meat from juices. Slice and serve with warmed pan juices and pineapple on top. This will serve 4–5. In Honolulu, rice is usually served with the brisket.

Honolulu Hawaii Cooking

Covering half the Big Island of Hawai'i, Mauna Loa is the largest active volcano on the earth, with an elevation of 13,680 feet above sea level and a summit about 56,000 feet above its ocean floor base. With its most recent eruption in 1984, Mauna Loa is also among the earth's most active volcanoes, having erupted 33 times since its first well-documented eruption in 1843. The Hawaiian name "Mauna Loa" means "long mountain."

Marinated Beef Slices

1 pound lean sirloin beef, well
  trimmed and thinly sliced
½ cup lemon juice
2 tablespoons oil
1 cup fresh, thinly sliced
  mushrooms

½ cup chopped green onions
½ cup thinly sliced green
  pepper
¼ teaspoon pepper

Marinate beef in lemon juice for 10 minutes. While beef is marinating, heat oil in large skillet and add mushrooms, onions, and
green pepper. Cook until tender. Remove from skillet and keep
warm. Drain meat, reserving lemon juice. Place meat in skillet
and brown. Return vegetables to skillet; add lemon juice and
pepper. Heat through. Yields 4 servings.

Favorite Recipes for Islanders

Easy Beef Stroganoff

1½ pounds top sirloin, cubed
½–1 pound mushrooms,
  sliced
1 large onion, diced
2 tablespoons oil
1 (10½-ounce) can beef
  consommé

2 tablespoons flour
1 cup sour cream
Salt and pepper to taste
1 (8-ounce) package egg
  noodles, cooked

Sauté cubed beef, mushrooms, and onion in oil until soft and
the meat is browned. Add consommé and simmer for 20 minutes. Mix flour with sour cream. Add to beef mixture. Heat,
but do not boil, until thickened. Add salt and pepper to taste.
Serve over egg noodles. Yields 4 servings.

Seasoned with Aloha Vol. 2

Butter Yaki

Butter or margarine
Sukiyaki beef or any good
   steak, sliced thin
Chicken, sliced thin
Onions, sliced thin

Won bok (Chinese
   cabbage), sliced
Bean sprouts
Watercress, chopped

Heat butter and stir-fry meats quickly, just until done. Arrange meat on large serving platter and keep warm. Add more butter and stir-fry vegetables, one type at a time; place on platter. Serve with dipping sauce.

BUTTER YAKI DIPPING SAUCE:

1 cup soy sauce
½ cup sugar
⅓ teaspoon minced garlic

¼ cup lime juice
¾ cup grated daikon or turnips

In a saucepan, combine all ingredients except daikon and heat. Pour sauce in 4 individual dipping bowls; add daikon to taste. Can be increased for more servings.

Island Flavors

Creamed Corned Beef

1 can cream soup (such as
  cream of mushroom)
½ can milk
Dash of pepper
1 can corned beef, chopped

1 cup frozen vegetables (such
  as peas and carrots or mixed
  vegetables)
Hot cooked rice

Heat soup, milk, and pepper. Add corned beef and vegetables.
Serve on top of hot rice.

Hawai'i's Spam Cookbook

Marinated Beef for 10 or More

A party pleaser.

1 (5-pound) rump roast (long cut,
  not triangle cut)

Start recipe 24 hours before serving. Cook rump roast at 325° for
4 hours for medium well, less for rare. Cool and slice thinly.

SAUCE:

¼ cup vinegar
1½ cups water
½ cup sugar
4 teaspoons prepared mustard
½ cup catsup
¼ teaspoon cayenne pepper
¼ teaspoon black pepper

1 teaspoon salt
3 teaspoons Worcestershire
  sauce
¼ cup red wine (optional)
¼ cup light soy sauce
2 medium Maui onions, sliced
2 slices lemon (very important)

Mix all Sauce ingredients. Place meat slices in a large pan, over-
lapping diagonally. Pour marinade over meat, making sure
Sauce gets between slices. Cover and refrigerate for 24 hours.
Bake at 325° for 1 hour under aluminum tent.

Cook 'em Up Kaua'i

Hawaiian Teriyaki Burger

This is definitely a local favorite.

1½ pounds ground beef	2 cloves garlic, minced
1 small onion, chopped	½ teaspoon minced fresh
1 egg	ginger
¼ cup shoyu	2 stalks green onions, chopped
¼ cup sugar	1 tablespoon sesame oil

Combine all ingredients; mix well. Form into patties. Fry, grill, or broil.

Hawai'i's Best Local Dishes

Stuffed Aburage

½ pound ground beef or chicken	½ onion, finely chopped
½ pound ground pork	1 tablespoon cornstarch
1 egg	1 teaspoon salt
2 stalks green onions, finely chopped	1 teaspoon shoyu
	2 packages aburage wrappers

Mix all ingredients in bowl. Stuff aburage wrappers with mixture and cook in Sauce for 1½ hours. (Be careful it does not burn.)

SAUCE:

1 cup beef broth	3 tablespoons sugar
2 tablespoons sake or wine	¼ cup shoyu

Combine ingredients in saucepan large enough to handle stuffed aburage.

Classic Cookbook Recipes

Lazy Loco Moco

1 tablespoon oil
1 pound ground beef
1 clove garlic, minced
3 tablespoons shoyu
2 stalks green onions, chopped

1 cup hot water
2 tablespoons cornstarch
2 tablespoons cold water
4 eggs
3 cups hot cooked rice

In a large skillet, heat oil and brown beef with the garlic. Add shoyu, green onions, and hot water. Let mixture come to a boil and cook 2–3 minutes. Mix cornstarch with cold water and add to the beef mixture. Cook until sauce thickens. Reduce heat to simmer.

Using a large spoon, make 4 holes in the beef mixture and break an egg into each hole. Cover and cook until eggs are cooked the way you like them. Serve the beef-egg mixture over hot rice. Serves 4.

Aunty Pua's Keiki Cookbook

Loco moco is Hawai'i's original homemade fast food and can be found at just about any fast food restaurant, roadside diner, or lunch wagon. Legend has it the dish was created in Hilo on the island of Hawai'i in 1949 by the owners of the Lincoln Grill, Mr. and Mrs. Inouye. Their goal was to create a fast, easy dish for hungry teenaged customers. So they took a bowl, spooned in two scoops of rice, a hamburger, and a fried egg, and then topped it with brown gravy. Today, the loco moco basics are two scoops of rice, a big burger or two regulars, an over-easy egg, and brown beef gravy. Usually it is accompanied by a scoop of macaroni salad on the side.

Arabian Night's Delite

1 pound ground beef
1 tablespoon butter or
  margarine
1 small round onion, chopped
4 full sprigs parsley, chopped
  fine
1 teaspoon salt
½ teaspoon pepper

1 teaspoon cinnamon
5 eggs
1 (10-ounce) box frozen,
  chopped spinach, thawed,
  and drained
1 box filo leaves (approximately
  12 leaves in a box)

Fry ground beef in butter. Add onion, parsley, salt, pepper, and cinnamon. Drain and set mixture aside in a bowl. Beat eggs in a bowl and add spinach, stirring lightly. Fry eggs-spinach mixture in a large frying pan, turning over carefully so that the omelet is flat. Slide it out from the pan onto a large platter; slice into rectangles about 1½ x ¾ inches in size, and set aside.

Assemble the following items in a cool part of the kitchen or dining room (so that the filo leaves won't dry out so quickly): beef and egg mixtures, large tray on which to put the rolled Delites, a large pastry board on which to roll the pastry, a small sharp knife, a tablespoon, and the filo leaves. Then, carefully unpack the leaves (detailed instructions are on the box) and lightly cover them with a slightly damp towel to prevent them from drying out and becoming too brittle to roll nicely.

Carefully take a filo leaf and cut it in half. For each Delite, use a half sheet and place about 2 tablespoons ground beef at the bottom of the strip, and put an egg rectangle on top. Fold the bottom of the filo over the filling, rolling twice, then fold the left and right edges of the filo over about ½ inch. Roll up the filo leaf to the end. Place roll seam-side-down on the large tray. Continue making rolls until all the filling is used. Deep-fry each roll until golden brown. Drain on paper towels. Serve. Serves 6–8 people.

Note: To prevent seam from separating when frying, seal the roll with a dab or two of water.

Friends and Celebrities Cookbook II

Veal Anna O'Neal

4 slices peeled eggplant, cut
  lengthwise, salted, rinsed
Flavored bread crumbs
Egg wash (one beaten egg)
¼ cup garlic-flavored extra
  virgin olive oil
1 pound mushrooms, sliced

4 (6-ounce) scallopine of veal
½ cup mozzarella cheese
4 teaspoons Parmesan cheese,
  divided
20 ounces marinara sauce if
  served without pasta (1 quart
  with pasta)

Preheat oven to 400°. Dredge eggplant in egg wash and bread crumbs. In a cast-iron skillet, sauté in oil. Set aside.

Sauté mushrooms over low heat; set aside. Dredge veal scallopine in egg wash and bread crumbs. Sauté and set aside.

In a baking dish brushed with olive oil, layer veal, eggplant, marinara sauce, and 1 teaspoon Parmesan per serving. (Just use skillet as baking pan if preparing for fewer than 4 people.) Bake until cheese melts over top and sauce bubbles. Serve with pasta.

Cooking Italian in Hawaii

Lamb Shanks
Roasted in Red Wine

¼ cup oil
2 onions, sliced thin
3 cloves garlic, minced
4 carrots, sliced thin
2 celery stalks, sliced thin
1 bay leaf, crushed
3 sprigs fresh oregano or 1
  teaspoon dried

3 sprigs fresh rosemary
½ cup chopped parsley
1½ cups dry red wine
1 (10½-ounce) can tomato
  sauce
Salt and freshly ground pepper
6 lamb shanks, trimmed of fat
8 mushrooms, sliced thinly

Heat oil in large roasting pan and sauté onions and garlic until tender. Add carrots, celery, bay leaf, oregano, rosemary, parsley, wine, and tomato sauce. Simmer. Season to taste with salt and pepper. Add lamb shanks and baste with sauce.

Cover and cook in a 375° oven 1½–2 hours, basting every 20 minutes. Uncover, add mushrooms, and cook additional 30 minutes or until shanks are tender, turning shanks to keep moist. Arrange lamb shanks on a large platter with vegetables and sauce. Serves 6.

Shaloha Cookbook

Poultry

'Iolani Palace is the only royal palace on American soil. King David Kalākaua built the Palace in 1882. After the Hawaiian government was overthrown, it became the capitol building and now serves as a museum.

Guava Chicken

5 pounds chicken thighs, skinned and boned

MARINADE:

½ cup soy sauce
½ cup catsup
½ cup oyster sauce
2 cloves garlic, minced

½ cup brown sugar
½ cup guava juice concentrate
½ teaspoon salt

Mix Marinade ingredients thoroughly. Marinate chicken in sauce overnight, turning occasionally. Bake at 350° for 30–45 minutes. Yields 8–10 servings.

Note: Guava juice concentrate can be found through the Internet.

Favorite Island Cookery Book V

Baked Guava Chicken

12 small chicken breasts, or
  5 pounds chicken parts
1 (10-ounce) jar guava jelly
1 tablespoon cornstarch
1 cup water
½ cup lemon juice

1½ teaspoons Worcestershire
  sauce
¼ cup shoyu
1 teaspoon allspice
½ teaspoon Hawaiian salt
½ teaspoon white pepper

Place chicken in baking pan. Mix all other ingredients in a saucepan and simmer for 5 minutes. Pour over chicken. Bake in preheated 350° oven for 40 minutes to 1 hour. Baste frequently. Add water if necessary.

We, the Women of Hawaii Cookbook

Sesame Chicken

6 chicken thighs, boned and cut into 1- to 1½-inch cubes
Cornstarch
Peanut oil
Chopped green onions for garnish

Coat chicken thoroughly with cornstarch and refrigerate for at least one hour. Coat again lightly just before frying. Deep-fry the chicken pieces in peanut oil at 350° for 3 minutes or until light golden brown. Drain and dip in Sauce. Serve over rice. Spoon on any unused Sauce and garnish with green onions. Serves 6.

SAUCE:
¼ cup soy sauce
¼ cup sugar
1 tablespoon sesame seeds, toasted
1 (1-inch) piece fresh ginger, finely grated
2 green onions, finely sliced
½–1 teaspoon sesame oil

In a saucepan, mix soy sauce, sugar, sesame seeds, and ginger. Cook over low heat until sugar is dissolved. Stir in green onions and sesame oil.

Another Taste of Aloha

Not your ordinary newspaperman, this one is a mime on the busy streets of Waikiki who beckons you to sit beside him and hold his hand. The dog, however, is not real.

Chicken Lū'au

2 cups coconut milk
2 pounds chicken
2 tablespoons oil
2 cloves garlic, crushed

1½ teaspoons salt, divided
2½ cups water, divided
2 pounds taro leaves (lū'au)

Prepare fresh coconut milk or use canned coconut milk. Cut chicken into bite-sized pieces. In saucepan, heat oil; add crushed garlic. Add chicken and brown. Sprinkle with 1 teaspoon salt and add 1 cup water. Cover and simmer until chicken is tender.

Wash taro leaves; remove tough stems. Place leaves in a pan with 1½ cups water and ½ teaspoon salt. Simmer, partially covered, for one hour. Drain and squeeze water out. Drain chicken; combine with lū'au leaves. Add coconut milk and bring to a boil. Serve immediately. Serves 4–6.

Note: Fresh spinach may be substituted if lū'au is not available.

Ethnic Foods of Hawai'i

Quick Chicken Lū'au

1 (10-ounce) package frozen
  leaf spinach
1 (10¾-ounce) can cream of
  chicken soup

8 chicken thighs (or breasts)
1 (12-ounce) can coconut milk

Thaw spinach by leaving it at room temperature for several hours, or defrost in the microwave (3–4 minutes). Squeeze water out of it, using your hands. Spread spinach out in a greased, 9x13-inch baking pan. Spread soup over it. Place chicken over the soup. Pour coconut milk over chicken. Bake in a 350° oven for one hour. Serves 4.

Note: Traditional chicken lū'au is made out of taro tops called lū'au leaves. Spinach is a quick substitute.

Aunty Pua's Keiki Cookbook

Lū'au Chicken

2 (3- to 4-pound) fryers, cut-up
4 tablespoons butter
1½ tablespoons salt
1½ cups water
Salt and pepper to taste

½ teaspoon MSG (optional)
3 pounds fresh spinach
3 cups coconut milk, fresh or
　canned, divided

Brown chicken in butter. Add salt and water and simmer until chicken is tender. Remove chicken from broth. Add salt, pepper, and MSG to season broth.

Wash spinach and break into large pieces. Cook without additional water in covered saucepan over low heat until tender. Add 2 cups of hot—but not boiling—coconut milk to the spinach and simmer for 2 minutes. Arrange chicken on the center of a large deep dish. Arrange spinach in coconut milk around the chicken pieces. Heat the remaining cup of coconut milk with chicken broth and pour over chicken and spinach.

Joys of Hawaiian Cooking

Chicken Adobo

1 frying chicken
½ cup rice vinegar
½ cup soy sauce
2 garlic cloves, minced

6 peppercorns
1 bay leaf
2 cups water
Cooking oil to brown

Cut chicken into pieces and put in heavy pot. Mix vinegar, soy sauce, minced garlic, peppercorns, and bay leaf. Add water. Pour mixture on chicken and marinate for 20–30 minutes. Bring to a boil, then simmer until chicken is tender and mixture is almost dry. Add cooking oil and brown chicken. Serve hot or cold.

We, the Women of Hawaii Cookbook

Pete's Roasted Teriyaki Chicken

Teriyaki is a classic island sauce used on everything from beef and chicken to fish.

1 cup shoyu	4 cloves garlic, peeled and
1 cup sugar	crushed
1 (3-inch) piece ginger, peeled	2 tablespoons bourbon
and sliced	1 (3½-pound) chicken

Cook the shoyu and sugar in a small saucepan over medium-low heat until sugar dissolves, about 2 minutes. Stir in ginger, garlic, and bourbon, and cook 30 minutes. Remove ginger and garlic. Pour ¼ cup of the sauce into a small mixing bowl and store the additional for later use. It will keep in the refrigerator for up to one week. Makes 2 cups sauce.

Preheat oven to 375°. Rinse chicken and pat dry. Tie the legs together with kitchen string. Using a brush, coat the chicken with sauce inside the cavity and out. Place chicken in a baking pan and roast for one hour, basting every 15 minutes. If you want a darker bird, baste more often. The chicken is done when you pierce the leg with a knife and the juice runs clear. Take the chicken out and allow it to rest for 15 minutes before carving. Serves 4.

Hawaiian Country Tables

The longest and deepest explored lava tube is Kazumura Cave, on the island of Hawai'i. It is 25 miles long and descends 3,600 feet down the eastern side of Kilauea volcano. Lava tubes are natural channels that lava travels through beneath the surface of a lava flow. Tubes form by the crusting over of lava flows.

Teri Chicken

½ cup sugar
⅔ cup shoyu
2 tablespoons water
3 cloves garlic, minced

1 thin slice fresh ginger,
  crushed
3 stalks green onions, chopped
4–5 pounds chicken pieces

In a mixing bowl, stir together all ingredients except chicken. Place chicken in baking pan and pour sauce over it. Place pan in the refrigerator and soak chicken for several hours or overnight.

When you are ready to cook, turn chicken over and place pan in a 325° oven for 1 hour and 15 minutes. During this time, turn chicken once, using tongs. If you prefer, chicken may be cooked outside on a charcoal grill. Serves 6–8.

Aunty Pua's Keiki Cookbook

Yaki Tori

¼ cup sugar
5 tablespoons shoyu
½ teaspoon salt
1 clove garlic, crushed

1 tablespoon sherry or sake
1 teaspoon sesame oil
2 pounds chicken thighs,
  deboned

Blend sugar, shoyu, salt, garlic, sherry, and sesame oil together. Soak chicken in sauce overnight.

Cook on charcoal grill, or skewer, if desired, with onion and green pepper, and broil or pan fry. Delicious either way. Double sauce if using more chicken.

Favorite Recipes for Islanders

Sweet Ginger Chicken

2 tablespoons honey
1½ cups orange juice
½ teaspoon grated orange
  peel
1 teaspoon minced garlic
⅛ teaspoon white pepper

1 tablespoon grated fresh
  ginger
4 whole skinless chicken
  breasts, cut in half
1 teaspoon cornstarch or flour

Mix honey into orange juice until well dissolved. Add all other ingredients except chicken and cornstarch, and mix well. Put marinade into a double plastic ZipLoc bag, add chicken, and place in bowl in refrigerator. Turn bag to coat chicken a few times while marinating.

Take chicken out of plastic bag, reserving marinade. Spray large skillet with cooking spray. Brown chicken lightly in skillet; add reserved marinade, and about 1 teaspoon of cornstarch or flour to thicken. Cook just until chicken is tender and marinade is warmed. Makes 8 servings of ½ breast each. Serve over steamed brown rice, and add a green vegetable and rolls for a hearty meal.

Nutritional analysis per serving: Cal 142; Fat 3.1g; Chol 71mg; Sod 30mg

Note: It is best to marinate the chicken overnight, but for 3 hours at least before cooking.

The Best of Heart-y Cooking

Cold Ginger Chicken

Water to cover
1½ pounds boneless, skinless
  chicken breasts

1 tablespoon whiskey or sake
Large slice ginger
1 stalk green onion

Boil water in a pot large enough to hold chicken pieces. When water boils briskly, add whiskey, ginger, and green onion. Put chicken pieces in, one at a time. Bring to a boil again; turn off heat. Cover pot and allow chicken to stand in the liquid for 30–35 minutes. Remove chicken; cool, then refrigerate. When cold, slice chicken and top with Sauce.

SAUCE:

6 tablespoons oil
2 tablespoons sesame oil
  (optional, may use all
  vegetable oil)
3 tablespoons grated ginger

¼ cup finely chopped green
  onions
¾ teaspoon salt
1 teaspoon sugar

Heat the oils, then cool. Add remaining ingredients and spread on the chicken. Serves 4–6.

Note: Traditionally, this dish is made with whole chicken, with skin left on. You may use a whole chicken if you prefer; however, boneless, skinless breasts have less fat.

Ethnic Foods of Hawai'i

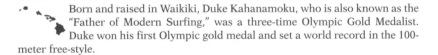

Born and raised in Waikiki, Duke Kahanamoku, who is also known as the "Father of Modern Surfing," was a three-time Olympic Gold Medalist. Duke won his first Olympic gold medal and set a world record in the 100-meter free-style.

Chicken Sciliano

4 large potatoes, peeled and
   cut in eighths
¼ cup garlic-flavored extra
   virgin olive oil
1 teaspoon kosher salt
Freshly ground black pepper
⅛ teaspoon powdered thyme
1 tablespoon oregano
1 medium yellow onion,
   peeled and quartered
2 pounds boneless fresh
   chicken, cut in 2-inch slices

½ cup herbed flour for
   dredging
1 green bell pepper, seeded and
   julienned
1 red bell pepper, seeded and
   julienned
½ pound mushrooms, sliced
4 Greek olives, pitted
¼ cup Italian white wine
¼ cup chicken stock
Tomato wedges
Parsley

In a cast-iron skillet, simmer potatoes in oil for 20 minutes at low heat, covered. Add salt, pepper, thyme, and oregano. Add onion and simmer 10 minutes. Dredge chicken in flour. Add chicken to skillet and sauté 10 minutes on each side, then add peppers, mushrooms, and olives. Simmer 10–15 minutes. Add wine and cook down. Add stock. Simmer 5 minutes. Serve garnished with tomato wedges and parsley.

Cooking Italian in Hawaii

Editor's Extra: A good blend for herbed flour: 1 cup flour, 1 teaspoon salt, 2 teaspoons black pepper, 2 teaspoons paprika, 1 teaspoon garlic powder, 1 teaspoon onion powder, 1 teaspoon dried marjoram, and 1 teaspoon dried parsley. Mix and store in freezer bag until ready to use.

Nearly 200 motion pictures have been filmed in Hawai'i since 1913, including six of the top grossing films of all time: *Jurassic Park, Lost World: Jurassic Park, Raiders of the Lost Ark, Godzilla* (1998), *Dinosaur,* and *Waterworld*. Between them, these films generated nearly $3 billion in gross receipts, fifteen Academy Award nominations, and nine Oscars.

Minute Chicken

3–4 pounds chicken
3 tablespoons flour
2 cloves garlic, crushed
¼ teaspoon pepper
1 teaspoon sugar
¼ cup hoisin sauce
½ cup chopped green onions

½ cup chopped Chinese
  parsley
2 tablespoons wine
1 (1-inch) piece ginger, crushed
2 tablespoons oyster sauce
¼ cup oil

Chop chicken in bite-size pieces. Marinate chicken in mixture of flour, garlic, pepper, sugar, hoisin sauce, green onions, parsley, wine, ginger, and oyster sauce. Heat oil in large skillet until sizzling hot. Add chicken and quickly stir at highest heat until brown. Lower heat and cook 10 minutes.

Favorite Island Cookery Book I

Chicken with Hoisin Sauce

MARINADE:
2 tablespoons sherry
1½ tablespoons cornstarch
1 tablespoon shoyu

1 clove garlic, grated
½ teaspoon salt

Mix all ingredients well.

1 fryer, cut in bite-size pieces
3 tablespoons oil
2 teaspoons sesame oil

1 piece ginger, mashed
2–3 tablespoons hoisin sauce
Green onion, chopped

Marinate chicken for 10 minutes. Heat oils in large skillet. Add ginger and marinated chicken, and cook. If chicken sticks, add some water. Cover. Cook until tender. Do not overcook. Add hoisin sauce. Garnish with green onion. Serve on bed of boiled broccoli, won bok (Chinese cabbage), and watercress. Yields 3–4 servings.

Favorite Island Cookery Book III

Chicken with Mushrooms

4–5 dried mushrooms
Water
1 tablespoon oil
2 pounds chicken thighs,
  skinned and boned
2 cloves garlic, crushed

⅓ cup oyster sauce
½ pound Chinese green peas
¼ teaspoon Chinese five-spice
  powder
2 tablespoons cornstarch

Soak dried mushrooms in water until soft; cut in half; save water. Heat oil in pan, and slightly brown chicken. Add garlic, oyster sauce, and mushrooms. Parboil Chinese peas in salted water. To retain color, rinse in cold water. After chicken is cooked, add the five-spice powder. Mix ¼ cup mushroom water and cornstarch, and add to thicken. Add Chinese peas. Serve immediately. Yields 4 servings.

Note: Sliced bamboo shoots and green onion may be added.

Favorite Island Cookery Book IV

Five Spices Shoyu Chicken

½ cup shoyu
½ cup water
2 teaspoons sugar
1 teaspoon oyster sauce
1 clove garlic, crushed

1 (1-inch) piece fresh ginger,
  grated
Dash of Chinese five-spice
  powder
3–4 pounds chicken

Bring to a boil all ingredients, except chicken. Add chicken to mixture and bring to a boil again. Lower heat and simmer 40–45 minutes, or until chicken is tender. Yields 6 servings.

Serving suggestion: Parboil 3 cups of Chinese cabbage cut into 1½-inch lengths. Drain and place on a serving platter. Place cooked chicken on Chinese cabbage. Add 3 tablespoons cornstarch mixed with 3 tablespoons water to sauce to thicken. Pour over chicken and garnish with Chinese parsley.

Hawai'i's Best Local Dishes

Huli Huli Chicken

This aromatic chicken turned (huli huli) on the spit is a staple at beach picnics, roadside stands, and at fundraisers.

SAUCE:

¼ cup catsup
¼ cup shoyu
½ cup chicken broth
⅓ cup sherry
½ cup fresh lime juice
¼ cup frozen pineapple
  juice concentrate

½ cup brown sugar
1 tablespoon crushed fresh
  ginger
1 clove garlic, crushed
1 teaspoon Worcestershire
  sauce

Mix Sauce ingredients in bowl.

**3 chicken fryers, halved
  or quartered**

**Hawaiian sea salt and pepper
  to taste**

Thread chicken onto rotisserie spit. Use clean 1½-inch paintbrush to coat Sauce over cleaned chicken pieces, then sprinkle with salt and pepper. Grill on rotisserie, turning and basting frequently with Sauce until done, 45–60 minutes.

For grilling, place on rack over coals, turning and basting for about 45 minutes. Or roast in 325° preheated oven, basting frequently, for 90 minutes. Serves 6.

Kona on My Plate

Mochiko Chicken

3 pounds chicken, cut in
  pieces and deboned
  (thighs are good)
4 tablespoons mochiko
4 tablespoons cornstarch
4 tablespoons sugar

5 tablespoons shoyu
2 beaten eggs
¼ cup chopped green onions
2 cloves garlic, minced
½ teaspoon salt and
  ajinomoto (MSG)

Soak chicken in remaining ingredients at least 5 hours or overnight. Fry in skillet with a little oil.

The Friends of 'Iolani Palace Cookbook

Chicken Long Rice

1 (3-pound) chicken
Water
1 (½-inch) slice ginger,
  crushed
1 (1¾-ounce) bundle long rice
  (bean threads), soaked in
  water to soften

Salt to taste
3 stalks green onions, chopped

Place chicken in a large pot and cover with water. Add ginger and bring to a boil; lower heat and simmer about 45 minutes to an hour, or until meat falls away from the bones. Remove chicken from broth and discard bones. Return chicken to the broth and add long rice. Simmer until about half the broth is absorbed by the long rice. Season with salt and add green onions just before serving. Serves 4–6.

Note: Although this dish is not "native Hawaiian," it is frequently served at modern Hawaiian lū'aus. To make the dish lower in fat, after chicken is cooked, refrigerate the broth overnight, or until the fat can be skimmed off the top.

Ethnic Foods of Hawai'i

Chicken Waikiki

2–3 pounds chicken pieces
Flour
Salt and pepper to taste
1 (20-ounce) can sliced
 pineapple, or about 2 cups
 fresh pineapple chunks

1 large green pepper, cut
 crosswise (in circles)

Shake the chicken in a paper bag with flour, salt and pepper. Brown in a skillet, then place uncovered in glass baking dish. Bake in 350° oven for 1–1¼ hours. While chicken is baking, make the Sauce. Place pineapple and green pepper over chicken during last half hour of baking time. Serve with rice and a tossed salad or cooked vegetables.

SAUCE:

½ cup sugar
2 tablespoons cornstarch
⅜ cup cider vinegar
⅜ cup pineapple juice

1 tablespoon soy sauce
½ teaspoon ginger
1 chicken bouillon cube

Combine ingredients in a saucepan; cook, stirring constantly and boil 2 minutes until Sauce thickens. Pour immediately over chicken while it is baking.

Friends and Celebrities Cookbook II

"Wai" means water and "kiki" means to spurt, thus Waikiki translates as "spurting water."

'Ono Sweet-Sour Chicken Spareribs

In this dish, the meat is just a medium for the flavor of the sauce—which is classic plantation Hawai'i. This recipe was probably once Chinese, but over the years changed to become simply "local." It's still a favorite at potluck gatherings and becomes a quick weekday dinner when served with steamed rice. You can substitute chicken drumettes for appetizers.

2 tablespoons vegetable oil
2 pounds chicken thighs
½ cup water
⅓ cup shoyu
⅓ cup firmly packed brown sugar
¼ cup apple or orange juice
2 tablespoons ketchup
1 tablespoon cider or rice wine vinegar
1 clove garlic, pressed
1 green onion, thinly sliced

½ teaspoon crushed red pepper
1 tablespoon freshly grated gingerroot
1 tablespoon cornstarch
1 tablespoon water
1 tablespoon black bean sauce (dau see) (optional)
Green onion, sliced diagonally, for garnish
Sesame seeds, toasted, for garnish

Add oil to a large frying pan with nonstick finish. Heat pan over medium-high heat until a few drops of water sprinkled on the surface sizzle. Add chicken pieces and sauté about 5–7 minutes, turning frequently until lightly browned on all sides.

Combine next 10 ingredients and add to chicken. Bring to a boil, cover, and reduce heat to simmer for 20 minutes. In a small bowl, mix together cornstarch and water. Add to chicken and cook, stirring until sauce thickens and glazes. If you like black bean flavor, you can add a tablespoon of black bean sauce at this point. Garnish with green onion slices and sesame seeds. Serves 4–6.

Hawaiian Country Tables

Chicken Spareribs

Flour
2–3 pounds chicken wings
   or drummettes
¼ cup oil
1 cup water
¼ cup vinegar

¾ cup brown sugar
3 teaspoons salt
4 tablespoons shoyu
1 slice ginger
3 cloves garlic, crushed

Lightly flour chicken; brown in oil in saucepan. Drain oil and add remaining ingredients to saucepan; simmer for one hour, turning wings occasionally.

Classic Cookbook Recipes

Mandarin Chicken Wings

2 pounds chicken wings
2 eggs, beaten
1 cup cornstarch

1 clove garlic, minced
½ teaspoon salt
½ teaspoon ajinomoto (MSG)

Dip chicken wings in beaten eggs; shake in combination of cornstarch, garlic, salt, and ajinomoto. Deep-fry until golden brown. Pour Sauce over and bake for 30 minutes at 350°.

SAUCE:
⅓ cup sugar
¼ cup water
¼ cup vinegar

2 teaspoons shoyu
Ajinomoto (MSG)
2 tablespoons catsup

Combine Sauce ingredients and pour over chicken wings. Bake for 30 minutes.

A Lei of Recipes

 There's fog and there's smog . . . but have you ever heard of vog? Actually, vog is the volcanic fog that occurs when a volcano erupts.

Golden Marinade Chicken on Sticks

½ cup soy sauce
½ cup gin (or sherry)
¼ cup honey
½ teaspoon black pepper
1 teaspoon grated gingerroot

1 clove garlic, grated
About a pound of boneless
 chicken
1 can large button mushrooms
Barbecue bamboo sticks

Combine first 6 ingredients and set aside. Cut chicken into small pieces that would hold on sticks, then marinate in sauce for at least half an hour. Place chicken pieces on sticks (that have been soaked in water) with mushrooms in between. Broil.

Cook 'em Up Kaua'i

Macadamia Stuffed Chicken Breasts

4 large chicken breasts
¼ cup coarsely chopped
 macadamia nuts
2 tablespoons finely chopped
 celery
1 teaspoon finely chopped
 onion

1 tablespoon soft butter
⅛ teaspoon salt and pepper
1 whole egg, slightly beaten
¼ cup flour, seasoned with
 salt and pepper
4 tablespoons butter

Bone and skin breasts and flatten with cleaver. Mix nuts, celery, onion, butter, salt and pepper. Slice chicken breasts in half. Put ¼ of the mixture on each breast, and roll up, turning in ends to secure filling. Pin with skewers. Dip into egg and then flour. Fry until brown and done in a medium-hot skillet.

Joys of Hawaiian Cooking

Chicken and Pineapple Curry

The chicken and pineapple are curried together. The result is a mild, yellow curry. Raw, not roasted, spices are used in the curry to add fragrance without altering the desired yellow color. Serve this curry with hot rice.

1½ pounds skinless, boneless
  chicken breasts
2 tablespoons olive oil
2 yellow onions, peeled and
  minced fine
2 teaspoons minced garlic
2 teaspoons minced ginger
1 teaspoon ground coriander
1 teaspoon ground turmeric
½ teaspoon cayenne pepper
⅛ teaspoon ground cinnamon

⅛ teaspoon ground cloves
⅛ teaspoon ground nutmeg
¼ cup water
Fresh lemon juice
Salt to taste
1 cup diced pineapple
½ cup coconut milk
½ cup unsalted, roasted
  cashew nuts
½ cup chopped Chinese
  parsley

Cut chicken into 1-inch squares. Heat oil and sauté onion on low heat, about 10 minutes or until golden. Add garlic, ginger, and spices, and cook 3–4 minutes. Stir chicken in with the spices. Add water and season with lemon juice and salt to taste. Cover and simmer on very low heat for 6–7 minutes. Stir in pineapple and simmer 3–4 minutes. Stir in coconut milk and sprinkle in cashew nuts and Chinese parsley. Cook for one minute and remove from heat. Serve hot with rice. Makes 4 servings.

Burst of Flavor

Chinese Style Roast Chicken

1 (3-pound) fryer

SAUCE:

4 cups water	1 cup soy sauce
3 stalks green onions, chopped	1 tablespoon sugar
4 gingerroot, sliced	1 teaspoon salt
½ cup sherry	

Wash and drain chicken. In a large pot, bring Sauce ingredients to a boil. Place chicken in boiling Sauce; cover and simmer for 30 minutes. Remove chicken and place on rack in roasting pan. Roast in 325° oven for 30–45 minutes or until chicken is brown. Serve hot Sauce separately for dipping chicken. Yields 4 servings.

Favorite Island Cookery Book IV

West Indian Curry Powder

¼ cup coriander seeds	1 tablespoon brown mustard
¼ cup black peppercorns	seeds
½ cup white cumin seeds	4 tablespoons ground Jamaican
1 tablespoon whole cloves	ginger
1 tablespoon poppy seeds	½ cup ground turmeric

Mix all seeds in a heavy skillet and dry-roast the spices, stirring, over low heat until they begin to pop and emit their aroma. Remove from pan and grind in a blender to a fine powder. Sieve and keep grinding, add turmeric and swirl all together again. Store in an air-tight jar up to a month.

Paradise Preserves

Curried Pineapple-Mango Chicken

Elements such as raisins, mango chutney, and pineapple would normally be served as condiments to top a curry dish; here, they're cooked along with the chicken and spices.

3 skinless, boneless chicken breasts
4 teaspoons sunflower oil, divided
1 cup sliced onion
2 tablespoons peeled and minced ginger

2 tablespoons curry powder
1 teaspoon cinnamon
⅓ cup raisins
3 tablespoons mango chutney
½ cup orange juice
2 cups fresh pineapple chunks
Salt and pepper to taste

Slice chicken into ½-inch-thick strips and place in a small bowl. Toss with 2 teaspoons sunflower oil. Heat skillet to hot and sear chicken for about 30–45 seconds on each side (until pink is just gone). Remove to a plate.

Add remaining oil and sauté onion and ginger together over medium heat until onions are translucent and caramelized. Add curry powder, cinnamon, raisins, mango chutney, orange juice, pineapple chunks, and seasoning to taste, and heat until it just reaches a boil. Return chicken to sauce, stir, and cover for about 2 minutes. Serve over rice or a grain dish like barley. Serves 4.

Hawai'i's Favorite Pineapple Recipes

Cornish Game Hens
with Tropical Fruit Garnish

Cornish game hens make a most attractive dish for a special party. They are easy to make and quite impressive. In this recipe, the hens are first marinated in a soy-ginger sauce. They are then roasted and garnished with your choice of tropical fruits before serving.

2 Cornish game hens	2–3 tablespoons freshly minced
¼ cup peanut or sesame oil,	ginger
or a mixture of both	2 cloves garlic, finely minced
½ cup soy sauce	Tropical fruit for garnish
¼ cup sherry	

You will usually find, inside the hens, a little packet containing the liver, neck, and gizzard. Remove these "insides." They may be discarded or used in soup. Rinse inside of hens and drain. Mix the oil, soy sauce, sherry, ginger, and garlic. Place hens in a bowl and cover with marinade. Refrigerate for several hours or overnight, turning now and then so the marinade covers all parts of the hens.

Drain marinade from hens and reserve. Place hens on a rack in a roasting pan. If desired, an onion or orange may be placed in the cavity for extra flavor. Tie the legs together. Brush with marinade. Bake at 375° for one hour, basting occasionally.

To serve, remove from pan and untie strings. Serve each person a half or whole hen, depending on their appetites. For the garnish, mix fresh pineapple, papaya, or mango cut in small dice, and spoon on top of the hens. Another garnish often used in Honolulu is lime juice mixed with minced fresh cilantro leaves, and some lime wedges.

Honolulu Hawaii Cooking

Seafood

PHOTO BY KIRK LEE AEDER / HAWAI'I VISITORS AND CONVENTION BUREAU

O'ahu's North Shore, where waves can top 30 feet, is popular for its outstanding surfing conditions. Since 1971, O'ahu has been the site of the Triple Crown of Surfing, the longest-running professional surfing competition in the world.

The World's Best—Bistro Scampi

¼ pound butter cube, frozen	Linguini pasta, cooked
1 pound (16- to 20-count) shrimp	½ cup dry white wine
1 tablespoon light olive oil	Bread crumbs
2 whole lemons	Paprika
Garlic cloves to taste	Parsley

Freeze cube of butter ahead of time in its wrapper. Prepare shrimp by removing heads (if you don't have headless shrimp); leave body shells and legs intact. With a sharp paring knife, carefully butterfly shrimp through top of shell (leave both halves joined). Carefully cut a small slot through body just above the tail with the point of the knife. (This will make the tail stand up when cooked.) Rinse shrimp under cold, running water to remove vein and any sand.

Heat oil in skillet over medium-high heat. Dry shrimp with a paper towel to avoid splatter, and sauté quickly to retain crispness, or snap, of the fresh shrimp.

Slice lemons in half. Peel and mince garlic. Shred frozen butter with a hand grater and then refreeze.

When shrimp have been cooked just enough, pour remaining oil from skillet over cooked linguini (while still in strainer) for flavor. Add garlic, to taste, to shrimp in pan, and sauté briefly while stirring. Next, add white wine and squeeze lemon juice over the sautéing shrimp (about ½ lemon to 4 shrimp). Reduce slightly by continuing to cook. Add bread crumbs to thicken slightly. Add paprika for taste and color.

Finally, add a generous amount of frozen shredded butter. Stir in quickly. Do not overcook or you will lose the creamy effect of the frozen butter.

Arrange a bed of linguini on each serving plate. Spoon shrimp and sauce mixture over linguini; garnish with parsley, and serve. Serves 4.

Fresh Catch of the Day...from the Fishwife

Island Scampi

Scallops or white fish like mahimahi may be substituted for scampi in this recipe.

Flour
6–8 ounces scampi
½ stick butter or margarine
⅓ teaspoon salt
½ ounce white wine
1 teaspoon grated Parmesan cheese

⅓ teaspoon chopped fresh parsley
2 medium cloves garlic, chopped fine

Flour scampi lightly. In saucepan melt butter; sauté scampi, adding salt, wine, Parmesan cheese, parsley, and garlic. Do not overcook.

Classic Cookbook Recipes

It had taken her a month of steady weaving to finish the part she was sitting on, and it would take another several weeks to entirely finish the mat. Demonstrations of Polynesian cultures are both informative and entertaining when talking to the natives at the Polynesian Cultural Center on O'ahu's North Shore.

Shrimp with Black Bean Sauce

2 tablespoons peanut oil
1 pound shrimp, cleaned and deveined
1 small clove garlic, finely chopped
1 tablespoon black beans, washed and mashed

2 stalks green onions, finely chopped
Salt and pepper to taste
1 tablespoon cornstarch
½ cup water

Heat oil in large frying pan. Sauté shrimp for 5 minutes. Add garlic, black beans, onions, salt, pepper, and cornstarch mixed with water. Cover and cook for a few minutes. Serve hot. Yields 3 servings.

Favorite Island Cookery Book IV

Shrimp Molokai

2 pounds raw shrimp
1 cup pineapple juice
1 cup sherry
3 tablespoons lemon juice
1 clove garlic, crushed

6 peppercorns
1 whole bay leaf
Hot pepper sauce to taste
1 stick (¼ pound) butter, melted
Sesame seeds

Shell and devein shrimp. Place in a bowl together with a mixture of all the ingredients except the butter and sesame seeds. Marinate for 2–3 hours.

Strain shrimp and brush with melted butter. Roll shrimp in sesame seeds and cook lightly in a buttered pan until they turn pink. Boil remaining marinade liquid for 10 minutes to reduce it, then strain and use as a dip for the shrimp.

Joys of Hawaiian Cooking

Aiea Shrimps with Basil Butter

On the porch of our friend's condo in the hills overlooking Pearl Harbor, there is a huge pot of basil. I was amazed at the large size and fullness of the plant. It seems basil thrives in the Honolulu climate. We sat drinking wine as we watched the sunset over the Pacific, and then were served this superb basil-flavored shrimp.

4 tablespoons butter, room temperature
1 tablespoon finely cut basil
Juice of one medium lemon
1 teaspoon chopped parsley

2 tablespoons olive oil
1 pound large, raw shrimp, peeled and deveined
Salt and pepper to taste

In a bowl, blend the butter, basil, lemon juice, and parsley. Heat the olive oil in a frying pan. Over medium heat, cook the shrimp just until pink. Add the butter mixture and stir to combine flavors. Add salt and pepper to taste. Garnish with a few sprigs of fresh basil. This will make 2 generous servings.

Honolulu Hawaii Cooking

Hawai'i's importance to the United States grew as the U.S. Navy established a huge military base at Pearl Harbor. The Japanese attack on Pearl Harbor on December 7, 1941, was the pivotal event that persuaded the United States to enter World War II. During the war, the port became a strategic naval base and a staging area for U.S. forces in the Pacific. Pearl Harbor is Hawai'i's largest harbor and the nation's only naval base designated as a National Historic Landmark.

Party Shrimp Curry

Honolulu parties often have curry as a main dish. Pale pink shrimp in a coconut-accented sauce, surrounded with pretty bowls of condiments, is impressive. The host or hostess can prepare the dinner ahead of time and with only a few last-minute touches, it will be ready for guests.

6 tablespoons butter (⅓ cup)
1 medium-size onion, finely
  chopped
⅓ cup flour
2 tablespoons grated fresh
  ginger, or 1 tablespoon dry
  ginger
2–3 tablespoons curry
  powder

2 cups milk
1 cup canned or fresh coconut
  milk
1 pound medium, raw shrimp,
  peeled and deveined
Salt to taste
Dash of cayenne pepper
  (optional)

Melt butter in large saucepan. Cook onion just until limp (do not brown). Add flour, ginger, and curry. Stir over a low flame to blend. Gradually add regular and coconut milk, stirring until the mixture is smooth. Add shrimp, with salt to taste, and the cayenne, if used. Cook over a low flame just until shrimp turn pink. This will take about 5 minutes. At this point the curry may be refrigerated until party time.

The condiments for the curry might include chopped peanuts or macadamia nuts, minced green onions, finely diced cucumbers, chutneys, and grated coconut. Curry is served with plenty of hot steamed rice. A dish of sliced fresh tropical fruits is often added to the festive table. Individual portions of curry may be served in papaya shells. This will serve 4, and can be increased for large parties.

Honolulu Hawaii Cooking

Shrimp, Chicken or Lamb with Coconut Curry Sauce

¼ pound butter or margarine
1 large onion, finely chopped
½ cup flour
2 tablespoons curry powder (adjust to taste)
1 cup milk
1 stalk of lemon grass (optional)
2 cans unsweetened coconut milk
3 cups shelled, deveined, and cooked shrimp (or shredded chicken or cubed lamb)

Salt and pepper to taste
Hot cooked rice
Condiments: chutney; chopped, hard-cooked egg; chopped, cooked bacon; chopped peanuts or macadamia nuts; chopped green onion; unsweetened, shredded coconut; raisins

Melt butter or margarine in large skillet or heavy pot. Add onion and cook until translucent. Stir in flour slowly to make a roux. Add curry powder. Slowly add plain milk, blending into roux. Add stalk of lemon grass whole, if desired.

Cook on low heat, stirring constantly, until mixture becomes very thick. Slowly add coconut milk, stirring until consistency of thick cream sauce. Do not boil. If sauce does not thicken sufficiently, mix more flour in separate bowl with milk or water and add, stirring until sauce thickens. More curry powder may be added in the same way. Remove lemon grass. Add shrimp, chicken, or lamb, and season. Serve over hot rice with condiments on the side. Very nice accompanied by baked or fried bananas and green salad. Serves about 8.

The Friends of 'Iolani Palace Cookbook

Queen Lili'uokalani, the last reigning Hawaiian monarch, is best known to the world as the composer of many beautiful songs, including "Aloha Oe."

Sweet and Sour Shrimp

The colorful mix of fresh, golden pineapple and green beans makes this a tempting stir-fry.

1 cup teriyaki sauce
⅓ cup pineapple juice
1 tablespoon rice vinegar
¼ teaspoon hot sauce
¼ teaspoon cornstarch
2 teaspoons canola oil, divided
1 teaspoon peeled and minced fresh ginger
1 cup fresh pineapple chunks
2 tablespoons minced green onion
2 cups (1½-inch pieces) long beans or fresh, young green beans
1 pound fresh or frozen, peeled and deveined shrimp
Cooked rice
Toasted sesame seeds for garnish

Whisk together teriyaki sauce, pineapple juice, vinegar, and hot sauce. Mix into cornstarch and set aside.

In saucepan, heat 1 teaspoon oil, and sauté ginger. Add pineapple chunks and green onion and heat until pineapple begins to brown. Stir occasionally. Add teriyaki-pineapple mixture and long beans. Simmer for about 5 minutes.

In a separate heavy skillet or wok, heat remaining oil and sauté shrimp until they just turn pink. Add to sauce and remove from heat. Serve over a bed of rice, and garnish with toasted sesame seeds. Serves 4.

Hawai'i's Favorite Pineapple Recipes

Hot Spicy Shrimp with Lemon Grass

2 tablespoons oil
1 tablespoon minced ginger
1 tablespoon minced garlic
1 teaspoon sugar
1 tablespoon finely minced lemon grass
1 tablespoon red curry paste
1 pound shrimp (25- to 30- count), peeled and deveined
2 egg whites
¼ cup cornstarch

¼ pound snow peas, cut on diagonal
2 red peppers, sliced into triangles
⅓ can bamboo shoots, sliced into triangles
1 can straw mushrooms
1 tablespoon oyster sauce
1 teaspoon fish sauce
1 tablespoon sesame oil
Chinese parsley for garnish

Heat oil in wok or frying pan. Add ginger, garlic, sugar, lemon grass, and red curry paste. Stir-fry until aroma is apparent. Coat shrimp with egg whites, then cornstarch. Add to wok. When the shrimp are cooked about halfway, add snow peas, red peppers, bamboo shoots, and mushrooms. Cook until vegetables are tender. Add oyster sauce, fish sauce, and sesame oil. Mix well and remove from heat. Garnish with Chinese parsley. Yields 5 servings.

Friends and Celebrities Cookbook II

On O'ahu, at Hanauma Bay's Toilet Bowl you can find out what it might be like to be flushed down a toilet—that is, if the conditions are right. The Toilet Bowl is a circular rock formation where waves "flush" in and out of an opening. The pool of water rises and falls with the tide, simulating the flushing of a toilet.

Garlic Shrimp with Nuts

2 tablespoons olive oil
3 cloves garlic, minced
¼ cup chopped scallions
  (white and green parts)
½ cup chopped nuts
  (macadamias or cashews)
1 tablespoon Worcestershire
  sauce

Dash of bottled hot sauce
Dash of cayenne pepper
½ cup dry white wine, or
  vermouth
24 large or jumbo shrimp,
  shelled and deveined

Heat olive oil in a skillet or wok over medium heat. Add garlic, scallions, nuts, Worcestershire, hot sauce, and cayenne pepper. Sauté for 1 or 2 minutes. Add wine and shrimp, and cook just until shrimp are done (pink). Serves 4.

Fresh Catch of the Day...from the Fishwife

Crisp Fried Shrimp

1 pound shrimp or prawns

Remove shells but retain tails. Set aside.

¼ cup mochiko
2 tablespoons cornstarch
½ teaspoon sugar or honey
3 cloves garlic, chopped fine
1 tablespoon finely chopped
  Chinese parsley
1 stalk lemon grass, chopped
  fine, or 1 tablespoon
  lemon zest

1 teaspoon seeded and finely
  chopped red chile peppers
1 teaspoon shoyu
1 teaspoon fish sauce, or ½
  teaspoon salt
1 egg
¼ teaspoon black pepper
¼ cup cold water

Combine all ingredients except cold water; blend well. Stir in cold water and mix well. Preheat enough oil for deep-frying on medium heat. Coat shrimp with mochiko mixture. Deep-fry until golden brown. Drain on paper towels.

Hawai'i's Best Mochi Recipes

Shrimp Shack's "Pan Fried Shrimp"

1 gallon water
¼ cup garlic powder
¹⁄₁₆ cup cayenne powder
4 pounds shell-on black tiger
  shrimp

½ cup margarine to cook and
  dip in
5 tablespoons chopped fresh
  garlic
Rice

Bring water to a boil; add garlic powder and cayenne to water. Drop in shrimp; return to a boil; drain. In sauté pan, heat margarine and chopped garlic. Sauté shrimp till golden brown, serve with rice, garlic butter, and cocktail sauce.

Shrimp Shack
(in Punalu'u, O'ahu)

On the drive up the North Shore on O'ahu (in Punalu'u), you can't miss the bright yellow Shrimp Shack truck. Irene serves up delicious pan-fried shrimp herself, delivering it personally to you on her umbrella-topped picnic tables. A big sign says, "Suck, peel, dip, eat," and, believe me, you will not need encouragement to do so. Her recipe has been written up in magazines, and she has been featured on the Food and Travel channels. I asked her if she would share her recipe, and she sweetly agreed. We all thank you, Irene. Barney and I licked our fingers and ordered more.

Colorful Stir-Fry

SAUCE:

2 mangoes, peeled and sliced
2 tablespoons frozen orange concentrate
2 tablespoons frozen apple concentrate
1 cup chicken broth mixed with 1 tablespoon cornstarch

2 cloves garlic, minced
¼ teaspoon curry powder
1 teaspoon grated ginger
1 teaspoon chili powder
1 teaspoon cumin seeds

Mix all ingredients in a saucepan and heat until just boiling and thickened.

1 pound large shrimp or chicken pieces (skin and fat removed)
Garlic powder
Paprika
Cayenne pepper
1 teaspoon peanut oil

¾ cup sliced onion
4 or 5 fresh mushrooms, sliced
1 large red bell pepper, cored, seeded, and sliced
¼ cup ground unsalted macadamia nuts
Hot cooked rice

Season shrimp (or chicken) with garlic powder, paprika, and cayenne pepper to taste. Marinate shrimp or chicken in Sauce in the refrigerator at least one hour.

Heat wok and add peanut oil. Add onion slices and mushrooms and sauté until tender. Remove shrimp or chicken from marinade and add to wok along with the red pepper slices. Stir and cook 1 or 2 minutes. Sprinkle with ground macadamia nuts and serve over hot rice.

Tropical Taste

Each island has its own official color: Niʻihau, white; Kauaʻi, red; Oʻahu, yellow; Molokaʻi, green; Lanaʻi, orange; Kahoʻolawe, gray; Maui, pink; Hawaiʻi, red.

Grilled Shrimp
with Mango Dipping Sauce

Skewered, coconut-marinated shrimp with lots of taste nuances. Terrific.

1 (14-ounce) can unsweetened
  coconut milk
1 tablespoon minced garlic
3 Hawaiian chili peppers,
  minced
Zest of 1 lime, grated
½ teaspoon paprika

1 pound large shrimp, shelled
  with tail intact
Wooden skewers, soaked
  overnight
Salt and cracked pepper to
  taste
¼ cup vegetable oil

In medium bowl, whisk together coconut milk, garlic, chili, zest, and paprika. Add shrimp and marinate overnight in refrigerator. Also soak wooden skewers overnight.

Heat grill. Drain shrimp and season with salt and pepper. Add vegetable oil and toss lightly until coated. Thread soaked skewers with 4 shrimp. Grill 1½ minutes on both sides or until shrimp are opaque. Serve with Mango Dipping Sauce. Makes 4–5 main-course servings.

MANGO DIPPING SAUCE:

1 cup red wine vinegar
½ cup sugar
½ mango, puréed
1 lime, juiced

½ red bell pepper, small dice
½ green bell pepper, small
  dice

In medium saucepan, bring vinegar and sugar to a boil, then lower heat to medium and cook until syrupy consistency. When cooled, combine in blender with mango purée and lime juice. Stir in diced peppers. Reserve.

Kona on My Plate

Goi Cuon
Fresh Spring Rolls

¾ pound lean pork
Water
16 medium shrimp, cleaned
  and boiled
2 ounces rice vermicelli,
  or ½ bundle somen noodles
2–3 carrots, shredded

8 large rice-paper rounds
  (bahn trang)
Leaf lettuce leaves, cut in half
  if large
Bean sprouts
Mint leaves
Chives or green onions

Cook pork in salted water for 25 minutes. Chill, then slice very thinly. Cook shrimp. Boil noodles, rinse under cold water, and drain. Shred carrots. Assemble ingredients on a work surface. Have a shallow pan of water ready to moisten the rice-paper rounds. Place a dry dish towel on the work surface.

Dip rice-paper in water and place it on the towel. Lay a piece of lettuce on the bottom third of the round (the side opposite your body). On lettuce, place some noodles, carrots, pork slices, bean sprouts, and mint leaves. Roll rice-paper round up halfway; fold ends of round over the filling. Place shrimp along the crease. Place chives or green onion (cut to 2-inch lengths) under the shrimp at one end, allowing some of the green to extend over the fold line. Continue rolling. Put on a plate and cover with a damp towel. Serve with peanut sauce. Makes 8 rolls.

Note: Rolling these takes some practice. Try not to put too much of each ingredient in the rolls. The shrimp should be seen through the rice-paper round when you are finished.

Ethnic Foods of Hawai'i

Sparkling Mahimahi

This is a very elegant way to serve fish for company.

2 pounds mahimahi fillets
¼ cup lime juice
1 tablespoon coarsely ground
  black pepper
Ti leaves
1 green onion, sliced

1 shallot, sliced fine
2 tablespoons olive oil
2 tablespoons all-purpose flour
2 cups champagne
½ cup liliko'i pulp and seeds
Watercress sprigs for garnish

Marinate fish in lime juice at least 15 minutes. Remove fish from marinade, and sprinkle with pepper. Broil fillets in oven 4 inches from heat for 6 minutes (we like to grill them, too), or until fish flakes easily. Transfer fish into a ti-leaf-lined platter. Sauté onion and shallot in olive oil over medium heat. Add flour and stir until smooth (this is called making a roux). Cook one minute. Gradually add champagne, stirring until mixture thickens. Stir in fruit pulp and seeds, and warm. Do not bring to a boil. Spoon warm sauce over fish and garnish with watercress.

Tropical Taste

Baked Mahi

8 mahimahi fillets
8 tablespoons mayonnaise
8 tablespoons lime juice

8 dill sprigs
Black pepper
Lime wedges

Pat fillets dry. Place in aluminum foil, smear top with mayonnaise and dribble over with lime juice. Add sprigs of dill and sprinkle with pepper before sealing the edges of foil. Bake in preheated 350° oven for 20 minutes. Unwrap; garnish with lime wedges. Serves 6–8.

Favorite Island Cookery Book V

Spicy Blackened Mahi

Use spices according to your own taste, and serve with rice or potatoes and a green salad.

1 pound fresh mahi fillets
  (4 pieces, may substitute
  any mild fish)
Sweet paprika
Salt (optional)
Onion powder

Garlic powder
Cayenne pepper
White pepper
Black pepper
Oregano
Dried thyme

Season fish by sprinkling spices on one by one and pressing into fish. Let stand in refrigerator to absorb spices for about one hour.

Preheat cast-iron skillet to high heat and sear fish on both sides. Turn down heat and cook for about 5–8 minutes or until fish is done. Makes 4 servings.

Nutritional analysis per serving: Cal 132; Fat 1.73g; Chol 77mg; Sod 252mg

The Best of Heart-y Cooking

Peppered 'Ahi
with Dijon-Wasabi Sauce

2 tablespoons freshly cracked
  black peppercorns
½ teaspoon paprika

½ teaspoon chili powder
1 (2x6-inch) 'ahi block

Heat skillet until very hot. In a pie plate, combine pepper, paprika, and chili powder; coat 'ahi block and sear in hot pan on all sides, about one minute. Reserve.

DIJON-WASABI SAUCE:

1 teaspoon minced fresh
  ginger
1 clove garlic, minced
2 tablespoons soy sauce
¼ cup Dijon mustard

1 tablespoon mirin sake
1 tablespoon brown sugar
1 tablespoon wasabi paste,
  to taste
Sesame seed oil

In the same skillet over medium heat, add ginger, garlic, soy sauce, mustard, mirin sake, and sugar; heat until sugar dissolves. Add wasabi paste and sesame seed oil to taste. Spoon sauce onto serving platter; top with sliced 'ahi. Serves 2.

Dd's Table Talk

Each year hundreds of the North Pacific 30- to 40-ton endangered humpback whales migrate to the main Hawaiian Islands during the months of November through May. The round-trip distance is approximately 6,000 miles, one of the longest migration distances of any animal species. While in Hawai'i, they do not feed, but rely upon stored energy. The humpbacks have become renowned for their various acrobatic displays.

Seared 'Ahi with Miso Sauce

Seared 'ahi is one of those dishes that has come to define Hawaiian regional cuisine. On the mainland 'ahi is marketed as yellowfin or albacore tuna, and is often found as sashimi in Japanese sushi bars. 'Ahi can also be marinated and grilled.

3 tablespoons cooking oil
12 ounces (2 blocks) sashimi-
  grade 'ahi, or thick 'ahi steaks

Heat oil in skillet until very hot, and sear the block of 'ahi on all four sides until the outside is cooked and the center remains pink and raw (only about 20 seconds on each side). Drain on paper towels and cool. You may also wrap the 'ahi in plastic wrap and place in the freezer while you prepare the sauce. This will firm it up and make it easier to slice. If block sashimi 'ahi is not available, use the thickest 'ahi steaks you can find, and sear on two sides for approximately 15 seconds.

MISO SAUCE:

4 tablespoons miso	**2 tablespoons honey**
½ cup Japanese rice vinegar	**2 teaspoons finely minced fresh**
2 tablespoons Korean hot	**ginger**
sauce (ko choo jung)	**2 teaspoons sesame oil**
2 tablespoons chopped green	**White sesame seeds to garnish**
onion	

Prepare sauce by mixing together the miso, vinegar, and hot sauce until smooth. Then add the onion, honey, ginger, and sesame oil. To serve, spoon sauce onto a platter, slice the 'ahi, and arrange on top of the vinaigrette. Garnish with sesame seeds. Serves 6.

Hawaiian Country Tables

Seared Sashimi

1 (2-ounce) piece of fresh
  yellowfin tuna, top fillet
1 tablespoon macadamia
  nut oil

1 tablespoon chopped basil
1 tablespoon chopped mint
1 tablespoon chopped cilantro

Coat fish in macadamia nut oil, and roll fish in herbs. Sear fish for 5 seconds on each side in a very hot pan. Remove, and slice ⅛-inch slices on the bias.

SAUCE:

4 ounces Chardonnay wine
1 ounce shiitake mushrooms,
  sliced
¼ ounce ginger, chopped
¼ ounce garlic, chopped
1 tablespoon butter

¼ ounce sweet onion,
  chopped
1 tablespoon Marumasa soy
  sauce
1 tablespoon green onion

Reduce the first 7 sauce ingredients over high heat until halved in volume. Add green onions. Nap plate (lightly coat the center of the plate with sauce), and fan sashimi over sauce. Serves 1.

Fresh Catch of the Day...from the Fishwife

Steamed 'Ōpakapaka with Shiitake Mushroom and Butter Shoyu

4 (6-ounce) 'ōpakapaka fillets (pink snapper)
¼ cup oil
3 tablespoons soy sauce, divided
1 teaspoon minced ginger

2 tablespoons butter
2 cups sliced fresh shiitake mushrooms
¼ cup chopped cilantro
Salt and pepper to taste
Fresh ti leaves

Marinate 'ōpakapaka fillets for one hour in a combination of oil, 2 tablespoons soy sauce and ginger.

Steam fillets 8–10 minutes, or until fish flakes easily when tested with a fork. Set fish aside on a heated platter.

Melt butter in a heavy skillet; add shiitake mushrooms, and sauté until mushrooms are just limp. Add remaining 1 tablespoon soy sauce and cilantro. Season to taste with salt and pepper. Pour shiitake mushroom mixture over fillets. Serves 4.

LUALUA METHOD:

Take 2 ti leaves, and lay them across each other. Place 1 'ōpakapaka fillet in the middle, top with shiitake mushrooms, and pour 1 tablespoon of the butter sauce on it; top with cilantro. Tie ti leaves together to form a basket. Steam 8–10 minutes.

Recipe by Chef Sam Choy, Sam Choy Restaurants of Hawai'i
Fresh Catch of the Day...from the Fishwife

The hukilau was an ancient Hawaiian celebration of the bounty of the sea. Hukilau means to "pull (huki) the leaf (lau)," and refers to a leaf-lined net that was cast into a bay or lagoon. Anyone who helped drag the massive fish-laden net onto the beach received a portion of the catch.

Baked 'Ōpakapaka
in Orange Citrus Sauce

¼ cup fresh orange juice
1 teaspoon grated orange rind
1 tablespoon soy sauce
1 tablespoon sesame oil
2 tablespoons minced green
  onion tops

Salt and pepper to taste
'Ōpakapaka (pink snapper)
  fillets

Combine all ingredients, except fish, in a shallow baking dish large enough to fit the fish in one single layer. Stir with fork to blend. Add the fish and cover with the marinade. Place in a cool place in the kitchen for one hour.

Heat oven to 400°. Place pan in oven, uncovered, for 10 minutes or until the fish is cooked. Baste once with the sauce while cooking. Be careful not to overcook. To serve, place fish with sauce on warmed plates. You may wish to add a few orange slices for garnish. Serves 2.

Note: This dish is also good served chilled for hot-weather dining.

Honolulu Hawaii Cooking

Opah Curry Kabobs

2 pounds opah fillets
  (moonfish)
¼ cup oil
2 tablespoons lemon juice
2 tablespoons grated or
  minced onion

¼ teaspoon dried mustard
1 teaspoon curry powder
Salt and pepper to taste
½ teaspoon dried thyme
Onion chunks, mushrooms, and
  zucchini wheels

Cut fillets into bite-sized pieces, and place in a nonaluminum bowl or dish. Combine oil, lemon juice, onion, dried mustard, curry powder, salt and pepper, and thyme and pour over fish. Marinate fish for one hour. Stir mixture a few times during marinating process.

When ready to cook, thread fish pieces, onion chunks, mushrooms, and zucchini wheels on skewers. Cook 4 inches from coals. Baste fish pieces often with marinade, and turn kabobs once while cooking. Serves 4.

Fresh Catch of the Day...from the Fishwife

Opah and Zucchini Sauté

1⅓ pounds opah (moonfish),
sliced into serving-sized
pieces
Salt and freshly ground
pepper
1 tablespoon olive oil
1–2 zucchini, cut in half
lengthwise, then across into
quarters ⅓ inch thick
1 large clove garlic, minced
1 tablespoon balsamic vinegar
1 teaspoon lemon zest
¾ teaspoon minced green
onion
2 teaspoons minced fresh mint

Sprinkle opah with salt and pepper. Heat oil in a large, nonstick skillet over medium-high heat. Sauté the fish quickly on each side. Remove to a plate before the fish is fully cooked.

Lower heat under skillet to medium low. Add zucchini, garlic, and balsamic vinegar, and sauté for a minute. Stir in lemon zest and green onion. Salt and pepper to taste. Return fish to skillet, and cook briefly. Remove from heat and serve topped with zucchini and fresh mint. Serves 4.

Fresh Catch of the Day...from the Fishwife

Shoyu Butterfish

1 cup shoyu
1 cup water
½ cup sugar
2 cloves garlic, crushed
1 slice ginger
2 butterfish fillets, rinsed in
warm water
Hot rice

In large pan with cover, add all ingredients, except fish; bring to a boil. Add fish. Reduce heat and simmer until fish flakes. Serve with rice.

Note: Butterfish has a tender texture and a rich, sweet flavor. In some regions they are called dollarfish, Pacific pompano, or pomfret.

Classic Cookbook Recipes

Casian-Spiced Taape with Papaya Relish

Casian is Chef Elmer Guzman's version of blackened fish—a blend of Cajun and Asian. Taape can withstand the bold spices and goes very well with the refreshing papaya relish.

4–6 (6-ounces each) whole taape (blue-striped snapper), scaled and gutted	**Chef E Spice to taste (see recipe below)** **6 tablespoons oil**

Season fish moderately with Chef E Spice. Heat oil in sauté pan over medium heat. Cook fish 3–4 minutes on each side until done. Serve with Papaya Relish. Serves 4–6.

PAPAYA RELISH:

1 whole ripe papaya, skinned, seeded, and diced	**Juice from ½ lime** **2 tablespoons oil**
½ cup diced red onions	**Salt and pepper to taste**
¼ cup sliced green onions	

Combine all ingredients and chill. Recommended wine: Pino Grigio.

The Shoreline Chef

Chef E Spice

6½ cups iodized salt	**1½ cups onion powder**
3¼ cups paprika	**4 cups dried oregano**
½ cup cayenne	**4 cups dried thyme**
2½ cups ground black pepper	**¾ cup togarashi (Japanese**
2½ cups granulated garlic	**seasoning)**

Combine all ingredients. Keeps well in tightly sealed jars.

The Shoreline Chef

Baked Snapper with Ginger Salsa

Fresh 'ōpakapaka (snapper) from Kona waters is the star of this easy, succulent dish.

GINGER SALSA:

3 medium tomatoes, peeled and diced

2 tablespoons chopped scallions

2 tablespoons chopped fresh cilantro

2 tablespoons diced jícama

3 tablespoons fresh lime juice, divided

2–3 teaspoons minced Hawaiian chili pepper

2 teaspoons peeled and minced fresh ginger

Combine tomatoes, scallions, cilantro, jícama, 2 tablespoons lime juice, chili pepper, and ginger in bowl. Cover and let sit for at least one hour.

4 (6-ounce) fresh red snapper fillets

1 cup dry white wine

Preheat oven to 425°. Place snapper fillets in a shallow pan and cover with wine and remaining one tablespoon lime juice. Cover pan with aluminum foil and bake for 25 minutes or until fish flakes easily with a fork. Arrange fish on serving plate and spoon Ginger Salsa on top. Serves 4.

Kona on My Plate

Quite a mouthful, Hawai'i's state fish, the humuhumu nukunuku a pua'a, is pronounced hoo-moo-hoo-moo noo-koo-noo-koo ahh poo-ah-ah.

Kaua'i Fillet of Sole

4 fish fillets (about 1 pound)
Salt and pepper
2 tablespoons lime juice,
  divided
Flour for dredging
3 or 4 tablespoons butter
¼ cup heavy cream
1 avocado, peeled, and sliced
¼ cup coarsely chopped
  macadamia nuts
Lime wedges

Sprinkle fish with salt and pepper and 1 tablespoon lime juice; let stand 10 minutes. Dredge with flour. Sauté in butter 1–3 minutes on each side until nicely browned. Remove to warm platter, sprinkle with remaining lime juice. Keep warm.

To the pan, add cream and bring to rapid boil, scraping brown particles free; spoon over fish. Top with avocado slices, macadamia nuts, and lime wedges. Serves 2.

Cook 'em Up Kaua'i

Gwen and Barney take a hikers' break at one of the memorable overlooks, where rainbows of colors dance along the canyon peaks of Waimea Canyon in Kaua'i. Dubbed by Mark Twain, the "Grand Canyon of the Pacific," it is ten miles long and about 3,600 feet deep.

Scallops with Oranges

This recipe is actually the result of some experimentation with different herbs and spices. Scallops are a nice change from 'Ahi or Ono, and cook in a matter of minutes. The scallops and sauce are all prepared in the same skillet, so cleaning up is a snap. I serve this with steamed brown rice and a spinach salad.

3 teaspoons flour dissolved
in 3 teaspoons warm water
1 teaspoon safflower oil
margarine
2 teaspoons olive oil
1 pound scallops, rinsed and
drained
1 teaspoon freshly minced
ginger

1 teaspoon minced shallots
½ cup canned, no-salt chicken
broth
¼ cup dry sherry
¼ teaspoon grated lemon peel
1 tablespoon fresh lime juice
Dash red pepper
1 medium sweet orange, peeled
and sliced

Dissolve flour in warm water and set aside. In 11- or 12-inch nonstick skillet, combine margarine and olive oil, and heat until hot. Brown scallops for about 4 minutes until firm. Remove scallops and keep warm. Combine ginger and shallots and sauté until soft. Add broth, sherry, lemon peel, lime juice, and pepper. Stir to combine, and bring to a boil. Add the dissolved flour and quickly stir in to combine well. Cover and reduce heat to simmer. Stir occasionally, and cook until sauce is thickened (about 6–10 minutes). Return scallops to skillet and add sliced orange. Cook for about 5 minutes, or until heated through. Makes 4 servings.

Nutritional analysis per serving: Cal 240; Fat 5g; Chol 40mg; Sod 250mg

The Best of Heart-y Cooking

Microwave Chinese Steamed Fish

2 pounds fish ('ōpakapaka, mullet, or any good steaming fish)
1 teaspoon garlic salt
Ti leaves

1 cup chopped green onions,
1 cup thinly sliced fresh mushrooms, and
1 cup chopped Chinese parsley for garnish

Score cleaned fish and rub with garlic salt (in cavity and outside of fish). Line the microwavable dish and top of fish with ti leaves. Cover with plastic wrap and microwave at 6 minutes per pound of fish. Turn the fish over about half-way through the cooking time and finish cooking in microwave.

SAUCE:

½ cup peanut oil
½ cup shoyu
1 teaspoon sugar

¼ cup slivered or grated ginger
Chile pepper flakes (optional)

While fish is cooking, prepare the Sauce by heating the oil until very hot (but not smoking). Mix the shoyu, sugar, and ginger together. When the fish is done, pour the hot oil over the fish first and then the shoyu mixture. Garnish by scattering green onions, fresh mushrooms, and Chinese parsley over the fish.

Friends and Celebrities Cookbook II

Imitation Crab Patties with Thai Chili Sauce

1 pound imitation crab,
  coarsely chopped
1 cup bread crumbs
2 eggs
1 clove garlic, minced
½ cup minced onion
2 stalks green onions, chopped

Vegetable oil
1 red bell pepper, seeded and
  chopped
¼ cup mayonnaise
2 ounces cream cheese,
  softened
Salt and white pepper

In a mixing bowl, combine crab, bread crumbs, and eggs. Reserve. In a skillet over medium-high heat, sauté garlic and onions in oil. Add bell pepper and sauté until tender. Remove from heat and cool. Add with remaining ingredients to reserved crab mixture, blending well, seasoning with salt and pepper. Cover and refrigerate for one hour.

Form crab mixture into patties and fry until golden brown. Drain on paper towels. Serve with Thai Chili Sauce. Serves 4.

THAI CHILI SAUCE:

1 cup sugar
½ cup water
½ cup rice wine vinegar
1 clove garlic, minced

1 teaspoon salt
1 tablespoon garlic chili paste
2 teaspoons chopped fresh
  cilantro

In a small saucepan, combine all ingredients; simmer until syrupy; cool. Stir in cilantro. Set aside. Makes 1½ cups.

Variation: Form mixture into 1-inch balls. Combine 1 egg and ¼ cup milk. Dip crab balls into egg wash. Wrap with shredded won ton pi, pressing firmly. Deep-fry until golden brown. Drain on paper towels; serve with your favorite sauce.

Dd's Table Talk

Tofu Patties

1 (20-ounce) block firm tofu
1 (6⅛-ounce) can tuna in
  water, drained
½ cup egg substitute
½ cup chopped green onions
¼ cup shredded carrot
½ teaspoon salt
1 tablespoon oil for frying

Drain tofu. Mix together with flaked tuna, egg substitute, green onions, carrot, and salt. Form into patties. Brown on both sides in a small amount of oil. Pour Sauce over patties just before serving. Yields 8 patties.

SAUCE:

3 tablespoons soy sauce
2 tablespoons sugar
1 clove garlic, minced
1 teaspoon grated gingerroot
1 tablespoon sesame oil
1 teaspoon sesame seeds,
  toasted
⅔ cup water mixed with
  1 tablespoon cornstarch

Heat Sauce ingredients, stirring constantly until thickened.

Favorite Island Cookery Book VI

Cakes

As part of performances, these natives adeptly climb these 40-foot coconut trees showing remarkable strength and ability. If you really want some fresh coconuts . . .

Banana-Pineapple Upside-Down Cake

³⁄₈ cup butter, softened
¾ cup sugar
1 egg
2 cups flour
2 teaspoons baking powder
½ teaspoon salt
¾ cup milk

1 banana, mashed
⅓ cup butter
⅔ cup brown sugar
1 cup crushed pineapple, drained
½ cup chopped nuts

Cream ³⁄₈ cup butter and sugar; add beaten egg. Sift flour, baking powder, and salt; add gradually with milk to butter mixture. Fold in mashed banana. Melt ⅓ cup butter in 8-inch-square pan or small tube pan. Sprinkle brown sugar over butter; add well-drained crushed pineapple and chopped nuts. Pour batter over this mixture and bake in 350° preheated oven for 25–30 minutes. Serves 6–8.

Cook 'em Up Kaua'i

Mango Upside-Down Cake

2 tablespoons lemon juice
2 cups sliced, ripe mangoes
1 tablespoon margarine
⅓ cup packed brown sugar
¼ cup oil
¾ cup sugar

1 egg, well beaten
1¼ cups flour
2 teaspoons baking powder
¼ teaspoon salt
½ cup milk

Sprinkle lemon juice over sliced mangoes. Melt margarine in an 8-inch cake pan. Sprinkle brown sugar evenly over the margarine. Place mangoes on top of brown sugar. In a mixing bowl, cream oil and sugar thoroughly. Add egg and mix again. Sift dry ingredients and add alternately with milk. Pour batter over mangoes. Bake about 1 hour in a 375° oven. When cake is done, remove from oven and turn it upside-down. Serve warm.

Variation: Bake in muffin tins for individual servings. Serve with whipped cream.

Joys of Hawaiian Cooking

Orange Cake

½ cup butter, softened
1 cup sugar
3 eggs, separated
¼ teaspoon salt
½ orange rind, grated

½ cup orange juice
1½ cups flour
1½ teaspoons baking powder
Orange Frosting

Cream butter and sugar and add beaten yolks of eggs, salt, and grated rind of orange. Beat in orange juice and flour which has been sifted with the baking powder. Fold in stiffly whipped egg whites. Bake in loaf pan at 350° for 25–30 minutes, and when cool, spread with Orange Frosting.

ORANGE FROSTING:
½ orange, juiced, and rind grated

Powdered sugar

Mix juice and grated peel with enough powdered sugar to make stiff enough to spread on cake.

How to Use Hawaiian Fruit

The production of sugar was first introduced in the early 1800s on Kaua'i. By 1877, there were eight plantations on Kaua'i, and over the years a total of 32 plantations operated at one time or another. By 2001, only two plantations were left in the state, one in Kaua'i, and one in Maui.

Boiled Orange Honey Cake

4 large oranges, peeled
4 cups sugar, divided
1 pound honey
1 teaspoon cloves
1 teaspoon ginger
1 teaspoon cinnamon
1 teaspoon allspice
1 teaspoon nutmeg
Dash of salt and pepper

½ cup oil
4 eggs, beaten well
5 cups flour plus 1 cup to dust
  boiled oranges
2 teaspoons baking soda
2 teaspoons baking powder
1½ cups cold, black coffee
2 cups chopped nuts

Cook the oranges in water to cover about 1 hour, or until soft. When cool, cut into small pieces and return pieces to pot. Add 2 cups sugar and cook slowly until water has evaporated. Cool and set aside.

Mix honey and remaining 2 cups sugar well. Add spices and mix well. Add oil and well-beaten eggs. Sift 5 cups flour with baking soda and baking powder. Add flour mixture and coffee alternately and mix well.

Dust orange pieces with 1 cup flour and add to the batter. Stir in nuts. Pour into 3 loaf pans lined with parchment or wax paper and sprinkle with water. Bake in a preheated 325° oven for 1½–2 hours.

Shaloha Cookbook

Butter Cake

1 cup butter, softened
1¾ cups sugar
4 eggs, separated
3 cups flour

1 teaspoon salt
1 teaspoon baking soda
1 cup milk
2 teaspoons cream of tartar

Cream together butter and sugar. Add egg yolks. Sift together flour, salt, and baking soda. Add alternately with milk. Beat egg whites, add cream of tartar, and beat until frothy. Fold into batter. Pour into greased 9x13-inch pan or Bundt pan. Bake in 350° oven for 25–30 minutes.

A Lei of Recipes

Coconut Broiled Oatmeal Cake

1½ cups boiling water
1 cup old-fashioned oats
½ cup butter, softened
1 cup sugar
1 cup firmly packed brown
  sugar
2 large eggs
1 teaspoon vanilla extract

1½ cups all-purpose flour
1 teaspoon baking powder
1 teaspoon baking soda
1 teaspoon cinnamon
½ teaspoon ground ginger
½ teaspoon salt
¼ teaspoon allspice
¼ teaspoon nutmeg

Preheat oven to 350°; lightly grease a 9x13-inch baking pan. In a mixing bowl, combine water and oats; let stand 15 minutes. In a mixing bowl, cream together butter and sugars. Add eggs and extract. Stir in oats and remaining ingredients. Pour mixture into prepared pan; bake 30–35 minutes. Serves 12.

FROSTING:

½ cup butter, melted
1 cup firmly packed brown
  sugar

6 tablespoons cream
1 cup chopped walnuts
1 cup flaked coconut

In a mixing bowl, combine ingredients. Spread onto hot cake. Place under broiler until bubbly.

Dd's Table Talk II

Pumpkin Pie Cake

1 (29-ounce) can pumpkin	½ teaspoon salt
1 (13-ounce) can evaporated	½ teaspoon ginger
milk	½ teaspoon cloves
3 eggs, beaten	1 (18¼-ounce) box yellow
1¼ cups sugar	cake mix
2 teaspoons cinnamon	1 cup chopped walnuts
1 teaspoon nutmeg	1 cup butter, melted

Combine all ingredients except cake mix, nuts, and butter. Pour into greased, 9x13-inch pan. Sprinkle dry cake mix over pumpkin mixture. Pat down gently with spoon. Sprinkle with chopped nuts. Drizzle melted butter over cake. Bake 50–60 minutes in 350° oven.

Favorite Island Cookery Book III

'Ono Coconut Cake

3 cups cake flour	1½ cups fresh coconut milk
1½ cups sugar	(if not available, use canned)
5 teaspoons baking powder	1½ cups freshly grated coconut
½ teaspoon salt	(or packaged)
8 egg whites	

Sift flour, sugar, and baking powder together. Add salt to egg whites and beat until stiff but not too dry. Add coconut milk to dry ingredients and beat till smooth. Fold in coconut and egg whites. Put into 2 (9-inch) cake pans that have been greased and floured. Bake for 40–45 minutes at 350°. Cool.

Frost with white frosting and sprinkle generously with additional freshly grated coconut.

Friends and Celebrities Cookbook II

Coconut milk is not the liquid inside a coconut (but you can drink this "water"). To make coconut milk, grate the flesh of a coconut in a food processor or blender. Add an equal amount of boiling water (or combination of coconut water and water), and blend till liquefied. Strain through a fine strainer.

Glazed Sponge Cake

1 cup butter or margarine,
 softened
1½ cups sugar
4 eggs, beaten
1 teaspoon vanilla, lemon,
 or almond extract

2 cups flour, unsifted
½ can pie filling (cherry,
 blueberry, apple, etc.)

Cream butter and sugar till fluffy. Add eggs a little at a time (3 pourings). Add extract. Blend in flour. Spread batter in well-greased 10½x15½x1-inch pan. Score lightly with knife in 24 pieces. Drop a teaspoonful of pie filling in center of each square. Bake at 350° for 30 minutes.

Favorite Island Cookery Book II

Light as Feather Chiffon Cake

9 eggs, separated
1 teaspoon cream of tartar
1½ cups sugar, divided
1½ cups cake flour
½ teaspoon salt

1 tablespoon baking powder
½ cup water
½ cup cooking oil
1 teaspoon lemon or vanilla
 extract

Beat egg whites with cream of tartar until soft peaks form. Gradually beat in ½ cup sugar until stiff and glossy; set aside. Combine flour, remaining 1 cup sugar, salt, and baking powder. Make a well, and add egg yolks, water, oil, and extract. Beat until smooth. Fold egg yolk mixture gradually into beaten egg whites. Pour into a greased tube pan. Bake 45 minutes at 350°. Turn pan upside down to cool. Use knife to separate cake from pan.

Favorite Island Cookery Book III

Three Layered Mochi

3½ cups mochiko
2½ cups white sugar
1 teaspoon baking powder
1 can coconut milk

2 cups water
2 teaspoons vanilla
3 different food coloring dyes,
any color

Preheat oven to 350°. In a large mixing bowl, combine mochiko, sugar, and baking powder. Add coconut milk and water. Mix until well blended. Add vanilla. Mix. Divide batter into 3 parts. Put several drops of the first food coloring into the first. Mix. Pour batter into a greased, 9x13-inch pan. Cover pan with foil tightly. Bake for 15 minutes.

While the first layer is baking, add the second and third color choices to the last 2 bowls. Mix. Pour the second color layer over the first baked layer. Cover tightly with foil and bake for 20 minutes.

Pour the third layer over the second baked layer. Cover tightly with foil and bake for 30 minutes. Remove from oven and cool before cutting.

Unbearably Good! Mochi Lovers' Cookbook

Coconut Custard Mochi

½ cup butter, softened
3 cups sugar
4 eggs
Water
1 (12-ounce) can coconut milk
1 (13-ounce) can evaporated
  milk

4 cups mochiko (2 [10-ounce]
  packages)
3 teaspoons baking powder
2 teaspoons vanilla
Toasted sesame seeds
  (optional)

Using an electric mixer, beat butter and sugar. Add eggs and beat well. Add water to coconut milk to make 2 cups liquid. Also add water to evaporated milk to make 2 cups liquid. Put all the milk, mochi flour, baking powder, and vanilla into the creamed mixture, and mix well. Pour batter into greased and floured 9x13-inch pan. Sprinkle toasted sesame seeds over batter. Bake at 350° for one hour.

Hawai'i's Best Mochi Recipes

Cocoa Mochi

1 (1-pound) box mochiko
1¾ cups white sugar
3 tablespoons cocoa powder
1 tablespoon baking soda
2 eggs, beaten

1 (12-ounce) can evaporated
  milk
1 can coconut milk
¼ cup butter, melted
1 teaspoon vanilla

Preheat oven to 350°. Grease and flour a 9x13-inch pan. Sift mochiko, sugar, cocoa, and baking soda into a large mixing bowl. Add eggs, milks, butter, and vanilla. Mix until batter is smooth. Pour batter into prepared pan. Bake for 1 hour and 10 minutes. Cool completely and cut with a plastic knife or it will stick.

Unbearably Good! Mochi Lovers' Cookbook

Jell-O Mochi

2 (10-ounce) packages
  mochiko
2 (3-ounce) packages Jell-O
  (any flavor)
2 cups white sugar
3 teaspoons baking powder

2 cans soda water (same
  flavor as Jell-O)
3 eggs, beaten
½ cup butter, melted
Kinako (soy flour) or
  katakuriko (potato starch)

Preheat oven to 350°. Grease a 9x13-inch pan and line it with wax paper. Combine mochiko, Jell-O, sugar, and baking powder in large mixing bowl. Add unchilled soda water, eggs, and butter. Mix well. Pour batter into prepared pan and bake for one hour. Cool, cut, and roll mochi in kinako or katakuriko.

Unbearably Good! Mochi Lovers' Cookbook

Bibingka Royale
(Coconut Rice Dessert)

¾ cup brown sugar
1¼ cups coconut milk
1 teaspoon vanilla
2 cups mochiko
4 teaspoons baking powder

3 eggs, beaten until light
¼ cup melted butter
Wilted banana leaves
2 cups shredded coconut

Preheat oven to 350°. Mix sugar, coconut milk, and vanilla together in a large mixing bowl. Sift mochiko and baking powder together. Add mochiko mixture to milk mixture. Beat until dough is smooth. Add eggs and melted butter to batter. Beat mixture until smooth. Pour batter into a greased, 9x13-inch pan that has been lined with wilted banana leaves. Bake for 45 minutes. Remove from oven and sprinkle with shredded coconut while still hot. Cool completely before cutting.

Unbearably Good! Mochi Lovers' Cookbook

Peach Refrigerator Cake

FILLING:

1 (13-ounce) can evaporated
  milk
1 (26-ounce) can sliced
  peaches, undrained

½ cup sugar
1 (3-ounce) box orange Jell-O
1 envelope unflavored gelatin

Put can of evaporated milk in freezer. Heat peaches with syrup and sugar and remove from heat. Add Jell-O and mix well. Add gelatin which has been softened in ¼ cup water. Cool. Beat icy cold can of evaporated milk until whipped. Fold into peach mixture gradually.

1 large chiffon cake   Whipped cream

Coat a 9x13-inch pan generously with butter. Break cake into bite-size pieces. Put in buttered pan. Layer cake pieces and Filling, starting with cake first. Frost with whipped cream. Chill.

Favorite Island Cookery Book I

Michelle Wie was born in Honolulu in 1989 and began playing golf at the age of four. At age seven, she played her first 18-hole round and finished 14-over par. At age 10, she shot a 64, and later became the youngest player to qualify in a USGA amateur championship event. Among her many accomplishments, at age 11, Wie won the Hawaii State Women's Stroke Play Championship, the Jennie K. Wilson Invitational, and reached the third round of match play at the US Women's Amateur Public Links Championship—a tournament she won at age 13. Michelle, who is over six feet tall, is now competing strongly in major tour events. Here's what Fred Couples says after playing with her: "When you see her hit a golf ball . . . there's nothing that prepares you for it. It's just the scariest thing you've ever seen."

Piña Colada Cake

1 (18¼-ounce) package
  yellow cake mix
1 (3¾-ounce) package vanilla
  pudding
1 (15-ounce) can Coco Lopez
  Cream of Coconut, divided
½ cup plus 2 tablespoons
  rum, divided

⅓ cup vegetable oil
4 eggs
1 (8-ounce) can crushed
  pineapple, drained
Whipped cream, pineapple
  chunks, maraschino cherries,
  and toasted coconut for
  garnish

Preheat oven to 350°; well grease and flour a 10-inch Bundt or tube pan. In a large mixing bowl, combine cake mix, pudding mix, ½ cup cream of coconut, ½ cup rum, oil, and eggs. Beat well. Stir in pineapple. Pour into prepared pan; bake for 50–55 minutes. Cool 10 minutes.

With a table knife or skewer, poke holes about 1 inch apart in cake almost to the bottom. Combine remaining cream of coconut and remaining 2 tablespoons rum; slowly spoon over cake. Chill thoroughly. Store in refrigerator. Garnish as desired. Serves 12.

Dd's Table Talk

Paradise Cake

1 cup vegetable shortening
2 cups sugar
4 eggs, beaten
3 bananas, mashed (by hand, not in a processor)
1 ripe mango or papaya, peeled, seeded, and mashed
2 teaspoons salt
1 teaspoon baking soda
3 teaspoons baking powder
4 cups flour
6 tablespoons sour milk or cream
2 tablespoons lemon juice
Grated lemon rind from 1 lemon
2 cups chopped macadamia nuts

Cream shortening and sugar. Add beaten eggs, bananas, and mango or papaya. Sift salt, baking soda, baking powder, and flour, and add to fruit mixture with milk, lemon juice, rind, and nuts. Mix well and turn into a well-greased Bundt pan. Bake at 350° for one hour. Cool in pan.

Note: You may make sour milk by adding one tablespoon lemon juice to regular milk and mixing.

TOPPING:

1 (8-ounce) package cream cheese, room temperature
2 cups whipped cream topping
½ (6-ounce) can unsweetened pineapple juice
1 cup ground macadamia nuts

Mix cream cheese and whipped cream topping. Add pineapple juice slowly until reaching a light consistency, about half the can. Top cooled cake with mixture and sprinkle with nuts. May be made a day ahead.

Hawaii's Best Tropical Food & Drinks

Italian Ricotta Cheesecake

Be sure to bake the bottom of the cheesecake until it's evenly browned—before you form and bake the rest of the cheesecake. Otherwise, the moist filling will make the bottom crust soggier than you'd like. Ricotta cheese produces a lighter, more granular cheesecake. If you prefer it thicker and smoother, substitute mascarpone or a good American cream cheese. But don't forget; using ricotta helps keep the calories down.

FILLING:

1½ cups sugar	5 whole eggs
3 pounds ricotta cheese	2 egg yolks
1 teaspoon vanilla	6 ounces heavy cream

Cut sugar in mixer with ricotta. Blend well. Add vanilla and whole eggs, one at a time, while increasing mixer speed. Add egg yolks and further increase mixing speed. Blend for 10 minutes. Remove from mixer, fold in cream, and set aside.

TART DOUGH:

3 ounces butter	1 egg yolk
9 tablespoons sugar	1 grated rind of lemon
1½ cups flour	Milk or water as needed

Preheat oven to 350°. Cut butter, sugar, and flour together. Add egg yolk. Add lemon zest and milk or water to form thick dough. Cover and refrigerate dough (½ hour or so).

Spray and dust a 12-inch springform pan with flour. Cut dough ball in half. Roll out one half to fit pan, but bake on a cookie sheet for 15 minutes. Remove to rack and allow to cool. Put baked dough inside of springform pan.

Cut and roll out remaining dough and evenly press around sides of pan, starting thick on bottom and tapering up to thin edge at top. Fill pan with Filling mix. Bake 10 minutes at 350°. Reduce oven temperature to 200° and turn pan. Bake 1 hour with door slightly open. Remove from oven and allow to cool in springform pan. Carefully remove from pan. Trim top of excess dough. Refrigerate at least 3 hours before cutting and serving.

Cooking Italian in Hawaii

Tropical Cheesecake

Cheesecake is one of the most popular desserts around the world, and Hawaii's abundance of fruits makes it a refreshing end to any meal. This can be made a day ahead, adding the fruit just before serving.

4 (3-ounce) packages cream cheese, room temperature
2 large eggs
1 teaspoon vanilla
½ cup plus 5 tablespoons sugar, divided
Dash cinnamon (optional)

1 (9-inch) graham cracker crust
3 ounces macadamia nuts, ground
1 pint sour cream
Fruit of choice
Apple jelly

Using an electric mixer or whisk, beat cream cheese with eggs until smooth. Add vanilla, ½ cup sugar, and cinnamon, and beat. Cover graham cracker crust with macadamia nuts and top with cream cheese mixture. Bake at 325° for 25 minutes, or until set. Cool. Add 5 tablespoons sugar to sour cream and pour on pie. Bake at 325° for 20 minutes until set. Cool.

Just before serving, top cheesecake in a decorative pattern with your choice of sliced or whole fruit. Melt apple jelly and brush over fruit.

Note: If you are using bananas, brush with lemon juice to prevent discoloration.

Hawaii's Best Tropical Food & Drinks

Panaewa Zoo, located inside a forest reserve on the island of Hawai'i, is the only tropical rainforest zoo in the United States. This 12-acre zoo is home to more than 75 species of animals, birds, and reptiles. Among the rainforest animals are the native Hawaiian gallinule (wading bird from Rallida family), 'io (hawk), and nene (goose).

Liliko'i Cheesecake

CRUST:

1⅔ cups graham cracker
  crumbs (or 22 squares
  finely rolled)

3 tablespoons honey
¼ cup butter or margarine,
  softened

Mix together crumbs, honey, and margarine, and press firmly into a 9-inch springform pan.

CHEESECAKE:

1 envelope or 1 tablespoon
  gelatin (unflavored)
½ cup liliko'i (passion fruit)
  juice, divided

½–¾ cup sugar
½ cup boiling water
2 (8-ounce) packages cream
  cheese, softened

In a large bowl, soften gelatin in a little of the fruit juice; mix in sugar. Add boiling water and remaining liliko'i juice, and stir until gelatin is completely dissolved. With electric mixer, beat in cream cheese until smooth. Pour into Crust; chill until firm (about 2 hours). Makes about 8 servings.

Note: For a sweeter cake, use ¾ cup sugar.

Cook 'em Up Kaua'i

Liliko'i cheesecake is like no other. This was even more delicious than it looks!

Lemon Cheesecake

1 package Pillsbury Lemon
  Cake Mix
3 eggs
1 cup plus 3–4 tablespoons
  sour cream, divided

1 (3-ounce) package cream
  cheese, softened
⅓ cup oil

Preheat oven to 350°. Lightly grease bottom only of 9x13-inch baking pan. In large bowl, blend cake mix (reserving glaze mix from package), eggs, 1 cup sour cream, cream cheese, and oil until moistened. Beat 2 minutes on medium speed (portable mixer can use highest speed). Pour into prepared pan. Bake at 350° for 30–40 minutes or until toothpick inserted in center comes out clean.

Cool cake in pan on cooling rack. Blend glaze mix with remaining sour cream. Drizzle over cooled cake. Refrigerate leftovers.

Classic Cookbook Recipes

Chocolate Chip Cheesecake

Soooooo yummy!

1½ cups graham cracker
  crumbs
⅓ cup Hershey's Cocoa
⅓ cup sugar
⅓ cup butter, melted
3 (8-ounce) packages cream
  cheese, softened

1 (14-ounce) can sweetened
  condensed milk
3 eggs
2 teaspoons vanilla
1 cup mini chocolate chips
  (semisweet), divided
1 teaspoon all-purpose flour

Heat oven to 300°. In bowl, combine cracker crumbs, cocoa, sugar, and butter. Press evenly in bottom of 9-inch springform pan. Beat cream cheese until fluffy. Add sweetened condensed milk; beat until smooth. Add eggs and vanilla. Mix well. Toss ½ chips with flour to coat. Stir into cheese mixture. Pour into pan. Sprinkle remaining chips over top. Bake one hour, then turn oven off and leave cheesecake in one additional hour. Refrigerate until firm.

Seasoned with Aloha Vol. 2

Chocolate Cheesecake

Cheesecake so creamy and chocolatey, you'll want to make it for every occasion!

CRUST:

1 cup chocolate macadamia
  nut cookie crumbs

¼ cup white sugar
¼ cup unsalted butter, melted

Combine and mix well; press mixture into a 9-inch springform pan.

4 squares chocolate, or
  4 ounces semisweet
  chocolate chips
1 (8-ounce) package cream
  cheese, softened
½ cup white sugar
1½ cups sour cream, divided

2 large eggs
1 teaspoon vanilla extract
¼ cup finely diced macadamia
  nuts
2 tablespoons firmly packed
  brown sugar

Melt chocolate in microwave on HIGH and stir; keep warm. Whip cream cheese and white sugar together until creamy. Add ½ cup sour cream and eggs. Blend in 3 ounces of the melted chocolate (reserving some for drizzle) and vanilla. Pour mixture into prepared Crust. Bake at 325° for 35–40 minutes or until cheesecake center is set.

Blend remaining 1 cup sour cream, macadamia nuts, and brown sugar and spread over cheesecake. Bake for 5 more minutes. Cool to room temperature. Drizzle remaining one ounce melted chocolate over cheesecake. Chill for 4 hours. Makes 8 servings.

Sugar and Spice–Cookies Made with Love

Cookies

PHOTO BY JIM STEINHART / WWW.PLANETWARE.COM

This statue of King Kamehameha I stands in front of the Judiciary Building in Honolulu. King Kamehameha I was the first ruler to unite all the Hawaiian Islands under one rule. He was king from 1795 to 1819.

Guava Crispies

¾ cup butter, divided
⅓ cup guava jelly
2 tablespoons lemon juice
2 tablespoons sugar
¼ teaspoon salt
1 egg yolk, slightly beaten
¼ cup chopped macadamia
  nuts

1 cup flour
½ teaspoon salt
½ teaspoon baking soda
½ cup brown sugar
1 cup quick oats

Combine ¼ cup butter, guava jelly, lemon juice, sugar, and salt in the top of a double boiler. Heat until the guava jelly has dissolved. Stir a part of this into slightly beaten yolk, then return the egg mixture to the rest of the jelly mixture. Heat and stir until the mixture thickens. Add nuts. Remove from heat and cool.

Sift flour, salt, and soda over brown sugar and remaining ½ cup butter. Cut together with 2 knives until coarse crumbs form. Add oatmeal and mix well. Pat half of the mixture into the bottom of a 9-inch-square pan. Spread guava mixture on top and sprinkle remaining oatmeal mixture on top. Bake in a 350° oven for 25 minutes. Cool and cut into squares. Makes 3 dozen.

Joys of Hawaiian Cooking

Hawaiian Vowel Pronunciation Guide:

a – Pronounced "ah" and never "ay." Kamehameha, for example, starts off "kah...," not "Kam..." (as in the word camera).

e – Pronounced "ay" as in the long "a" in the English language. Kamehameha, for example, is roughly pronounced "kah may hah may hah."

i – Pronounced "ee" as in the long "e" in the English language. Waikiki, for example, is pronounced "wah ee kee kee." "Wah" and "ee" are slurred to sound like "wye." Try it. Likewise, "kai," as in Hawai'i Kai, is pronounced "kah ee." When slurred, it sounds like "kye."

o – Pronounced "oh," never differently.

u – Pronounced "oo" as in "goo," never differently.

Almond Cookies

3 cups all-purpose flour
1 cup sugar
½ teaspoon salt
½ teaspoon baking soda

1 cup margarine, softened
1 egg, slightly beaten
1 teaspoon almond extract
⅓ cup whole almonds

Preheat oven to 350°. Combine flour, sugar, salt, and baking soda. Add margarine and mix until mixture resembles cornmeal. Add in egg and almond extract. Roll mixture into walnut-size balls. Place a whole almond on each ball, pressing down slightly. Place on greased cookie sheet. Bake for 12–15 minutes or until light brown.

Hawai'i's Favorite Firehouse Recipes

Famous Cookies

2 sticks butter, softened
¾ cup sugar (brown or white)
1 teaspoon baking soda
1 teaspoon water
1 egg
½ teaspoon salt

1 teaspoon vanilla
3 cups flour
½ cup shredded coconut
1 cup chopped nuts
2 cups chocolate chips

Cream butter and sugar. Mix soda with water and add to cream mixture, along with egg, salt, and vanilla. Mix in flour and remaining ingredients. Chill for an hour. Preheat oven to 350°. Drop dough by spoonfuls onto cookie sheet and bake 12 minutes.

Island Flavors

Pernod-Pistachio Cookies

Melt-in-your-mouth madness. Pernod adds a cool touch to this sultry cookie.

1 cup golden raisins or
  currants
1 cup Pernod
2 sticks unsalted butter,
  melted
1 cup sugar
2 large eggs

2½ cups all-purpose flour
1 tablespoon poppy seeds
1 teaspoon baking soda
½ teaspoon salt
1 cup lightly salted shelled
  pistachio nuts

Soak raisins in Pernod for 3 hours. In a large bowl, mix together butter, sugar, and eggs. In a separate bowl, sift together flour, poppy seeds, baking soda, and salt. Combine Pernod mixture with butter mixture. Gradually stir in dry ingredients. Add pistachios. Scoop spoonfuls of dough onto oiled baking sheets and bake in a 350° oven for 20–25 minutes, or until you smell the Pernod wafting out of the oven. Makes about 3 dozen.

Sugar and Spice–Cookies Made with Love

Lemonade Cookies

1 cup butter or margarine,
  softened
1 cup sugar
2 eggs, beaten
3 cups flour

1 teaspoon baking soda
1 (6-ounce) can frozen
  lemonade concentrate,
  thawed, divided
Colored sugar for sprinkling

Cream butter with sugar and well-beaten eggs. Mix flour and baking soda, and add alternately with ½ of the thawed lemonade concentrate to butter mixture.

Drop by teaspoonfuls onto greased cookie sheets. Bake at 375° until slightly brown—about 10 minutes. Remove to rack to cool and brush hot cookies with remaining lemonade concentrate. Sprinkle tops lightly with colored sugars for a decorative effect.

Hilo Woman's Club Cookbook

Samurai Shortbread Cookies

1 cup butter or margarine,
  softened
1 cup sugar
1 cup mochiko

4 cups flour
2 teaspoons vanilla extract
⅛ teaspoon salt

Preheat oven to 350°. Combine butter with sugar and mix until smooth. Add other ingredients (but do not overmix, as cookies may become rock hard). Form dough into balls and flatten, or roll into ¼-inch thick sheet and cut with cookie cutter. Bake on ungreased pan for 20–30 minutes.

Hawai'i's Favorite Firehouse Recipes

Coconut Macadamia Nut Crisps

¾ cup butter, softened
¾ cup sugar
½ cup firmly packed brown
  sugar
1 large egg
1 teaspoon vanilla extract
2 cups all-purpose flour

1 teaspoon baking powder
1 teaspoon baking soda
½ teaspoon salt
1 cup chopped macadamia nuts
1 cup old-fashioned oats
½ cup flaked coconut

Preheat oven to 375°; lightly grease baking sheets. In a mixing bowl, cream together butter and sugars until fluffy. Add egg and extract. Stir in remaining ingredients until well blended. Drop by teaspoonfuls 1 inch apart on prepared sheets. Bake 8–10 minutes until edges are brown. Makes 5 dozen.

Dd's Table Talk II

Fresh Coconut Macaroons

1 fresh coconut (about 1½
  pounds)
4 egg whites

½ cup sugar
¾ teaspoon almond extract

Remove coconut from shell; grate it and measure 3 cups. In a mixing bowl, combine grated coconut, unbeaten egg whites, sugar, and almond extract. Stir until well blended. Drop batter by teaspoons, about 1 inch apart, onto a lightly greased baking sheet or a cookie sheet lined with parchment paper. Lightly press down each cookie with the back of a spoon.

Bake in 325° oven for 25–35 minutes, or until lightly browned. Cool on a wire rack, then store in an airtight container. Yields 2 dozen cookies.

Tropical Taste

White Chocolate Coconut Cookies

These are especially light and heavenly cookies with a distinctively coconut-y flavor.

1 cup butter, softened
1 cup white sugar
2 large eggs
1 teaspoon rum extract or
  dark rum
3 cups all-purpose flour

½ teaspoon baking soda
1 teaspoon salt
1 cup shredded coconut
1 (12-ounce) package white
  chocolate chips

Preheat oven to 350°. Oil baking sheet. Cream together butter and sugar until light. Add eggs and rum extract or rum. Sift together flour, soda, and salt, and gradually mix into egg-butter mixture. Fold in coconut and white chocolate chips.

Drop mounds of dough onto oiled baking sheet. Bake for 35–40 minutes in 350° oven. Remove cookie sheet from oven and let cool.

Variation: Add ½ cup chopped, dried pineapple to coconut mixture for a piña colada cookie.

Sugar and Spice–Cookies Made with Love

Chocolate Macadamia Nut Cookies

1 cup whole macadamia nuts
5 ounces semisweet chocolate
½ cup butter
2 large eggs
½ cup white sugar
1 teaspoon vanilla extract
2 cups all-purpose flour

¾ cup cocoa
1 teaspoon baking soda
1 teaspoon salt
¾ cup semisweet chocolate
  chips
Beaten egg white

Preheat oven to 350°. Oil a baking sheet. Place whole macadamia nuts in another pan and bake in oven for 5–8 minutes or until golden brown; set aside. When cool, chop, reserving ¼ cup for garnish.

Combine chocolate and butter in microwave-proof dish. Melt in microwave 1–2 minutes; cool, then add eggs, sugar, and vanilla. Sift together flour, cocoa, soda, and salt. Mix into egg batter. Fold in macadamia nuts (except ¼ cup for garnish) and semisweet chocolate chips until well blended.

Scoop out spoonfuls of mixture onto oiled baking sheet, about 1 inch apart. Brush with beaten egg white and sprinkle with chopped macadamia nuts. Bake on the middle rack of a 350° oven for 30 minutes or until edges are browned. Remove cookie sheet from oven and let cool. Serve with coffee ice cream. Makes about 3½ dozen.

Sugar and Spice–Cookies Made with Love

Kilauea Lighthouse, located on Kaua'i, is the northernmost point of the main Hawaiian Islands. It has the world's largest clamshell lens, sending a beacon 90 miles out to sea. (Compared to other lenses, a clamshell lens has only two flash panels and sends light beams in only two directions as it rotates.) Built in 1913, the lighthouse was in use until 1976.

Judy's Macadamia Nut Bars

These easy-to-make cookies are some of the most addictively delicious morsels you can imagine. Macadamia nuts give a taste of Hawaiian crunch and flavor. This recipe, from a special family friend, is a winner.

FILLING:

2 eggs
1 teaspoon vanilla
1¼ cups brown sugar
2 tablespoons flour
¼ teaspoon baking powder
¼ teaspoon salt

½ cup flaked coconut
1 (3½-ounce) can (1 cup)
 toasted macadamia nuts,
 coarsely chopped
Powdered sugar for topping

Beat the eggs, vanilla, and brown sugar together until smooth. Sift flour with baking powder and salt; stir into egg mixture and blend well. Fold in coconut and nuts to complete the Filling.

BUTTER CRUST:

½ cup butter
¼ cup sugar

1 cup flour

Blend butter, sugar, and flour together with a fork to make a crumbly texture. Press into a 9-inch-square pan. Bake at 350° for 20 minutes or until light brown. Remove from the oven.

Gently spread Filling over crust. Bake an additional 25 minutes at 350°. Remove from oven and place on a rack. Sprinkle with powdered sugar. Cool 5 minutes, then cut with a knife into desired size squares. For a romantic dessert, serve with chilled champagne!

Honolulu Hawaii Cooking

Calabash Cousins Coconut Bars

Rich with coconut and macadamias, these bars won't last long in your household. They are named after the volunteer support group for the Daughters of Hawai'i who maintain our beloved Hulihe'e Palace.

**1½ cups plus 1 tablespoon
  all-purpose flour, divided
1½ cups firmly packed brown
  sugar, divided
½ cup butter, softened
2 eggs, beaten**

**½ teaspoon baking powder
¼ teaspoon salt
½ teaspoon vanilla extract
1¼ cups shredded coconut
½ cup chopped macadamia
  nuts**

Combine 1½ cups flour and ½ cup brown sugar in medium bowl. Cut in butter with 2 knives or pastry cutter until mixture resembles coarse meal. Press into bottom of a lightly greased 9-inch-square pan. Bake in preheated oven at 350° for 15 minutes.

Meanwhile, combine eggs, remaining one cup brown sugar, 1 tablespoon flour, baking powder, salt, and vanilla in large bowl, mixing well. Stir in shredded coconut and chopped macadamia nuts. Spread coconut mixture over crust. Bake at 350° for 20 minutes. Remove and cool. Cut into 2-inch-square bars. Yields 20.

Kona on My Plate

Pineapple Bars

2 cups sugar
½ cup butter, softened
1 (20-ounce) can
 crushed pineapple, drained
1 cup chopped walnuts

1 cup flour
½ teaspoon salt
½ teaspoon baking soda
6 eggs

Mix all ingredients well. Bake in greased 10x15x2-inch pan at 350° for 30–35 minutes. Cut into bars.

We, the Women of Hawaii Cookbook

Pineapple Squares

½ cup (1 stick) butter or
 margarine, softened
1⅓ cups sugar
4 eggs
1½ cups flour
1 teaspoon baking powder

½ teaspoon baking soda
¼ teaspoon salt
1 (20-ounce) can crushed
 pineapple, drained
Powdered sugar

Cream together butter and sugar with an electric mixer for 2 minutes on high speed. Mix in eggs. Add dry ingredients, except the powdered sugar, and mix.

Drain pineapple by pressing the top of the open can against the pineapple while draining the juice. Add pineapple to the ingredients in the bowl and stir with a spoon until blended. Pour batter into a greased, 9x13-inch pan and bake for 30–35 minutes at 350°. Cool; cut into 24 bars. Sprinkle with powdered sugar.

Aunty Pua's Keiki Cookbook

Editor's Extra: Don't throw the pineapple juice away. I like adding it to orange juice.

Mud Slide Brownies

2 cups all-purpose flour
½ teaspoon baking powder
½ teaspoon salt
⅔ cup unsalted butter
4 ounces unsweetened
  chocolate
3 eggs, beaten

1½ cups sugar
4 tablespoons Kahlúa
2 tablespoons Bailey's Irish
  Cream
1 tablespoon vodka
¾ cup chopped walnuts

Preheat oven to 350°; lightly grease a 9x13-inch baking pan. On wax paper, sift together dry ingredients. In a saucepan over medium heat, melt butter and chocolate, stirring to blend. Cool. In a mixing bowl, combine eggs and sugar. Stir in dry ingredients, then add chocolate mixture and liqueurs. Stir in nuts. Spread into prepared pan; bake for 25–30 minutes. Serves 12.

Dd's Table Talk

Da Kine Brownies

These brownies are a great finger dessert. Women eat them in two or three bites and most men pop the whole thing in their mouths. For a sophisticated dessert, serve brownie with vanilla ice cream drizzled with a little home-made raspberry sauce. (In Hawaiian slang, "Da Kine" means "the best.")

1 package Betty Crocker's
  Fudge Brownie Mix
½ cup unsweetened
  applesauce (instead of oil)

⅓ cup natural peanut butter
⅓ cup semisweet chocolate
  chips

Preheat oven to 325°. According to package directions, blend appropriate amount water and eggs, then applesauce, and peanut butter in a large bowl; add mix. Stir until moistened and fully blended. Add chocolate chips. Spoon batter into Teflon-coated mini-muffin pan without paper inserts. Instead, spray lightly with nonstick cooking spray. Bake for about 20 minutes, depending on oven, or until done. Do not overbake. Allow brownies to cool and pop them out onto a serving tray. Stand back so you won't get trampled.

Shaloha Cookbook

Coffee Glazed Brownies

A delicious treat with a nice cold glass of skim milk for an after-school treat!

1 cup unbleached flour
½ teaspoon baking soda
½ teaspoon baking powder
¼ cup oat bran
⅓ cup sugar
⅓ cup unsweetened cocoa
1 large ripe banana, mashed
  well

3 tablespoons canola oil
1 tablespoon applesauce mixed
  with 1 tablespoon strong
  coffee
3 tablespoons light corn syrup
2 egg whites, lightly beaten
¼ teaspoon almond extract
1 teaspoon vanilla

Preheat oven to 350°. Prepare 8-inch baking pan with cooking spray. Combine flour, baking soda, baking powder, bran, sugar, and cocoa; mix well and set aside. Combine banana, canola oil, applesauce-coffee mixture, corn syrup, egg whites, and extracts; beat for a few minutes and add to dry mixture, combining well. Pour into pan and bake for about 25 minutes, or until center is set.

GLAZE:

½ cup confectioners' sugar
3 teaspoons cocoa

3–4 teaspoons strong coffee
  blend

Mix sugar and cocoa. Gradually add coffee until mixture drizzles slowly from spoon. Drizzle Glaze in zig zag pattern over top of warm brownies. Cut into squares when cooled. Makes 12 squares.

Nutritional analysis per serving: Cal 180; Fat 3.5g; Chol 0mg; Sod 85mg

The Best of Heart-y Cooking

Hawai'i is the only state that grows cacao beans used to make chocolate. Cacao is the name of the tree that produces a 6- to 10-inch pod containing 20 to 40 seeds. To become chocolate, the seeds are fermented, dried, aged, lightly roasted, ground, and conched (the process of continuously mixing, grinding, and stirring).

Toll House Bars

1 cup butter, softened
1 cup brown sugar
1 large egg
1 teaspoon vanilla

2 cups flour
6 ounces chocolate chips
1 cup chopped nuts

Cream butter, sugar, and egg; add vanilla and flour; mix well. Stir in chocolate chips and chopped nuts. Preheat oven to 325°. Spread dough on greased 17x14-inch cookie sheet or jellyroll sheet. Roll with rolling pin or pat with hand to 1 inch from edge of pan. Bake for 25 minutes. Cut into 1½-inch bars. Makes about 48 bars.

Favorite Island Cookery Book IV

Chocolate Walnut Crumb Bars

1 cup (2 sticks) butter,
  softened
2 cups flour
½ cup sugar
¼ teaspoon salt
2 cups (12-ounce package)
  chocolate chips, divided

1¼ cups (14-ounce can)
  sweetened condensed milk
1 teaspoon vanilla
1 cup chopped walnuts

Preheat oven to 350°. Beat butter in large mixing bowl until creamy. Add flour, sugar, and salt, and mix until crumbly. With floured fingers, press 2 cups crumb mixture onto bottom of greased, 9x13-inch baking pan; reserve remaining mixture. Bake for 10–12 minutes until edges are golden brown.

Warm 1½ cups chocolate chips and sweetened condensed milk in small, heavy saucepan over low heat, stirring until smooth. Stir in vanilla. Spread chocolate mixture over hot crust. Stir walnuts and remaining chocolate chips into reserved crumb mixture; sprinkle over chocolate filling. Bake for 25–30 minutes until center is set. Cool in pan on wire rack. Cut with sharp knife into bars. Makes 24–30.

Kailua Cooks

The Best Date Bars

CRUST:
½ cup butter, softened   1 cup sifted flour
¼ cup sugar

Mix butter, sugar, and flour until crumbly. Press evenly in a 9x9-inch or 7x11-inch pan. Bake at 400° for 10–12 minutes. Do not brown the Crust.

FILLING:
⅓ cup flour   ½ cup chopped dates
½ teaspoon baking powder   1 teaspoon vanilla
¼ teaspoon salt   ½ cup chopped walnuts
2 eggs, beaten   Powdered sugar (optional)
1 cup brown sugar

Mix together the flour, baking powder, and salt. Set aside. Beat eggs, add brown sugar and dates, and blend well. Add flour mixture, vanilla, and nuts. Spread over baked Crust and bake at 350° for 30 minutes. Cut into squares or bars while hot. May dust with powdered sugar, if desired.

Favorite Recipes for Islanders

Mango Bars

CRUST:

2 cups flour   1 cup butter, softened
½ cup sugar

Preheat oven to 350°. Grease 9x13-inch baking pan. Combine flour with sugar. Add butter and press into prepared baking pan; bake 7 minutes.

FILLING:

4 cups chopped mangoes   1 teaspoon vanilla
¾ cup sugar   1 teaspoon cinnamon
⅓ cup water   3 tablespoons cornstarch
1 teaspoon lemon juice   3 tablespoons water

Combine mangoes, sugar, water, lemon juice, vanilla, and cinnamon in a saucepan. Simmer until the mangoes are tender, about 10 minutes. Combine cornstarch and water; stir into the mango mixture and cook until thickened. Remove from heat and cool slightly. Pour over prepared Crust.

TOPPING:

2 cups quick oats   ½ cup sugar
¼ cup flour   ⅔ cup butter, softened

Combine oats, flour, and sugar. Blend in butter and sprinkle over mango mixture. Bake for 50 minutes; cool and cut into bars. Store in refrigerator. Makes 2 dozen.

Kailua Cooks

Chien Doi
(Chinese Doughnuts)

FILLING:

½ cup chopped roasted
  peanuts

½ cup shredded coconut
3 tablespoons white sugar

Combine peanuts, coconut, and white sugar in a bowl.

DOUGH:

3¾ cups mochiko
1½ cups dark brown sugar

1¼ cups hot water
1 teaspoon sherry

Place mochiko into large mixing bowl. In a small bowl, dissolve brown sugar in hot water. Stir sugar water into mochiko. Make a stiff dough. Do not overwork dough. Add sherry and mix. Shape Dough into 1½-inch-diameter rolls. Cut rolls into ½-inch slices. Flatten each piece and place 1 tablespoon Filling into center of dough piece. Bring up edges and pinch together to seal.

¼ cup toasted sesame seeds   Oil for deep-frying

Roll balls in sesame seeds. Heat oil to 350°. Fry balls until golden brown. If you want hollow chien doi, press balls against side of pan while frying so balls will expand.

Unbearably Good! Mochi Lovers' Cookbook

Aloha shirts, or Hawaiian shirts, began their rise to popularity in the 1920s and 1930s. These brightly colored shirts with bold Hawaiian-themed prints actually got their start in the sugar cane and pineapple plantations. To keep cool, plantation workers created the original shirts by combining styles of clothing brought with them from the Philippines, Japan, and China.

Mochi Snowballs

1 (10-ounce) package mochiko
2 cups flour
1½ cups white sugar
4 tablespoons baking powder
½ teaspoon salt

1½ cups milk
3 eggs, beaten
Oil
Powdered sugar for sprinkling

Heat oil to 350° in deep fryer. Mix mochiko, flour, sugar, baking powder, and salt together in a large mixing bowl. Add milk and eggs and mix until well blended. Drop by tablespoons into hot oil and fry until golden brown. Sprinkle with powdered sugar while still warm.

Unbearably Good! Mochi Lovers' Cookbook

Hawaiian Snowflakes

I serve these all year because they are always a hit and so easy to make. They freeze well, too.

2 egg whites
⅔ cup granulated sugar

1 cup chopped walnuts
1 cup chocolate chips

Preheat oven to 350°. Beat whites until fluffy. Gradually add sugar and beat until stiff. Carefully fold in nuts and chocolate chips. Drop by teaspoonfuls onto foil-covered cookie sheet. Place in oven, close door, count to ten, and turn oven off. Do not open door until several hours later or the next day when oven has completely cooled. Makes about 4 dozen.

The When You Live in Hawaii You Get Very Creative During Passover Cookbook

Pies and Other Desserts

James Dole paid 1.1 million or $12 an acre for the island of Lana'i in 1922, and planted 16,000 acres of pineapples there. Today more than one-third of the world's commercial supply of pineapples comes from Hawai'i.

Fresh Mango Pie

For mango pie, you can use pretty ripe mangoes. If you prefer tart pies, use mangoes that are less ripe and add the juice from half a lemon.

4 cups mango slices
1 teaspoon lemon juice
½ cup sugar
3 tablespoons cornstarch

1 teaspoon cinnamon
Pastry for (8-inch) 2-crust pie
1 tablespoon butter or
   margarine

Put all ingredients except pastry and butter in a bowl and mix them gently. Line a pie pan with half the pastry. Pour mango filling into the pastry and dot with butter. Cover pie with top crust. Crimp edges and slit crust to allow steam to escape. Bake pie at 400° for about 45 minutes or until crust is golden brown and juice is bubbly.

Kau Kau Kitchen

Mango Chiffon Pie

5 cups half-ripe mango slices
1 cup sugar, divided
3 eggs, separated
6 tablespoons water, divided

2 teaspoons unflavored gelatin
1 tablespoon lemon juice
1 (9-inch) pastry shell, baked

Combine mango slices and ½ cup sugar. Let stand 20 minutes. Cook over low heat until tender. Cool. Put through sieve or purée in blender.

In a saucepan, beat egg yolks slightly. Add 3 tablespoons water and ¼ cup sugar. Cook over low heat until thickened. Soak gelatin in 3 tablespoons cold water. Stir into hot mixture until dissolved. Add lemon juice and mango sauce. Blend in. Refrigerate until slightly set.

Beat egg whites until foamy. Gradually beat in remaining ¼ cup sugar until stiff. Fold into mango mixture. Pour into baked pastry shell. Chill until firm.

Hawaii–Cooking with Aloha

Guava Chiffon Pie

4 eggs
½ cup sugar, divided
¼ teaspoon salt
1¼ cups frozen guava
  concentrate, divided

1 package unflavored gelatin
¼ cup water
1 tablespoon lemon juice
1 9-inch pie shell, baked
Whipped cream for garnish

Separate eggs. Beat egg yolks until light. Add ¼ cup sugar, ¼ teaspoon salt, and ½ cup guava concentrate. Cook mixture in top of double boiler until smooth and thickened slightly, stirring continually. Soak gelatin in water to soften and add to hot mixture. Remove from heat and cool to room temperature. Add lemon juice and remainder of guava concentrate. Chill until partly set.

Whip egg whites until stiffened. Add remaining ¼ cup sugar slowly while continually beating. Whip partly set gelatin mixture and fold in egg whites. Pour into pie shell and top with whipped cream.

Hawai'i's Island Cooking

Banana Crunch Pie

6 cups banana chunks
2 tablespoons lemon juice
1 cup flour
½ cup brown sugar
½ cup butter, cold

½ cup sugar
½ teaspoon cinnamon
½ teaspoon nutmeg
1 unbaked, 9-inch pie shell

Combine bananas and lemon juice and let stand 15 minutes. Preheat oven to 400°.

In a small bowl, combine flour and brown sugar. Cut in butter until mixture looks mealy. Add sugar, cinnamon, and nutmeg to bananas and mix gently. Pour into pie shell and top with flour crumb mixture. Spread crumbs to edge of pie. Bake 40 minutes.

Island Flavors

Pineapple Mincemeat

1 pint chopped meat
3 pints crushed pineapple
  with juice (canned or fresh)
1 extra cup pineapple juice
1½ cups raisins
1 cup currants
1 tablespoon salt
3 cups brown sugar
1½ cups molasses

Butter size of egg
2 teaspoons cinnamon
2 teaspoons allspice
1 teaspoon cloves
½ teaspoon pepper
1 tablespoon cornstarch
Cold water
1 cup wine or brandy
2 tablespoons brandy per pie

Simmer all ingredients, except cornstarch, water, and wine, for an hour, stirring often. Add cornstarch dissolved in a little cold water, and boil again. Then add 1 cup wine or brandy, and seal in glass jars. When making the pies, heat the meat, and add 2 tablespoons brandy to each pie.

How to Use Hawaiian Fruit

Macadamia Nut Pie

¼ pound (1 stick) butter,
  softened
¾ cup sugar
3 eggs, slightly beaten
¾ cup dark corn syrup

¼ teaspoon salt
1 teaspoon vanilla
1 cup chopped, unsalted
  macadamia nuts
1 unbaked pie shell

Cream butter; add sugar gradually. When light and lemon colored, add the beaten eggs. Blend in corn syrup. Add salt, vanilla, and nuts. Mix well, then pour into the unbaked pie shell. Bake in a 350° oven for 35–40 minutes.

Joys of Hawaiian Cooking

Haupia Pie

1 (10- to 12-ounce) can
  coconut milk
¼ cup sugar
¼ cup water

3 tablespoons cornstarch
1 (8-inch) prepared graham
  cracker crust

Put coconut milk and sugar in saucepan and heat. Measure water in a liquid measuring cup and add the cornstarch to it. Stir until smooth and add to the hot coconut milk. Cook on medium heat until mixture thickens, stirring constantly. Cool to room temperature and pour into prepared crust. Refrigerate at least 3 hours. Serves 6.

Aunty Pua's Keiki Cookbook

There are only twelve letters in the Hawaiian Alphabet:
  Vowels: A, E, I, O, U
  Consonants: H, K, L, M, N, P, W

Nancy Veracruz's Extra Special Liliko'i Pie

CRUST:

1½ cups flour
2 tablespoons wheat germ
2 tablespoons chopped
  walnuts or macadamia nuts

¾ teaspoon salt
½ cup shortening (or half
  shortening, half margarine)
2–3 tablespoons water

In a bowl combine flour, wheat germ, nuts, and salt. Cut in shortening. Gradually add water to blend, and form into ball. Roll out between 2 sheets of floured wax paper, place in 9-inch pie plate, and bake in 475° oven for 8–10 minutes.

FILLING:

1 package unflavored gelatin
¼ cup water
½ cup liliko'i (passion fruit)
  juice

½ teaspoon salt
1 cup sugar, divided
4 eggs, separated
Whipped cream

Sprinkle gelatin slowly into water to soak. In double boiler, cook liliko'i juice, salt, ½ cup sugar, and egg yolks. Stir constantly until thick, then add the gelatin. Let this cool.

Beat egg whites and slowly add remaining ½ cup sugar until it holds a peak. Fold into thoroughly cooled liliko'i mixture and pour into baked pie shell. Refrigerate 3–4 hours. Top with whipped cream at serving time.

Hawaii Cooks Throughout the Year

Liliko'i Pistachio Pie

CRUST:

3 cups flour
3½ tablespoons sugar
1⅛ teaspoons salt

1 cup oil
3⅓ tablespoons milk

Mix all together. Press in 9x13-inch pan. Prick shell. Bake at 325° for 45 minutes until golden brown. Cool.

FIRST LAYER:

1½ cups powdered sugar, sifted
2 (8-ounce) packages cream cheese, softened

2 cups Cool Whip

Beat sugar and cream cheese. Stir in Cool Whip. Spread on Crust. Refrigerate until set.

SECOND LAYER:

2 (3¾-ounce) boxes pistachio instant pudding

Follow pudding directions on box label. Spread over First Layer. Refrigerate.

THIRD LAYER:

2 packages unflavored gelatin
½ cup cold water
6 eggs, separated

1⅓ cups sugar, divided
1 cup fresh liliko'i juice

Soak gelatin in water. Beat egg yolks until light. Add 1 cup sugar and continue beating until light. Cook in double boiler, stirring continuously until thick. Remove from heat; add soft gelatin. Beat and cool to room temperature. Add liliko'i juice. Chill to partly set. Whip egg whites until stiff. Add remaining ⅓ cup sugar slowly while beating. Fold into whipped gelatin. Spread over Second Layer.

TOPPING:

1 (8-ounce) container Cool Whip

Finely chopped macadamia nuts, for sprinkling

Spread Cool Whip over Third Layer. Sprinkle with nuts.

Hawai'i's Best Local Desserts

Okinawan Sweet Potato Pie with Haupia Topping

A new favorite that combines the different textures of a light crust, dense sweet potato, and smooth haupia. A hands-down winner at any gathering.

CRUST:

4 tablespoons sugar
1½ cups flour
½ cup chopped nuts (optional)

¾ cup margarine or butter
   (1½ sticks)

Combine sugar, flour, and nuts. Cut margarine into flour mixture until texture is sandy. Press lightly into 9x13-inch pan. Bake at 325° for 20–25 minutes.

FILLING:

8 tablespoons butter or
   margarine, softened
1 cup sugar
2 eggs, beaten
2 cups Okinawan sweet potato,
   cooked and mashed

½ cup evaporated milk
1 teaspoon vanilla
¼ teaspoon salt

Beat butter and sugar. Add eggs and mix. Gradually mix in mashed sweet potatoes. Add evaporated milk, vanilla, and salt; mix well. Pour onto Crust. Bake at 350° for 30–35 minutes. Cool.

HAUPIA TOPPING:

½ cup sugar
½ cup cornstarch
1½ cups water

2 (12-ounce) cans frozen
   coconut milk, thawed

Combine sugar and cornstarch; stir in water and blend well. Stir sugar mixture into coconut milk; cook and stir over low heat until thickened. Cool slightly. Pour coconut milk mixture (haupia) over the pie filling and refrigerate.

Hawai'i's Best Local Desserts

The Okinawan sweet potato has a unique dark purple color and a dry texture and sweet flavor, making it unlike other types of sweet potatoes. Purple sweet potatoes contain a high fiber level.

Coconut Cream Pie

2 cups milk
1 cup sugar, divided
¼ teaspoon salt
¼ cup grated coconut
4 egg yolks
3 tablespoons cornstarch

1 tablespoon butter
1 teaspoon vanilla extract
2 drops almond extract
1 (9-inch) pie shell, baked
Sweetened whipped cream
    (optional)

Combine milk, ½ cup sugar, salt, and coconut in double boiler, and heat to near boiling. Mix together egg yolks, remaining ½ cup sugar, and cornstarch; add to milk mixture and cook until thickened. Add butter, vanilla, and almond extract. Cool and pour into baked pie shell. Top with whipped cream and additional coconut, if desired. Serves 6–8.

The Tastes and Tales of Moiliili

Frozen Lemon Pie

2 eggs, separated
⅓ cup lemon juice
Grated rind of ½ lemon

½ cup sugar, divided
1 cup whipped cream
½ cup cookie crumbs, divided

Beat egg yolks; add lemon juice, rind, and all but 2 tablespoons of sugar. Cook over low heat, stirring constantly for 15 minutes; cool. Beat egg whites until stiff; add remaining sugar. Fold into egg yolk mixture and mix. Beat cream and fold into mixture.

Line a 9-inch pan with wax paper. Sprinkle some crumbs on paper and add lemon mixture. Shake more crumbs on top. Cover with wax paper and freeze. Keeps well in the freezer.

Hilo Woman's Club Cookbook

Pumpkin Ice Cream Pie

1 pint vanilla ice cream
1 (9-inch) pie shell, baked
1 cup pumpkin
¾ cup sugar

¼ teaspoon ginger
¼ teaspoon salt
1 cup whipped cream
½ cup chopped nuts

Soften ice cream and spread in pie shell. Freeze until ice cream is solid. Combine pumpkin, sugar, ginger, and salt. Fold in whipped cream. Pour over ice cream. Top with nuts. Freeze.

A Lei of Recipes

Chocolate Macadamia Ice Cream Pie

This pie is more than a mouthful of seduction.

1 cup Chocolate Macadamia
   Nut Cookie crumbs (see
   page 218)
¼ cup unsalted butter,
   melted
½ gallon Kona coffee ice
   cream

½ gallon chocolate ice cream
½ gallon vanilla ice cream
½ cup Bailey's Irish Cream
Whipped cream, diced
   macadamia nuts, and cookie
   crumbs for garnish

Combine cookie crumbs and butter, and mix well. Press mixture into a 9-inch pie pan. Cover crust with and lay alternately the 3 ice creams. Pour Bailey's Irish Cream over ice cream. Freeze overnight.

Slice pie into 8 wedges and top with whipped cream, diced macadamia nuts, and chocolate macadamia nut cookie crumbs. Makes 8 servings.

Sugar and Spice–Cookies Made with Love

Kona Coffee Ice Cream Pie

3 pints vanilla ice cream
1½ cups heavy cream, divided
½ cup coarsely chopped
   macadamia nuts
2 tablespoons coffee liqueur
2 tablespoons instant coffee

1 (9-inch) pastry shell, baked
4 egg whites
¼ teaspoon cream of tartar
½ cup sugar
Maraschino cherries for
   garnish

Soften 1 pint ice cream in a medium-size bowl. Beat ½ of the heavy cream in a small bowl until stiff. Fold into softened ice cream along with nuts and liqueur. If very soft, place in freezer until mixture holds its shape.

Soften remaining 2 pints ice cream in large bowl. Stir instant coffee into remaining heavy cream. Beat until stiff. Fold into remaining softened ice cream. Spread ⅔ coffee mixture in pastry shell. Make a depression in center. Spoon macadamia mixture into center. Mound remaining coffee mixture on top. Freeze overnight or until firm.

Beat egg whites and cream of tartar until foamy. Beat in sugar until meringue forms soft peaks. Cover ice cream filling with meringue and maraschino cherries in proportions desired. Chill.

Hawaii–Cooking with Aloha

Hawai'i is the only state that grows coffee. The 10-day Kona Coffee Cultural Festival in Kona, started in 1970, is recognized as the oldest product festival in Hawai'i, and is the only coffee festival in the United States. Kona coffee is only grown on the Big Island of Hawai'i, and any coffee claiming to be Kona coffee must be at least 10% pure Kona.

Max's Apple Cobbler

Everyone loves this dessert, including Max, our guinea pig, who feasts on the peels and cores.

5 cups peeled, cored, and
   sliced apples
Scant ½ cup sugar
1 teaspoon cinnamon
½ teaspoon nutmeg
2 teaspoons lemon juice

¼ cup sugar
¾ cup matzo or cake meal
⅛ teaspoon salt (optional)
6 tablespoons margarine
1 cup chopped nuts

Combine apples with next 4 ingredients. Pour into greased 1½-quart casserole. In another bowl, blend ¼ cup sugar, matzo meal, salt, and margarine until crumbly. Add nuts and sprinkle over apples. Bake in preheated 350° oven for 45–60 minutes, until crust is nicely browned. Serve hot, warm, or cold. Serves 6.

The When You Live in Hawaii You Get Very Creative During Passover Cookbook

Unlike the volcanic craters on the Big Island, Haleakala Crater is an erosion crater. Its last eruption in 1790 filled enormous canyons and raised the summit floor. An awesome playground for the adventurous, Haleakala Crater is vast and desolate . . . and awesomely beautiful.

Pineapple Bread Pudding

Most bread puddings call for whole eggs and milk, which is the source of lots of fat and calories. Pineapple packed in its' own juice adds to the flavor without the calories of heavy sugar syrups, so you can enjoy the taste without the guilt.

6 slices whole-wheat bread,
lightly toasted and cut
into cubes
¼ cup chopped dates
¼ cup golden raisins
1 (8-ounce) can crushed
pineapple, drained
1 egg
2 egg whites

½ cup sugar
⅓ cup water
1 teaspoon vanilla
½ teaspoon nutmeg
½ teaspoon cinnamon
1 (13-ounce) can evaporated
skim milk
Cinnamon sugar to sprinkle on
top

Preheat oven to 350°. Spray 8x8-inch pan with cooking spray. Place half of the bread on bottom of baking pan. Sprinkle with chopped dates and raisins and spread crushed pineapple over all; cover with remaining bread. Beat egg and egg whites with sugar until frothy; add in water until blended. Add vanilla, spices, and milk, and beat until mixed well. Pour over bread mixture; sprinkle cinnamon sugar on top. Bake for about 40 minutes, or until center tests dry. Remove from oven and cool on wire rack. Cut into squares. Makes 9 servings.

Nutritional analysis per serving: Cal 175; Fat 2g; Chol 30mg; Sod 160mg

The Best of Heart-y Cooking

The Pineapple Garden Maze at the Dole Plantation was the "World's Largest Maze," according to The Guinness Book of World Records 2001. You can spend half an hour or half a day among its 1.7 miles of paths.

Tropical Bread Pudding

Quick and easy in the microwave.

**6 slices stale Portuguese sweet
bread or French bread,
cubed or torn in small
pieces (about 6 cups)**
½ cup raisins
2 apple bananas, chopped
**¼ cup chopped, dried papaya,
pineapple, mango, apricot,
or tropical trail mix, or half
a fresh papaya or mango,
chopped**

2 cups milk
1 tablespoon butter
2 eggs
¾ cup sugar, or more to taste
1½ teaspoons vanilla
½ teaspoon cinnamon
¼ teaspoon salt

Butter or oil-spray a 2-quart baking dish. Add bread and fruit and set aside. Put milk and butter in a 4-cup, glass measure and microwave on HIGH for 3 minutes. In a bowl, beat eggs and sugar. Stir in a little hot milk and then whisk that mixture into the rest of the milk. Add vanilla, cinnamon, and salt. Pour mixture over the bread and fruit. Microwave the whole dish for 7 minutes, turning once. If the middle isn't firm, microwave for another minute or two, or until it firms up. Cool a bit before serving. This is a custard-like version of bread pudding and makes a good breakfast. To use for dessert, serve with Butter Rum Sauce.

BUTTER RUM SAUCE (OPTIONAL):
½ cup butter   **2 tablespoons rum**
½ cup sugar

Add sauce ingredients to a 4-cup, glass measure and microwave 2 minutes on HIGH. Stir and serve with pudding.

Island Flavors

Ni'ihau Island is a 72-square-mile, privately owned island also known as the "Forbidden Island." Sheltered from the influences of the outside world, the Hawaiian language is spoken almost exclusively there, and there are no cars, roads, hotels, restaurants, or electricity.

Lemon Pudding

1 cup sugar
⅛ teaspoon salt
¼ cup flour
2 tablespoons margarine,
  melted

4–5 tablespoons lemon juice
1 tablespoon grated lemon peel
2 egg yolks, well beaten
1 cup milk, scalded
2 egg whites, stiffly beaten

Combine sugar, salt, flour, and melted margarine. Add lemon juice and peel. Stir in well-beaten egg yolks and scalded milk. Mix well. Fold in beaten egg whites; pour into a greased, 1½-quart casserole. Bake in larger pan with 1 inch of hot water for 1 hour in 325° oven. Sponge cake comes to top, and layer of lemon custard forms on bottom.

Note: If it curdles, it will be all right after baking.

Hawaii Cooks Throughout the Year

Haupia
(Coconut Pudding)

2 cups boiling water
6 cups grated coconut
  (2 coconuts)

3 or 6 tablespoons cornstarch
  (for soft or firm pudding)
3½ tablespoons sugar

Pour boiling water over coconut and allow to stand for 15 minutes. Strain through double thickness of cheesecloth, squeezing out as much of the milk as possible, about 3 cups. If not 3 cups, add milk poured from the coconut to equal 3 cups. Mix cornstarch (appropriate amount) with sugar and add sufficient coconut milk to make a smooth paste. Heat remaining milk to boiling and slowly stir in cornstarch paste. Boil until it thickens. Pour into mold and allow to cool. Cut into squares and serve on squares of ti leaves.

Joys of Hawaiian Cooking

Haupia Coconut Pudding

3 tablespoons cornstarch   ½ teaspoon salt
3 tablespoons sugar   2 cups coconut milk, divided

Combine dry ingredients. Add ½ cup of coconut milk and blend
to a smooth paste. Heat remaining milk on low heat. Add cornstarch mixture, stirring constantly until thickened. Pour into
shallow pan. Let it cool until firm. Yields 6 servings.

The Friends of 'Iolani Palace Cookbook

Coconut Tapioca Pudding

*This is without a doubt the simplest dessert recipe on record, and devoured
by everyone who tastes it. Its success depends on two things: the quality of
coconut milk used, and availability of especially fine, ripe fruit. If you are
able to find Mendonca's brand frozen coconut milk and a sweet, ripe, pineapple, or a couple of sweet mangoes, this is the dessert of the hour—made in
minutes.*

2½ cups frozen coconut   Egg-replacer for 1 egg (don't
  milk, thawed   use real egg here)
⅓ cup mild-flavored honey 3 cups seasonal fruit of your
3 tablespoons quick cooking   choice, chopped
  tapioca   6 sprigs mint (optional)
2 generous pinches salt

Put the coconut milk, honey, tapioca, salt, and egg-replacer in a
saucepan and let it stand 5 minutes. While it stands, prepare
the fruit, as necessary.

    Bring the pudding to a boil over medium heat, stirring often.
When it comes to a full boil, remove from heat. Let cool 20 minutes, then stir, and spoon pudding and ½ cup prepared fruit per
serving into 6 small bowls or parfait glasses, leaving an attractive sampling of fruit on top. Garnish with a mint leaf, if you
like. Serve warm. Yields 6 servings.

Vegetarian Nights

Berry Special Torte

Refreshing, light, relatively low in calories and it's made in advance.

MACAROON NUT CRUST:

5 ounces almond macaroons (about 1½ cups crumbled)

2 tablespoons unsalted margarine or butter, melted

½ cup chopped pecans or walnuts

Process macaroons and butter in food processor until coarsely ground. Add nuts and process until mixture begins to hold together. Press into bottom of 10x3-inch springform pan. Bake at 350° for 7–10 minutes or until golden. Cool.

FILLING:

2 egg whites, room temperature

1 cup sugar

1 tablespoon lemon juice

2 cups frozen, sliced strawberries

1 teaspoon vanilla extract

In large mixing bowl, place egg whites, sugar, lemon juice, strawberries, and vanilla. Blend on low speed. Increase to high and beat until stiff peaks form, about 10–15 minutes. Pour into cooled Macaroon Nut Crust. Cover and freeze until very firm, a minimum of 6 hours. The torte may be frozen at this point for 3 weeks. Cut into wedges and serve frozen.

STRAWBERRY SAUCE (OPTIONAL):

1 (10-ounce) package frozen, sliced strawberries

3 tablespoons frozen orange juice concentrate, undiluted, or 2 tablespoons orange marmalade

1 tablespoon currant jelly

1 cup sliced fresh strawberries

Slightly defrost strawberries and orange juice. Purée frozen berries and juice or marmalade in food processor; add currant jelly. Remove to a bowl and stir in fresh strawberries. Sauce may be refrigerated overnight. Serve with torte. Serves 12.

The When You Live in Hawaii You Get Very Creative During Passover Cookbook

Banana Soufflé

This is very simple and would be the perfect ending to a summer meal!

5 bananas	5 eggs, well beaten
1 pint whipping cream	½ teaspoon vanilla extract
¼ cup sugar	

Peel bananas and mash them smooth. Whip cream and sugar to stiff peaks. Mix mashed bananas, beaten eggs, and vanilla, until well incorporated. Carefully, fold the banana-egg mixture into whipped cream. Tape a parchment paper collar around a soufflé dish. Pour banana mixture into soufflé dish; bake at 350° until brown and light. Serve immediately.

Tropical Taste

Mango Dessert

CRUST:

1½ sticks margarine, softened	2 cups flour
	⅓ cup sugar

Mix softened margarine and flour; add sugar and mix well. Press in 9x13-inch pan and bake at 350° till lightly brown (10 minutes or so). Set aside.

FILLING:

2 packages gelatin	2 drops yellow food coloring
1 cup water	4 tablespoons lemon juice
1 cup hot water	4 cups sliced mangoes
¼ teaspoon salt	1 (8-ounce) carton Cool Whip
1 cup sugar	

Soften gelatin in cold water. Add hot water, salt, sugar, and food coloring. Mix. Add lemon juice and let cool. When it has congealed, add mangoes. Pour over Crust and refrigerate until firm. Cover with Cool Whip.

A Lei of Recipes

Orange Cream Dessert

CRUST:

¾ cup (1½ sticks) margarine
¼ cup firmly packed brown
  sugar

1½ cups flour
½ cup chopped nuts

Cream margarine and sugar. Add flour and nuts; mix well. Spread dough in 9x13-inch pan and bake at 375° for 10 minutes. Cool.

FILLING:

1 (8-ounce) package cream
  cheese, softened
¾ cup sugar or 1 cup
  powdered sugar

1 (4-ounce) carton Cool Whip

Beat cream cheese and sugar. Fold in Cool Whip. Spread Filling evenly on Crust. Chill for ½ hour.

TOPPING:

1 envelope unflavored gelatin
1 cup cold water, divided
1 (6-ounce) package orange
  Jell-O

2 cups hot water
1 pint orange sherbet
2 (11-ounce) cans Mandarin
  oranges, drained

Soften unflavored gelatin in ¼ cup water and set aside. In large bowl, dissolve Jell-O with hot water; add softened gelatin and remaining water and stir until dissolved. Fold in sherbet and Mandarin oranges. Pour Jell-O mixture over cream cheese mixture and refrigerate.

Friends and Celebrities Cookbook II

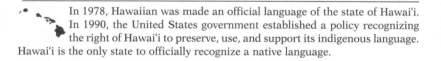

In 1978, Hawaiian was made an official language of the state of Hawai'i. In 1990, the United States government established a policy recognizing the right of Hawai'i to preserve, use, and support its indigenous language. Hawai'i is the only state to officially recognize a native language.

Grape Sponge

¼ package unflavored gelatin
¼ cup cold water
¾ cup sugar
1 cup grape juice

Juice of 1 lemon
2 egg whites, beaten
Cream or boiled custard

Soak gelatin in cold water and dissolve by standing dish or bowl in hot water. Dissolve sugar in fruit juices, and strain the gelatin into the mixture. Set in ice and water, and when it thickens, add beaten egg whites; beat with egg beater until it is light and spongy. Put into glass dish or shape in mold on ice. Serve with cream or boiled custard made from the yolk of the eggs.

How to Use Hawaiian Fruit

Grapes in Sour Cream

Green seedless grapes
Sour cream

Dark brown sugar

Prepare this the morning of serving. Pick over clusters of seedless grapes and pick each one off individually; discard any soft or bad ones. Cover them in enough whipped sour cream to really coat each grape, then sprinkle with dark brown sugar to taste. Refrigerate and keep stirring whenever you're at the refrigerator.

Just before serving, spread grapes on baking sheet and sprinkle brown sugar (¼ cup) over the top of grapes. Place under the broiler very briefly, just enough to caramelize the sugar.

Hawaii Cooks Throughout the Year

Kona Coffee Chocolate Pôt de Crème

12 ounces Hawaiian semisweet
  chocolate, finely chopped
2 large eggs
½ teaspoon salt
1½ cups fresh milk
1 tablespoon Irish cream or
  other liqueur

3 tablespoons instant Kona
  coffee
Whipped cream and chocolate
  shavings (optional)

Place first 3 ingredients in blender container. Scald together milk and liqueur over medium-high heat, stirring constantly. Remove from heat and stir in Kona coffee granules until dissolved. Add hot liquid to blender and immediately blend all ingredients for 5–8 seconds at high speed. Divide mixture among 8 small dessert ramekins or pôt de crème cups and chill until firm, at least 4 hours. Serve unadorned in traditional manner, or garnish with a dollop of slightly sweetened whipped cream and shaved chocolate. Almost any liqueur of choice is suitable for taste variations. Serves 8.

Kona on My Plate

Academy Café Chocolate Sauce

One of the loveliest spots in Honolulu to lunch is the courtyard restaurant at the Honolulu Academy of Arts.

1 (16-ounce) can chocolate
    fudge topping
8 ounces chocolate syrup
½ teaspoon cinnamon

Salt to taste
4 tablespoons Kahlúa liqueur
    or crème de cacao
Candied ginger for topping

In a medium bowl, mix all the ingredients (except ginger) together until well blended. Refrigerate until ready to serve. Serve on vanilla ice cream with chopped candied ginger.

Hawaiian Country Tables

Mai Tai Sundae Sauce

1 (12-ounce) jar pineapple-
    mango jam, or peach jam
3 tablespoons butter
2 teaspoons lime juice

¼ cup orange marmalade
½ teaspoon each: cinnamon,
    cloves, and nutmeg
¼ cup rum

Combine all ingredients, except rum. Cook over low heat until smoothly blended. Add rum. Serve warm over ice cream (macadamia flavor is best). Bananas may also be added just before serving.

The Friends of 'Iolani Palace Cookbook

Famous Hawaiians include Tia Carrere, Don Ho, Kelly Hu, Nicole Kidman, Jason Scott Lee, Bette Midler, Kelly Preston, Harold Sakata, James Shigeta, and Don Stroud.

Almond Float

2 packages Knox gelatin
3½ cups water, divided
1 cup evaporated milk
1 cup sugar

2 teaspoons almond extract
1 can lychees
2 cans Mandarin oranges

Soften gelatin in ½ cup water. Combine remaining water and milk in saucepan and bring to a boil. Add gelatin mixture; cook for 2 minutes. Cool slightly; add almond extract. Pour into 9x13-inch dish and refrigerate until firm.

Before serving, combine cans of fruit (juice included) in a bowl. Cut almond pudding into squares and place over fruit. Refrigerate.

Island Flavors

Vanilla Coconut Ball Treats

1½ cups sweetened coconut
  shreds
1 stick butter
1 cup condensed milk

1 large Symphony candy bar
Vanilla ice cream
Chopped nuts (optional)

Brown coconut shreds under broiler until golden brown. Set aside and cool. Melt butter, then add milk and chocolate bar a piece at a time, and heat slowly until the consistency is creamy. Make ice cream into balls and roll in coconut shreds. Top each ball with chocolate sauce; serve immediately. Nuts of your choice can be added to the top of each vanilla ball, if desired.

Recipe by Fire Fighter 3 Brian Derby
Hawai'i's Favorite Firehouse Recipes

Come to the Lūʻau!

Always held at sunset, usually near the beach where the sun sets beautifully over the ocean, a lūʻau typically lasts several hours. While you are enjoying the feast, talented performers entertain and educate you about Hawaiian culture with colorful and dramatic dances in traditional costumes. The hula is the most popular dance, where girls in grass skirts perform graceful movements to the strums of the ukulele. Usually the audience gets an opportunity to learn the dance as well.

The cooking of the kalua ("pit") pig typically goes like this: A large pit is dug in the sand early in the morning of the day of the lūʻau—this pit is called the "imu." The bottom of the imu has Kiawe logs, then river rocks. The fire is now started. A couple of hours later, moist banana stalks are placed on the hot coals and rocks, then a bed of banana leaves. Now here comes the pig! He is accompanied by sweet potatoes and laulau, then covered with more banana leaves and ti leaves. Wet burlap bags or the like add steam and moisture; a tarp covers this, then sand covers the pit. It cooks all day long—six to eight hours—and by sunset, it is ready!

Traditional Hawaiian lūʻaus feature hula dancers. After they perform, they usually invite people from the audience to come on stage and try their "hips" at it. The young ones are usually the most enthusiastic.

The ceremonial pig is ready! These "warriors" entertain nightly at the Hilton on Maui in their lūʻau performance called "Drums of the Pacific." No matter the place or size of the feast, a sunset lūʻau is the most famous and frequently attended event in Hawaiʻi.

TYPICAL LŪʻAU FOOD

Kalua Pig (Page 126)

Laulau (Page 131) – Chicken, pork, or fish wrapped in ti leaves and steamed

Poi – Pounded taro root

Lomi Salmon (Page 37) – Cold diced salmon with diced tomatoes, onions, and green onions

Chicken Long Rice (Page 154) – Opaque noodles

Chicken Lūʻau (Page 144) – Baked taro leaves

Mahimahi (Pages 177-178) – fish

Yams or Sweet Potatoes (Pages 94-96)

Tropical Fruit – Pineapples, mangoes, papayas

Sweet Potato or **Poi Rolls**

Haupia (Pages 243-244) – Coconut-flavored dessert; a stiff pudding

Mai Tais (Page 20) or other tropical drinks and punches

Glossary of Food Terms

aburage [ah-boo-rah-gay] – Found in Asian markets, Japanese-style fried bean curd is prepared in thin sheets, square or rectangular, and is sold frozen. The Chinese type, dow foo pok, comes in cubes. It can be kept frozen for months. Also known as a-ge.

'ahi [ah-HEE] – The Hawaiian name for yellowfin tuna. It is also called shibi in Japanese.

aji-mirin [ah-JEE MIHR-ihn] – Japanese sweet cooking rice wine.

ajinomoto [ah-JEE-noh-MOH-toh] – A popular flavor enhancer in Japanese and Chinese cooking. Commonly known as MSG, it has no pronounced flavor of its own, but it has the ability to intensify flavors.

apple banana – This small Hawaiian banana grows three to five inches long. The taste has a hint of apple and papaya and changes from tart-sweet to sweet-tart as it ripens. Apple bananas do not turn brown when peeled, and have a longer shelf life than regular bananas.

baking bananas – Also called plantains, cooking bananas, or Mexican potatoes. In tropical countries, these bananas play the role of the potato in cooking. Can be green, yellow, or red-like in color. They cannot be eaten raw.

char siu [char see-you] – Chinese for roast barbecued pork, it is reddish in color and slightly sweet in taste. It is used for topping saimin (Japanese noodle soup) and in many Chinese dishes.

chayote [chi-OH-tay] – This bland-tasting squash resembles a pale, wrinkled pear. It must be peeled and cooked before serving. The seed is edible. Look for those that are small, firm, and unblemished.

Chinese bean sauce – Salty sauce made from fermented soybeans.

Chinese wood ear – A variety of mushroom with a crunchy texture and bland taste. It absorbs the taste of other flavors. Also known as cloud ear, tree ear (the larger, thicker specimens), or silver ear (albinos). Found in Asian markets.

coconut syrup – A syrup made from coconut milk and sugar. It is usually found in 10-ounce bottles.

daikon [DI-kuhn; DI-kon] – Derived from the Japanese words dai (large) and kon (root). A large Asian radish, usually white in color. Shred raw for salads and garnishes, or cook similar to turnips in soups and stir-fry. Best when firm and unwrinkled.

enoki mushrooms [en-oh-kee] – Crisp, delicate mushrooms come with long, spaghetti-like stems topped with tiny, snowy white caps. Enoki mushrooms have a mild, almost fruity taste. They are good raw in salads and may be used as garnish for soups or other hot dishes. Add at last minute, if used as part of a cooked dish, to avoid making them tough. Also called enokitake and enokidake. Available in Asian markets and some supermarkets.

fish sauce – This condiment/flavoring can be flavored many ways depending on the use, but is based on the liquid flavoring from salted, fermented fish. Also known as: nam pla (Thai), nuoc nam (Vietnamese), patis (Filipino), and harm har (Chinese).

five-spice powder – Chinese ground spice mixture of equal parts cinnamon, cloves, fennel seed, star anise, and szechuan peppercorns. Can be found in Asian markets and most supermarkets.

groundnut oil – Peanut oil

haupia [ha-oo-pia] – Hawaiian name for coconut pudding. Also commonly used to refer to many coconut-flavored desserts.

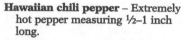

Hawaiian chili pepper – Extremely hot pepper measuring ½–1 inch long.

Hawaiian salt – Produced from the Hawaiian waters. Hawaiian, kosher, and sea salt adhere to food better than table salt. Noniodized table salt can be substituted for any of these, but only use half as much, since table salt is more dense.

hoisin sauce [hoy-sihn] – This thick, reddish-brown sauce is a mixture of soybeans, garlic, chile peppers, and various spices. It tastes sweet and spicy and is mainly used as a table condiment and flavoring for many meat, poultry, and shellfish dishes. Also called Peking sauce and Chinese miso sauce. It can be found in Asian markets and many large supermarkets.

'inamona [ee-nah-MO-nuh] – Seasoning mix made from grinding roasted kukui nuts and Hawaiian salt. Roasted salted cashew nuts can be substituted.

jícama [HEE-kah-mah] – This large, bulbous root vegetable has a thin brown skin and white crunchy flesh that has a sweet, nutty flavor. Can be eaten both raw and cooked. Available from November through May. Can be purchased in Mexican markets and supermarkets. Often referred to as the Mexican potato.

katakuriko [ka-ta-ka-REE-ko] – Japanese potato starch. This gluten-free starch is used to thicken soups and gravies and for coating food for frying. Cornstarch can be substituted. Can be found in supermarkets.

kim chee [KIHM chee] – Spicy-hot, pungent Korean pickled vegetables. Commercial kim chee can be purchased in Korean markets.

kinako [KEE-nah-koh] – Japanese for soy flour—finely ground flour made from soybeans. It is high in protein (twice that of wheat flour) and low in carbohydrates. Sold in health food stores and some supermarkets.

ko choo jung [koh choo CHANG] – Korean spicy-hot chile bean paste.

Kona coffee [KO-nah] – Rich coffee made from beans grown only in the Kona district on the island of Hawai'i. Must contain a minimum of 10% pure Kona coffee beans to be called "Kona blend" coffee.

laulau [lau lau'] – chicken, pork, or fish wrapped in ti leaves and steamed

liliko'i [lee-lee-ko-'ee] – Hawaiian for passion fruit. The common variety in Hawai'i is yellow-skinned with a tangy juice.

long rice – Translucent thread-like noodles made from mung bean flour.

lū'au [Loo-'ah-oo] – The Hawaiian word "lū'au" means "young taro tops," and also refers to a dish made with the leaves, cooked with coconut milk and chicken, octopus, or squid. Lū'au has come to be sononymous with a celebration at which these foods are served.

lumpia [LOOM-pee-ah] – The Philippine version of an egg roll. Consists of a thin shell, made of flour or cornstarch, eggs, and water, wrapped around a filling of chopped raw or cooked vegetables, meat, or a combination of the two, and fried. Can be served as an appetizer or side dish.

lychee [LEE-chee] – Also known as li chi, this small Southeast Asian fruit has a rough, bright red outer skin, creamy, juicy white flesh, and one seed. Good plain or in salads or desserts. When dried and crisp, they are called lychee nuts, and are eaten as a snack.

mahimahi [MAH-hee MAH-hee] – A type of dolphin, not to be confused with the dolphin that is a mammal. A moderately fat fish with firm, flavorful flesh, it ranges in weight from 3 to 45 pounds and can be purchased in steaks or fillets. Mahimahi is best prepared simply, as in grilling or broiling. Also called dolphinfish and dorado.

mai fun [MAAI-fun] – Chinese semi-transparent, thin noodles that turn white upon cooking. Made from long-grain rice powder and water, they can be deep-fried or softened in hot water. Can substitute vermicelli.

mānoa lettuce [mah-no-ah] – Ruffled, yellow-green leaves with crunchy, sweet flavor. Excellent for salads.

matzo meal – Ground matzo is available in fine and medium textures. It is used in a variety of foods, to thicken soups, and for breading foods to be fried. Can be found in Jewish markets and most supermarkets.

mirin sake [MIHR-ihn SAH-kee] – A Japanese low-alcohol, sweet, golden wine made from glutinous rice used to add sweetness and flavor. Substitute 1 tablespoon cream sherry or 1 teaspoon sugar for each tablespoon mirin.

miso [MEE-soh] – Japanese for fermented soybean paste, ranging from a mild white version to a stronger red version. It is often used as the base to a broth.

mochi [MOH-chee] – Japanese "cake" made of cooked, pounded mochi rice or of steamed sweet rice flour.

mochiko [MOH-chee-koh] – Flour made from sweet or mochi rice.

mung bean – A small dried bean that needs no presoaking. When cooked, they have a tender texture and sweet flavor. Mung beans have yellow flesh, and a skin that is normally green but sometimes yellow or black. Dried mung beans are ground into flour, which is used to make noodles in China and a variety of dishes in India. Most commonly used to grow bean sprouts.

naan [NAHN] – An East Indian flat, yeast bread that is lightly levened by a natural yeast starter developed from airborne yeasts. It has a soft center and smoky, crisp crust. Traditionally baked in a charcoal-fired clay oven called a tandoor, but a hot oven will work.

nori [NOH-ree] – Japanese for purple or greenish-black dried seaweed used to wrap sushi and rice balls. They can be cut into squares and eaten as a snack or appetizer, or finely cut or crushed for use as seasoning or as a garnish in soups and salads.

nori goma furikake [NOH-ree GOH-mah FOO-ree-kah-keh] – A seasoning of dried seaweed, sesame seeds, and assorted seasonings used for flavoring rice. Available in specialty markets.

nuoc nam [noo-AHK NAHM] – Commonly known as fish sauce, this Vietnamese condiment can be flavored many ways depending on the use, but is based on the liquid flavoring from salted, fermented fish. Also known as: nam pla (Thai), patis (Filipino), and harm har (Chinese).

ogo [OH-go] – The Japanese word for sea vegetable. Also known in Hawaiian as limu manauea, a term originally applied to plants that grow in wet places, but now used exclusively for edible seaweeds.

ono [OH-noh] – The Hawaiian word for wahoo, a fish with delicate white meat.

'ono [OH-noh] – The Hawaiian word for delicious.

opah [OH-pah] – Also called moonfish, the opah is a large fish that can grow up to 200 pounds. Its pinkish-colored flesh possesses a rich, full flavor and fine texture. Can substitute swordfish or tuna.

'ōpakapaka [oh-pah-kah-PAH-kah] – Commonly known as Hawaiian pink snapper, this fish is found in the waters surrounding the Hawaiian Islands. Its sweet, delicate flesh is firm in texture and ranges from white to pink in color.

oyster sauce – This Asian seasoning is made of oysters, brine, and soy sauce, cooked until thick and concentrated.

panko [PAHN-koh] – Bread crumbs used in Japanese cooking for coating fried foods. The texture is more coarse than typical bread crumbs used in the United States. Panko is sold in Asian markets.

patis [PA-teese] – Commonly known as fish sauce, this Filipino condiment can be flavored many ways depending on the use, but is based on the liquid flavoring from salted, fermented fish. Also known as: nam pla (Thai), nuoc nam (Vietnamese), and harm har (Chinese).

Pernod [pehr NOH] – A yellowish, licorice-flavored liqueur similar to absinthe.

poi [poh-ee] – A Hawaiian staple, this thick, gray paste is made from cooked taro root that is pounded to a paste. It can be eaten by itself, mixed with milk to make a porridge, or served as a condiment for meat and fish. It is available in some specialty markets.

poisson cru [pwah-SOHN crew] – Raw fish

poke [po-kay] – The Hawaiian word meaning to slice or to cut into small, bite-sized pieces. It is also a traditional Hawaiian dish of sliced raw seafood seasoned with seaweed, Hawaiian salt, or Hawaiian red chili peppers.

pūpū [poo-poo] – The Hawaiian term for any hot or cold appetizer, which can include a wide range of items such as macadamia nuts and won tons.

quinoa [KEEN-wah] – This tiny, bead-shaped, ivory-colored grain cooks like rice but in less time and expands to four or five times its size. Its flavor is delicate, almost bland. It contains more protein than any other grain and is also higher in unsaturated fats and lower in carbohydrates. Quinoa can be found in most health-food stores and some supermarkets.

sake [SAH-kee] – Japanese rice wine typically made from steamed glutinous rice. It has a relatively low alcohol content. Various types of this wine in Japan are known as sake and mirin, and in China as chia fan and yen hung.

sambal [SAHM-bahl] – Usually served as a condiment or side dish to rice and curried dishes. Various ingredients could include coconut, meat, seafood, or vegetables. Can be found in Indonesian markets and some Chinese markets.

sambal oelek [SAHM-bahl OH-leyk] – Indonesian ground chili paste. Very hot. Can be found in Indonesian markets and some Chinese markets.

sambol [SAM-bol] – Sri Lankan for sambal

seitan [SAY-tan] – This chewy, meat-like food is made from wheat gluten. It absorbs the flavors of the foods with which it is cooked. Available in health food stores and Asian markets.

shoyu [SHOH-yoo] – The Japanese word for soy sauce.

shrimp flakes, colored – Dried shavings of shrimp, colored red or green. Used to decorate sushi, and other foods.

soba [SOH-buh] – A Japanese noodle made of buckwheat and flour. Soba is a staple in areas of Japan where rice is difficult to grow.

somen [SOH-mehn] – A thin, white Japanese noodle made from wheat flour. It is almost always served cold. May substitute angel hair pasta or vermicelli.

sukiyaki [soo-kee-YAH-kee; skee-YAH-kee] – Consists of stir-fried bite-size pieces of meat, vegetables, and sometimes noodles and tofu. It is flavored with soy sauce, dashi (or other broth), and mirin, and is usually prepared at the table. Known in Japan as the "friendship dish."

sushi [SOO-shee] – A Japanese specialty made with boiled rice flavored with a sweetened rice vinegar. Once cooled the rice has a glossy sheen and separates easily. Sushi are designed to be finger food and can be served as appetizers, snacks, or a full meal. Soy sauce is often served with sushi for dipping. There is a wide variety of sushi including nigiri sushi (thin slices of raw fish seasoned with wasabi and wrapped around or layered with this rice), hosomaki (thin sushi rolls), and futomaki (thick sushi rolls).

tahini [tah-HEE-nee] – A thick paste made of ground sesame seeds.

takuwan [TAH-ku-wahn] – Pickled Japanese radish.

tamari [tuh-MAH-ree] – Dark Japanese sauce similar to soy sauce, but thicker. Made from soybeans, it is used in many dishes to enhance flavor, as a dipping sauce, for basting, and as a table condiment.

taro root [TAHR-oh; TEHR-oh] – A starchy, potato-like tuber with a brown, fibrous skin, and gray-white, sometimes purple-tinged flesh. Though acrid-tasting when raw, the root has a nut-like flavor when cooked. While extremely easy to digest, it should be noted that some varieties are highly toxic unless thoroughly cooked. Much like the potato, the taro root may be prepared in a variety of ways including boiling, frying, and baking. In Hawai'i, it is used to make poi. The taro root also has large, edible leaves (called callaloo in the Caribbean), which can be prepared and eaten like mustard or turnip greens. Available in ethnic markets and some specialty produce stores.

tempeh [TEHM-pay] – A fermented soybean cake with a texture similar to that of soft tofu. It has a yeasty, nutty flavor. Available at health food stores.

ti leaves [TEE] – Leaves used in Polynesia to wrap foods to be cooked. The leaves are removed before the food is eaten. Dried ti leaves must be soaked to soften before using.

tofu [TOH-foo] – This easy-to-digest, high-protein food made from soy beans has a bland, slightly nutty flavor which gives it the ability to take on the flavors it is cooked with. The texture is smooth and creamy. It is available in a number of shapes, including blocks, sheets, sticks, and pouches. It can be purchased fresh, dried, freeze-dried, deep-fried, pickled, and fermented. It is a versatile ingredient used in Asian cooking. Bean curd is marketed under the name tofu.

togarashi [toh-gah-RAH-shee] – Small, hot, red Japanese chile available fresh and in various dried forms—rounds, flakes and powder. Togarashi is also known as ichimi.

ume plum vinegar [oo-MEH] – Japanese pink brine with a deep, cherry aroma and a fruity sour flavor. It is a by-product of umeboshi, Japanese pickled plum, and is technically not a vinegar because it contains salt.

wasabi paste [WAH-sah-bee] – Japanese version of horseradish with hot, pungent flavor. It is available in specialty and Asian markets.

won bok [WAHN bahk] – Also known as Chinese cabbage and napa cabbage.

yaki [YAH-kee] – Japanese word for grilled.

yakitori [yah-kee-TOH-ree] – Japanese for grilled (yaki) fowl (tori), yakitori are small pieces of marinated chicken usually skewered and grilled.

yatsumi zuke [YAT-suu-mee ZU-kay] – Pickled cabbage

Catalog of
Contributing Cookbooks

For Hawaiians, the hula is more than just a dance; it is a way of life. Every movement and expression of the dancer's hands has a specific meaning as told through the accompanying chant. It is the means by which the culture, history, stories, and almost every aspect of Hawaiian life is expressed and passed down through generations.

PHOTO BY SRI MAIAVA RUSDEN / HAWAI'I VISITORS AND CONVENTION BUREAU

Catalog of
Contributing Cookbooks

All recipes in this book have been selected from the cookbooks shown on the following pages. Individuals who wish to obtain a copy of any particular book may do so by sending a check or money order to the address listed by each cookbook. Please note the postage and handling charges that are required. State residents add tax only when requested. Prices and addresses are subject to change, and the books may sell out and become unavailable. Retailers are invited to call or write to same address for discount information.

Another Taste of Aloha

The Junior League of Honolulu, Inc.   Phone 808-946-6466
1500 South Beretania Street, Suite 100   Fax 808-949-4617
Honolulu, HI 96826   www.juniorleagueofhonolulu.org

Another Taste of Aloha reflects the shift in cooking of trying to do more with less time, less cholesterol, and less fat. Recipes blend together the many ethnic backgrounds of the people of Hawaii and are flavored by the diverse cultures that create our aloha.

$19.95 Retail price   Visa/MC accepted
  $.80 Tax for Hawaii residents   ISBN 0-9612484-4-0
 $5.00 Postage and handling

Make check payable to The Junior League of Honolulu, Inc.

Aunty Pua's Keiki Cookbook

by Ann Kondo Corum
Bess Press   Phone 808-734-7159
3565 Harding Avenue   Fax 808-732-3627
Honolulu, HI 96816   www.besspress.com

Easy-to-make local dishes for kids with fun verses and illustrations for each recipe. Includes kitchen hints, a measuring guide, a list of necessary utensils, a glossary of cooking terms, and a Hawaiian pidgin glossary. 80 pages.

$4.95 Retail price   Visa/MC accepted
 $.21 Tax for Hawaii residents   ISBN 0-935848-88-6
$6.50 Postage and handling

Make check payable to Bess Press

The Best of Heart-y Cooking

by Diana Helfand   Phone 808-262-8029
962 Kainui Drive   Fax 808-261-3630
Kailua, HI 96734-2026

Organized compilation of recipes from popular television cooking host, nutrition instructor, and food columnist in Hawaii. Recipes are quick, easy, and lower in fat and cholesterol with nutrition information for each recipe. Handy reference section with substitutions, weights and measures, cooking hints, and more. 124 pages.

$12.95 Retail price   ISBN 1-886229-09-0
  $.53 Tax for Hawaii residents
 $3.50 Postage and handling

Make check payable to Diana Helfand

Burst of Flavor:
The Fine Art of Cooking with Spices

by Kusuma Cooray
University of Hawaii Press   Phone 808-956-8255
2840 Kolowalu Street   Fax 808-988-6052
Honolulu, HI 96822   www.uhpress.hawaii.edu

Includes over 200 recipes showcasing Chef Cooray's bold use of fresh herbs
and spices, from the familiar (nutmeg, fennel, basil) to the exotic (burnet,
ajowan, neem). The 280-page book contains 85 color photos and a glossary
explaining the characteristics and origins of the spices and herbs used within.

$24.95 Retail price   Visa/MC accepted
 $5.00 Postage and handling   ISBN 0-8248-2416-4

Make check payable to University of Hawaii Press

Classic Cookbook Recipes

by Christine Mayural   Phone 808-677-9238
94-637 Kaiewa Street
Waipahu, HI 96797

Island favorites at their best. Wonderful home-style cooking—Sweet Sour
Spareribs, Island Scampi, even Custard Mochi. Enjoy 63 pages of easy every-
day cooking.

$7.50 Retail price
$.30 Tax for Hawaii residents
$3.00 Postage and handling

Make check payable to Christine Mayural

Cook 'em Up Kaua'i

Kaua'i Historical Society Cookbook   Phone 808-245-3373
P. O. Box 1778   Fax 808-245-8693
Lihue, HI 96766   www.kauaihistoricalsociety.org

The Kaua'i Historical Society's 204-page *Cook 'em Up Kaua'i* reflects the native
foods of Chinese, Japanese, Korean, Filipinos, Portuguese, and Caucasians.
Some recipes retain their original ethnic flavor while others have been modi-
fied to become a favorite "local" food.

$13.00 Retail price   Visa/MC accepted
 $4.00 Postage and handling

Make check payable to Kaua'i Historical Society

Cooking Italian in Hawaii

by George Sabato "Cass" Castagnola
Watermark Publishing
Honolulu, HI

Cooking Italian in Hawaii provides nearly 100 innovative recipes and dozens of
suggestions for preparation and—most important—for shopping. Discover
how Castagnola's cuisine can translate into memorable Italian cooking right in
your own kitchen. This book is currently out of print.

Dd's Table Talk

by Deirdre Kieko Todd
Booklines Hawaii, Ltd.
269 Pali'i Street
Mililani, HI 96789

www.ddstabletalk.com
Phone 808-676-0116
Fax 808-676-5156
www.booklineshawaii.com

This best-selling cookbook is filled with 788 recipes in a 3-ring binder of 290 pages. Unique recipes of Japanese, Chinese, Vietnamese, Thai, Filipino, and more are easy to follow with step-by-step instructions for the novice to the experienced chef; recipes are sure to delight everyone for whom you cook.

$24.95 Retail price
$6.95 Postage and handling

Make check payable to Booklines Hawaii

Dd's Table Talk II

by Deirdre Kieko Todd
Booklines Hawaii, Ltd.
269 Pali'i Street
Mililani, HI 96789

www.ddstabletalk.com
Phone 808-676-0116
Fax 808-676-5156
www.booklineshawaii.com

This follow-up cookbook is filled with 794 recipes in a 3-ring binder of 352 pages. Unique recipes of Japanese, Chinese, Vietnamese, Thai, Italian, German, Filipino and more, some are re-creations of island favorite restaurant cuisine made simple for the home cook.

$25.95 Retail price
$6.95 Postage and handling

Make check payable to Booklines Hawaii

Eat More, Weigh Less™ Cookbook

by Terry Shintani, M.D., J.D., M.P.H.
Hawaii Health Foundation
P. O. Box 37337
Honolulu, HI 96837

Hate dieting? Eat MORE and lose weight. 392 pages. Over 175 tasty recipes help you lose weight without counting calories. Includes 77 "Eat More, Weigh Less™" tips; 6 steps to lower cholesterol in 30 days; much more.

$17.95 Retail price
$6.05 Postage and handling

ISBN 0-9636117-1-2

Make check payable to Hawaii Health Foundation

Ethnic Foods of Hawai'i

by Ann Kondo Corum
Bess Press
3565 Harding Avenue
Honolulu, HI 96816

Phone 808-734-7159
Fax 808-732-3627
www.besspress.com

Includes foods, cooking traditions, and celebrations specific to different ethnic groups in Hawaii. More than a cookbook, it gives readers an understanding of local traditions and introduces visitors and new residents to Hawaiian Island foods and customs. 240 pages.

$11.95 Retail price
$.50 Tax for Hawaii residents
$6.50 Postage and handling

Visa/MC accepted
ISBN 1-57306-117-4

Make check payable to Bess Press

Favorite Island Cookery Book I

Honpa Hongwanji Hawaii Betsuin
1727 Pali Highway   Phone 808-536-7044
Honolulu, HI 96813   Fax 808-536-0919

Compiled and published by members of Honpa Hongwanji Hawaii Betsuin (a
Buddhist temple of the Pure Land Sect). As the first in a series, this book offers
traditional, Japanese, local, and other ethnic favorite recipes contributed by
members. Includes everything from appetizers to desserts. 260 recipes. 143
pages.

   $8.50   Retail price
   $2.00   Postage and handling

Make check payable to Honpa Hongwanji Hawaii Betsuin

Favorite Island Cookery Book II

Honpa Hongwanji Hawaii Betsuin
1727 Pali Highway   Phone 808-536-7044
Honolulu, HI 96813   Fax 808-536-0919

Intended to preserve recipes used in preparation of important Buddhist obser-
vance, particularly, the vegetarian fare called "shojin ryori," this second edition
in the FAVORITE ISLAND COOKERY SERIES continues the theme of the first cookbook with an even greater selection of Japanese, local, and other ethnic
recipes. 420 recipes. 236 pages.

   $8.50   Retail price
   $2.00   Postage and handling

Make check payable to Honpa Hongwanji Hawaii Betsuin

Favorite Island Cookery Book III

Honpa Hongwanji Hawaii Betsuin
1727 Pali Highway   Phone 808-536-7044
Honolulu, HI 96813   Fax 808-536-0919

Enjoy the third in the FAVORITE ISLAND COOKERY SERIES which rejoices in the
ethnic diversity in Hawaii and typified in the culinary area. This edition provides quick and easy-to-prepare dishes and Hawaiian Island favorites with a
comprehensive guide to Buddhist practices, particularly Hongwanji religious
observances. 460 recipes. 280 pages.

   $9.50   Retail price
   $2.00   Postage and handling

Make check payable to Honpa Hongwanji Hawaii Betsuin

Favorite Island Cookery Book IV

Honpa Hongwanji Hawaii Betsuin
1727 Pali Highway   Phone 808-536-7044
Honolulu, HI 96813   Fax 808-536-0919

In addition to providing a cumulative index for books 1–4 and interesting illustrations, the fourth volume in the FAVORITE ISLAND COOKERY SERIES focuses on
the relationship between human nature and food, including Buddhist practices of showing reverence and gratitude for our daily sustenance. 461 recipes.
181 pages.

   $9.00   Retail price
   $2.00   Postage and handling

Make check payable to Honpa Hongwanji Hawaii Betsuin

Favorite Island Cookery Book V

Honpa Hongwanji Hawaii Betsuin
1727 Pali Highway
Honolulu, HI 96813

Phone 808-536-7044
Fax 808-536-0919

The fifth book in the FAVORITE ISLAND COOKERY SERIES was intended to preserve the peculiarities of culinary art contributed by immigrants from different prefectures or areas in Japan, in celebration of Honpa Hongwanji Betsuin's Centennial Anniversary. Includes maps of Japan and Hawaii. Over 450 recipes. 228 pages.

$9.00   Retail price
$2.00   Postage and handling

Make check payable to Honpa Hongwanji Hawaii Betsuin

Favorite Island Cookery Book VI

Honpa Hongwanji Hawaii Betsuin
1727 Pali Highway
Honolulu, HI 96813

Phone 808-536-7044
Fax 808-536-0919

The sixth book in the FAVORITE ISLAND COOKERY SERIES contains over 400 recipes of oriental and local favorites. Focusing on certain unique nutritional characteristics of different food items to assist you in making healthy choices each day, this edition includes the necessary tools to aid in dietary planning. 205 pages.

$10.00   Retail price
$2.00   Postage and handling

Make check payable to Honpa Hongwanji Hawaii Betsuin

Favorite Recipes for Islanders

Hilo Extension Homemakers Council, Inc.
Betty Jo Thompson
875 Komohana Street
Hilo, HI 96720

Dedicated to the Cooperative Extension Service and its 75 years of success, this book was compiled by members of the Hilo Extension Homemakers Council. Full of wonderful recipes which have been tested and tried many times, you are bound to find some favorites that will please the whole family!

$6.00   Retail price
$2.00   Postage and handling

Make check payable to Hilo FCE

Fresh Catch of the Day...from the Fishwife

by Shirley Rizzuto
Hawaii Fishing News/Chuck Johnston
P. O. Box 25488
Honolulu, HI 96825

Phone 808-395-4499
Fax 808-396-3474
www.hawaiifishingnews.com

Whether you're a novice cook or a gourmet seafood chef, you'll love the tempting simplicity of the more than 300 recipes offered here. From choosing fresh seafood, to safe handling preparation, to innovative cooking in the kitchen, and barbecuing and smoking seafood outdoors, this book has it all.

$ 19.95   Retail price
$26.00   per book includes postage

ISBN 0-944462-07-3

Make check payable to *Hawaii Fishing News*

Friends and Celebrities Cookbook II

Castle Performing Arts Center
c/o Mr. Ron Bright
45-386 Kaneohe Bay Drive
Kaneohe, HI 96744

Proceeds from the sales of this cookbook go toward helping a youngster achieve a dream of performing on the main stage at the annual Thespian Festival in Lincoln, Nebraska. Many thanks to CPAC friends, colleagues, celebrities, neighbors, co-workers, and relatives for donating their best recipes and supporting this project.

$10.00   Retail price
 $3.00   Postage and handling

Make check payable to CPAC

The Friends of 'Iolani Palace Cookbook

The Friends of 'Iolani Palace
P. O. Box 2259
Honolulu, HI 96804

Phone 808-532-1050
Fax 808-532-1049
www.iolanipalace.org

This cookbook contains recipes from Palace staff and volunteers. In November 1977 the first volunteer class held the first potluck on the Palace grounds to commemorate King Kalākaua's 141st birth date. Each attendee made a recipe and these recipes were exchanged, then later published and shared.

$8.50   Retail price
 $.35   Tax for Hawaii residents
$6.85   Postage and handling (one copy)

Visa/MC accepted
ISBN 1-886399-00-X

Make check payable to The Palace Shop

Hawaii–Cooking with Aloha

by Elvira Monroe and Irish Margah
Wide World Publishing
P. O. Box 476
San Carlos, CA 94070

Phone 650-593-2839
Fax 650-595-0802
www.wideworldpublishing.com

Illustrations by Don Blanding—Hawaii's legendary artist and poet • 8"x10" • 208 pages • 130 recipes including pūpūs • main dishes ranging from Kalua pig to curries • side dishes • salads • breads • beverages • special desserts • menus for a lū'au, dinners, suppers, barbecues, and brunches

$12.95   Retail price
 $1.06   Tax for CA residents
 $3.00   Postage and handling

Visa/MC accepted
ISBN 1-884550-25-8

Make check payable to Wide World Publishing

Hawaii Cooks Throughout the Year

by Maili Yardley
Editions Limited
P. O. Box 10150
Honolulu, HI 96816

Phone 808-735-7644
Fax 808-732-2164
editionslimited@hawaii.rr.com

This volume is more than a cookbook, it is literally a calendar of cooking. It tells when popular Hawaiian Island fruits are in season with a brief description and recipes. You'll find menus for summer picnics and long weekends, tea and cocktail parties, and holiday feasts—all in the appropriate months!

$18.95   Retail price
Inquire for postage and handling

ISBN 0-915013-13-4

Make check payable to Editions Limited

Hawai'i Tropical Rum Drinks & Cuisine

by Arnold Bitner and Phoebe Beach
Mutual Publishing   Phone 808-732-1703
1215 Center Street, Suite 210   Fax 808-734-4094
Honolulu, HI 96816   www.mutualpublishing.com

World traveler and celebrity restaurateur "Don the Beachcomber" was the inventor of the Mai Tai and more than ninety other exotic drinks that put Hawaii on the map. Tiki torches, rattan furniture, and superb cuisine set his Polynesian-theme restaurants apart, and you can re-create this magic with his book.

$12.95   Retail price   Visa/MC accepted
  $.54   Tax for Hawaii residents   ISBN 1-56647-491-4
$4.00   Postage and handling

Make check payable to Mutual Publishing

Hawaiian Country Tables

by Kaui Philpotts
Bess Press   Phone 808-734-7159
3565 Harding Avenue   Fax 808-732-3627
Honolulu, HI 96816   www.besspress.com

Take a nostalgic peek at traditions in Hawaiian Island hospitality, and learn to make new recipes with "local" Hawaiian foods. 144 pages.

$19.95   Retail price   Visa/MC accepted
  $.83   Tax for Hawaii residents   ISBN 1-57306-076-3
$6.50   Postage and handling

Make check payable to Bess Press

Hawai'i's Best Local Desserts

by Jean Watanabe Hee
Mutual Publishing   Phone 808-732-1709
1215 Center Street, Suite 210   Fax 808-734-4094
Honolulu, HI 96816   www.mutualpublishing.com

Treasured family favorites have been gathered in this special book to celebrate Hawaii's unique sweets. Passed from mother to daughter and friend to friend, recipes are simple to prepare but ever so good. Mangoes, pineapples, and other tropical ingredients imbue the desserts with the lush flavor of the Hawaiian Islands.

$10.95   Retail price   Visa/MC accepted
  $.46   Tax for Hawaii residents   ISBN 1-56647-518-X
$4.00   Postage and handling

Make check payable to Mutual Publishing

Hawai'i's Best Local Dishes

by Jean Watanabe Hee
Mutual Publishing   Phone 808-732-1709
1215 Center Street, Suite 210   Fax 808-734-4094
Honolulu, HI 96816   www.mutualpublishing.com

The rainbow of cultures in Hawaii has produced a rich heritage of home cooking shared from family to family at potlucks and beach barbecues. You can enjoy 140 favorite recipes from Hawaiian dishes like Lazy Style Laulau to international pleasures like Pork Adobo and Portuguese Bean Soup.

$13.95   Retail price   Visa/MC accepted
  $.58   Tax for Hawaii residents   ISBN 1-56647-570-8
$4.00   Postage and handling

Make check payable to Mutual Publishing

Hawai'i's Best Mochi Recipes

by Jean Watanabe Hee
Mutual Publishing   Phone 808-732-1709
1215 Center Street, Suite 210   Fax 808-734-4094
Honolulu, HI 96816   www.mutualpublishing.com

Chewy, moist and highly addictive, mochi (Japanese rice cake) is a favorite
food in Hawaii. This mouth-watering cookbook shows how to make all the traditional and current popular mochi desserts, and includes innovative main
course recipes such as Crisp Fried Shrimp. You'll love sharing these treats.

$10.95   Retail price   Visa/MC accepted
 $.46   Tax for Hawaii residents   ISBN 1-56647-336-5
$4.00   Postage and handling

Make check payable to Mutual Publishing

Hawaii's Best Tropical Food & Drinks

Hawaiian Service Inc., a division of Booklines Hawaii, Ltd.
Booklines Hawaii, Ltd.   Phone 808-676-0116
269 Pali'i Street   Fax 808-676-5156
Mililani, HI 96789   www.booklineshawaii.com

Beautiful full-color photos of twenty-four of *Hawaii's Best Tropical Food &
Drinks* along with the recipes for these tropical delights. Enjoy "Hawaii's Best"
wherever you are.

$4.95   Retail price   ISBN 0-930492-44-7
 $.21   Tax for Hawaii residents
$6.95   Postage and handling

Make check payable to Booklines Hawaii, Ltd.

Hawai'i's Favorite Firehouse Recipes

FilmWorks Press   Phone 808-585-9005
P. O. Box 61281   Fax 808-537-9272
Honolulu, HI 96839-1281   www.filmworkspacific.com

A compilation of recipes contributed from across the Hawaiian Islands from
municipal, state, and federal firefighters. Enjoy this wonderful collection of
recipes which includes some of their classic favorites, many of which have
been passed down through several generations of firefighters.

$9.00   Retail price   Visa/MC/Diners/Amex accepted
 $.38   Tax for Hawaii residents   ISBN 09706213-9-6
$3.50   Postage and handling

Make check payable to FilmWorks Press

Hawai'i's Favorite Pineapple Recipes

by Joannie Dobbs and Betty Shimabukuro
Mutual Publishing   Phone 808-732-1709
1215 Center Street, Suite 210   Fax 808-734-4094
Honolulu, HI 96816   www.mutualpublishing.com

No other food is more strongly associated with Hawaii than the pineapple. Like
bright, edible sunshine, its flavor is the essence of tropical fun. Have your taste
buds do the hula to frosty exotic drinks and refreshing salads. The pineapple will
work magic with main courses, too—just try the Sweet and Sour Shrimp!

$13.95   Retail price   Visa/MC accepted
 $.58   Tax for Hawaii residents   ISBN 1-56647-566-X
$4.00   Postage and handling

Make check payable to Mutual Publishing

Hawaiʻi's Island Cooking

by Bonnie Tuell
Mutual Publishing   Phone 808-732-1709
1215 Center Street, Suite 210   Fax 808-734-4094
Honolulu, HI 96816   www.mutualpublishing.com

Learn how to deliciously prepare the exotic produce of Hawaii. This easy-to-use guide gives you instructions for storing and preparing Hawaiian Island fruits and vegetables. The diverse collection of recipes includes favorite dishes of the Hawaiian, Chinese, Japanese, Filipino, Korean, and Portugese people.

$6.95 Retail price   Visa/MC accepted
$.29 Tax for Hawaii residents   ISBN 1-56647-137-0
$3.85 Postage and handling

Make check payable to Mutual Publishing

Hawaiʻi's Spam™ Cookbook

by Ann Kondo Corum
Bess Press   Phone 808-734-7159
3565 Harding Avenue   Fax 808-732-3627
Honolulu, HI 96816   www.besspress.com

Humorously illustrated recipes for Hawaii's favorite luncheon meat, as well as sardines, corned beef, and vienna sausages. *Hawaiʻi's Spam™ Cookbook* is a local and national bestseller with 30,000 copies sold to date. 160 pages; over 100 recipes.

$9.95 Retail price   Visa/MC accepted
$.42 Tax for Hawaii residents   ISBN 0-935848-49-5
$6.50 Postage and handling

Make check payable to Bess Press

Hawaiʻi's 2nd Spam™ Cookbook

by Ann Kondo Corum
Bess Press   Phone 808-734-7159
3565 Harding Avenue   Fax 808-732-3627
Honolulu, HI 96816   www.besspress.com

Readers will enjoy a second helping of fun recipes in Ann Kondo Corum's sequel to the best-selling *Hawaiʻi's Spam™ Cookbook*. 160 pages.

$9.95 Retail price   Visa/MC accepted
$.42 Tax for Hawaii residents   ISBN 1-57306-135-2
$6.50 Postage and handling

Make check payable to Bess Press

Hilo Woman's Club Cookbook

Hilo Woman's Club
Hilo, HI

Hilo women have developed a truly international cuisine. Included are many interesting dishes from members and friends of the Hilo Woman's Club. This book is currently out of print.

Honolulu Hawaii Cooking

by Betty Evans   Phone 310-379-5932
1769 Valley Park Avenue
Hermosa Beach, CA 90254

A unique collection of recipes from this captivating Pacific Rim state capital. Suggestions and information for visiting Honolulu make this book useful not only as a cookbook, but as a travel guide.

$7.95   Retail price   ISBN 0-931104-33-5
 $.64   Tax for CA residents
$2.00   Postage and handling

Make check payable to Betty Evans

How to Use Hawaiian Fruit

by Agnes Alexander
Petroglyph Press   Phone 866-666-8644
160 Kamehameha Avenue   Fax 808-935-1553
Hilo, HI 96720   www.basicallybooks.com

Originally published in 1912 with very simple recipes which call for basic ingredients. Petroglyph Press added illustrations by William D. Brooks in 1974, and a new cover design by Jan Moon in 1999. One recipe calls for 5-cent onions and 5-cent tomatoes—my how times have changed!

$7.95   Retail price   Visa/MC/Amex/Disc accepted
 $.33   Tax for Hawaii residents   ISBN 0-912180-53-6
$3.50   Postage and handling

Make check payable to Petroglyph Press

Incredibly Delicious: Recipes for a New Paradigm

Gentle World   Phone 808-884-5551
P. O. Box 238   Fax 808-884-5215
Kapa'au, HI 96755   www.gentleworld.org

A beautifully presented collection of over 500 incredibly delicious, plant-based recipes from beginner to gourmet. Its 311 pages include breads, soups, salads, dips, appetizers, holiday dishes, divine desserts, scrumptious entrées, as well as information on raw food preparation, feeding pets, vegan-organic gardening, inspirational quotes, informative reading, and color pictures.

$22.95   Retail price   Credit cards accepted online only (PayPal)
 $4.00   Postage and handling   ISBN 0-929274-25-3

Make check payable to Gentle World

Island Flavors

Historic Hawaii Foundation   Phone 808-523-2900
P. O. Box 1658   Fax 808-523-0800
Honolulu, HI 96806-1658   www.historichawaii.org

Historic Hawaii Foundation invites you to hele mai a'i (come and eat!). *Island Flavors* is a collection of recipes that preserve favorite family recipes to help chefs of the future carry on Hawaii's unique multiethnic food traditions. Where else can you find a recipe for Grandpa Kanaka's Stew?

$12.00   Retail price   Visa/MC accepted
 $.48   Tax for Hawaii residents
$4.00   Postage and handling

Make check payable to Historic Hawaii Foundation

Joys of Hawaiian Cooking

by Martin and Judy Beeman
Petroglyph Press
160 Kamehameha Avenue
Hilo, HI 96720

Phone 866-666-8644
Fax 808-935-1553
www.basicallybooks.com

This collection was compiled from recipes shared by some of the best cooks living on the Big Island of Hawaii. Some are passed down from generation to generation, and some are shared through friendships. All are family favorites that illustrate the great variety of dishes available in our Hawaiian paradise.

$7.95 Retail price   Visa/MC/Amex/Disc accepted
 $.33 Tax for Hawaii residents   ISBN 912180-41-2
$3.50 Postage and handling

Make check payable to Petroglyph Press

Kailua Cooks: Hana Hou

Le Jardin Academy
Island Heritage Publishing
917 Kalaianaole Highway
Kailua, HI 96734

Phone 808-261-0707
Fax 808-262-9339
www.lejardinacademy.com

Compiled by parents, families, staff, and friends of Le Jardin Academy, this 40th anniversary cookbook is a compilation of tried-and-true recipes and culinary pride. Enjoy such dishes as Red Bell Pepper and Cheddar Cheese Spread or Famous Kona Inn Banana Bread—from appetizers to desserts, this book has it all!

$20.00 Retail price   ISBN 0-89610-493-1
  $.83 Tax for Hawaii residents
$5.00 Postage and handling

Make check payable to LJA Parents' Association

Kau Kau Kitchen

by Dana Yuen
Press Pacifica, Ltd.
P. O. Box 47
Kailua, HI 96734

Phone 808-261-6594
Fax 808-261-6594

The best recipes of the first year of the "Kau Kau Kitchen Cooking Column," which was published in the *Hawaii Tribune Herald*, these recipes are from family collections and the community, and reflect the home cooking of the people of Hawaii. No Pacific Rim cuisine here, just plain old home cookin'.

$4.95 Retail price   ISBN 0-916630-50-1
 $.20 Tax for Hawaii residents
$1.42 Media Mail, $3.85 Priority Mail

Make check payable to Press Pacifica, Ltd.

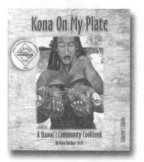

Kona on My Plate

Kona Outdoor Circle
76-6280 Kuakini Highway
Kailua-Kona, HI 96740

Phone 808-329-7286
Fax 808-334-9646
www.konacookbook.com

Kona on My Plate, first place national winner of the Tabasco Community Cookbook Awards, comprises a 456-page treasury of over 690 recipes that reflect the heritages and culinary traditions of Hawaii. This dazzling cookbook showcases simple as well as elegant dishes that rely primarily on fresh, flavorful island ingredients.

$28.50 Retail price   Visa/MC accepted
$10.00 Postage and handling   ISBN 0971949905

Make check payable to KOC Cookbook

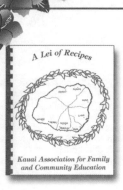

A Lei of Recipes

Kauai Association for Family and Community Education
3472 Maona Road
Lihue, HI 96766   Phone 808-245-2532

A Lei of Recipes was compiled by members of the Kauai Association for Family
and Community Education some years ago, and since then has undergone several reprints. It now contains over 880 recipes and 392 pages. The recipes
reflect the cultural and ethnic diversity of its members.

$15.00   Retail price
 $3.00   Postage and handling

Make check payable to KAFCE

Paradise Preserves

by Yvonne Hodgins
Press Pacifica, Ltd.
P. O. Box 47   Phone 808-261-6594
Kailua, HI 96734   Fax 808-261-6594

For condiment lovers, this book offers delectable recipes of the many preserves
served in Hawaii, the pickled fruits and vegetables, and the spicy relishes and
chutneys which complement the meal, plus jams and jellies.

$5.95   Retail price   ISBN 0-916630-63-3
 $.24   Tax for Hawaii residents
$1.42   Media Mail, $3.85 Priority Mail

Make check payable to Press Pacifica, Ltd.

Pupus–An Island Tradition

by Sachi Fukuda
Bess Press   Phone 808-734-7159
3565 Harding Avenue   Fax 808-732-3627
Honolulu, HI 96816   www.besspress.com

Over 200 mouth-watering appetizer recipes with easy-to-follow instructions
for beginning and experienced cooks. 184 pages.

$12.95   Retail price   Visa/MC accepted
  $.54   Tax for Hawaii residents   ISBN 1-57306-019-4
 $6.50   Postage and handling

Make check payable to Bess Press

Pupus from Paradise

Assistance League of Hawaii
Margie Van Swearingen
2600 Pualani Way #2001   Phone 808-923-8313
Honolulu, HI 96815   www.kokuawithaloha.org

Pupus from Paradise is filled with recipes for appetizers (pūpūs) and drinks
reflecting a casual Hawaiian lifestyle. Proceeds from the sales of this book
benefit the philanthropic projects of Assistance League of Hawaii. 90 pages;
spiral bound; 8½"x11".

$12.95   Retail price
 $4.00   Postage and handling

Make check payable to Assistance League of Hawaii

A Race for Life

by Ruth Heidrich, Ph. D.
Lantern Books
1415 Victoria Street #1106
Honolulu, HI 96822

Phone 808-536-4006
dr-ruth@hawaii.rr.com
www.ruthheidrich.com

Not just a cookbook, it's an eating guide used by Ironman Triathelete, Ruth Heidrich. Recipes follow the CHEF criteria, Cheap, Healthy, Easy, and Fat Free, keeping it simple with few ingredients and easy instructions. A diet and exercise program for super fitness, weight loss, and reversing the aging process.

$14.95 Retail price   Credit cards accepted online only (PayPal)
$ .60 Tax for Hawaii residents   ISBN 1-930051-00-X
$4.00 Postage and handling

Make check payable to Ruth Heidrich

Sam Choy's Kitchen

by Chef Sam Choy
Mutual Publishing
1215 Center Street, Suite 210
Honolulu, HI 96816

Phone 808-732-1709
Fax 808-734-4094
www.mutualpublishing.com

Join the star of the popular television show *Sam Choy's Kitchen* and learn to make scrumptious local Hawaiian food. Sam's treasury of detailed, step-by-step recipes will help you make your next dinner party a hit with your friends and family. Not only are these recipes easy to follow, they're quick, too.

$24.95 Retail price   Visa/MC accepted
$1.04 Tax for Hawaii residents   ISBN 1-56647-252-0
$4.00 Postage and handling

Make check payable to Mutual Publishing

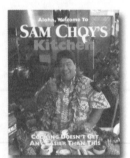

Sam Choy's Sampler

by Chef Sam Choy
Mutual Publishing
1215 Center Street, Suite 210
Honolulu, HI 96816

Phone 808-732-1709
Fax 808-734-4094
www.mutualpublishing.com

Celebrity Chef Sam Choy presents the perfect introduction to the exotic and sunny flavors of Hawaii's multiethnic cooking. Eighty easy-to-prepare recipes range from traditional favorites to dazzling new dishes created by Chef Choy. Learn to make poke, the Hawaiian seafood sensation, and much, much more.

$12.95 Retail price   Visa/MC accepted
$.54 Tax for Hawaii residents   ISBN 1-56647-344-6
$4.00 Postage and handling

Make check payable to Mutual Publishing

Seasoned with Aloha Vol. 2

VP-9 Officer Spouses' Club
Kailua, HI

Seasoned with Aloha Vol. 2 is a compilation of recipes from the officers' spouses of Patrol Squadron 9. Containing almost 400 recipes, this second volume celebrates the diversity within our group. With each volume published, a portion of the proceeds supports a charity within the local community. This book is currently out of print.

Shaloha Cookbook

Kona Beth Shalom
c/o Karen Breier
73-4548 Mahi Street
Kailua-Kona, HI 96740   klimes@aloha.net

Shaloha Cookbook has been featured in the *New York Times* "Food and Wine Section," February 2003. Shaloha—a combination of shalom (or peace), and aloha (or love) is our way of life on the Kona Coast of the Big Island. *Shaloha Cookbook* has over 225 pages filled with great recipes, wit, and wisdom to nourish your soul.

  $18.00 Retail price
    $5.00 Postage and handling

Make check payable to Kona Beth Shalom Cookbook

The Shoreline Chef
Creative Cuisine for Hawaiian Reef Fish

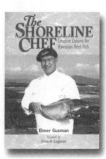

by Elmer Guzman   Phone 808-587-7766
Watermark Publishing   Fax 808-521-3461
1088 Bishop Street, Suite 310   sales@bookshawaii.net
Honolulu, HI 96813   www.bookshawaii.net

Chef Elmer Guzman demonstrates great ways to prepare some of Hawaii's best-eating fish. Here for the first time is a cookbook featuring 100 innovative recipes for Hawaiian reef and shoreline fish, complete with comparison chart, fish substitutions, wine pairings, and a fish-cutting guide.

  $12.95 Retail price   Visa/MC/Amex/Disc/Diner's Club/Carte Blanche
    $.54 Tax for Hawaii residents   ISBN 0-9720932-8-1
    $6.00 Postage and handling for 1st book, $3.00 for any additional

Make check payable to Watermark Publishing

Sugar and Spice–Cookies Made with Love

by Kelimia Mednick
4391A Kahala Avenue   Phone 808-735-1394
Honolulu, HI 96816   Fax 808-735-6673

Sugar 'n Spice–Cookies Made with Love is designed for everyone who would love to re-create the beloved cookie, as well as an exotic taste from around the world. This book contains 50 recipes from Hawaii in 53 pages of easy-to-follow format.

  $8.00 Retail price
  $2.00 Postage and handling

Make check payable to Kelimia Mednick

Tailgate Party Cookbook

by Kris Smith
1515 Nuuanu Avenue, Unit 68
Honolulu, HI 96817   ksmith@hpu.edu

Tailgate Party Cookbook is a collection of over 100 recipes that are perfect for events that require a portable feast. Hawaii is a blend of diverse cultures, and this book represents its rich culinary heritage.

  $6.95 Retail price   ISBN 0-935848-86-X
  $2.00 Postage and handling

Make check payable to Kris Smith

A Taste of Aloha

The Junior League of Honolulu, Inc.   Phone 808-946-6466
1500 South Beretania Street, Suite 100   Fax 808-949-4617
Honolulu, HI 96826   www.juniorleagueofhonolulu.org

The recipes in *A Taste of Aloha* are representative of Hawaii's colorful panorama of cultures, providing a vast and unique display of culinary delights. Our islands are blessed with a wide array of fresh ingredients that are complemented by oriental spices, European flair, and Yankee ingenuity.

$19.95 Retail price   Visa/MC accepted
  $.80 Tax for Hawaii residents   ISBN 0-9612484-0-8
$5.00 Postage and handling

Make check payable to The Junior League of Honolulu, Inc.

The Tastes and Tales of Moiliili

Moiliili Community Center
2535 South King Street   Phone 808-955-1555
Honolulu, HI 96826   Fax 808-945-7033

The cookbook is a collection of recipes and stories about the Moiliili community, "a place of the heart," in east Honolulu. The recipes, tested in the kitchens of the donors and edited by the cookbook committee, reflect the diversity and heritage of Moiliili. Tales evoke warm memories of a bygone era.

$14.95 Retail price   Visa/MC accepted
  $3.00 Postage and handling

Make check payable to Moiliili Community Center

Tropical Taste

by Sonia Martinez
P. O. Box 190   Phone 808-963-6860
Honomu, HI 96728   cubanwahine@hawaii.rr.com

Tropical Taste is a collection of recipes and articles first featured in Sonia's monthly column by the *The Hamakua Times*. Using her Cuban culinary heritage and Hawaii's produce and products, Sonia created her own adaptation of Latin Pacific fusion cuisine. Easy, impressive, and sure to bring you many rave reviews.

$12.00 Retail price
  $2.00 Media Mail, $4.00 Priority Mail

Make check payable to Sonia Martinez

Unbearably Good! Mochi Lovers' Cookbook

by Teresa DeVirgilio-Lam
5239 Kalanianaole Highway   Phone 808-373-5123
Honolulu, HI 96821

The first mochi cookbook published, it has 74 pages of mochi recipes and was on Hawaii's best-seller list for over a year. Over 40,000 copies have been sold. (Mochi is a popular Asian dessert and is enjoyed by millions.)

$6.00 Retail price   ISBN 0-9612484-0-8
$2.00 Postage and handling

Make check payable to Teresa DeVirgilio-Lam

Vegetarian Nights
by Bonnie Mandoe Gusto
825 Quesenberry Street
Las Cruces, NM 88005

Fabulous taste, gorgeous presentation, and healthy dishes all made EASILY using relatively few ingredients. How? Because they are the RIGHT ingredients. These are the recipes from Bonnie's catering business on Maui and her TV show, *Smart Cooking*, in New Mexico. Every one is a winner.

$18.95   Retail price   ISBN 0-89087-712-2
  $.55   Tax for NM residents
 $2.00   Postage and handling

Make check payable to Bonnie Mandoe Gusto

We, the Women of Hawaii Cookbook
We, the Women of Hawaii
Press Pacifica, Inc.
P. O. Box 47   Phone 808-261-6594
Kailua, HI 96734   Fax 808-261-6594

The most representative collection of family cooking in the Hawaiian Islands, from the sophisticated to the very easy, these 850-plus recipes come from Asian, Polynesian, and Caucasian cultures. This book has been one of the all-time bestsellers in Hawaii.

$9.95   Retail price   ISBN 0-916630-47-1
 $.40   Tax for Hawaii residents
$1.84   Postage and handling

Make check payable to Press Pacifica, Ltd.

West Kauai's Plantation Heritage
West Kauai Community Development Corp.   Phone 808-338-1900
P. O. Box 548   Fax 808-338-1619
Waimea, HI 96796   www.waimea-plantation.com/shop

This 247-page collection of recipes, images, anecdotes, and personal memoirs, reflecting the major ethnic groups of West Kauai, is now in its second printing. It is a cookbook and historical anthropology lesson, honoring a culture that found unity in its diversity and an appreciation for the struggles of its pioneers.

$15.00   Retail price   Visa/MC accepted
  $.63   Tax for Hawaii residents   ISBN 0-9728633-0-3
 $5.00   Postage and handling

Make check payable to WKCDC

The When You Live in Hawaii You Get Very Creative During Passover Cookbook
Cookbook Committee, Congregation of Ma'arav
Davida Skigen and Judy Goldman
P. O. Box 11154
Honolulu, HI 96828   http://uscj.org/pacsw/honolulu

This cookbook is an incredible collection of Passover recipes gathered by the members, families, and friends of Congregation of Ma'arav in Honolulu, Hawaii.

$16.95   Retail price
 $3.50   Postage and handling

Make check payable to Cookbook Committee, Congregation of Ma'arav

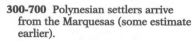

HAWAI'I TIMELINE

300-700 Polynesian settlers arrive from the Marquesas (some estimate earlier).

1627 Spanish sailors visit Hawai'i and describe volcanic eruption in ship's log.

1758 Paiea, later known as Kamehameha the Great, the Lonely One, born in Kohala on the island of Hawai'i.

1778 European discovery of Hawai'i by English Captain James Cook who names them the Sandwich Islands.

1782 Kamehameha inherits power in the northern part of the island of Hawai'i and later begins conquest of the other Hawaiian Islands.

1810 Kamehameha unifies all the Hawaiian Islands into one kingdom through a treaty with the King of Kaua'i.

1819 King Kamehameha dies; Prince Liholiho ascends the throne as Kamehameha II (1819-1824).

1843 Lord George Paulet seizes Hawai'i in the name of England for five months. Admiral Richard Thomas is dispatched to the islands to return the throne to Kamehameha III.

1850 United States and the Kingdom of Hawai'i ratify a treaty of friendship, commerce, and navigation.

1883 Princess Bernice Pauahi Bishop, the last direct descendant of Kamehameha I, executes her will which contains a trust to erect and maintain a school for boys and girls to be called Kamehameha Schools.

1884 United States and Kingdom of Hawai'i extend the 1875 Reciprocity Treaty for seven years in return for the United States receiving the exclusive right to use Pearl Harbor as a naval base.

1891 King Kalākaua dies in San Francisco. Lydia Kamaka'eha becomes Queen Lili'uokalani.

1893 Hawaiian monarchy overthrown by government ministers, planters, and businessmen with the assistance of the U.S. Consul. U.S. Marines and sailors sent ashore to maintain order and protect Americans.

1893 Sanford B. Dole and his provisional government request annexation of Hawai'i by the United States.

1894 July 4th, Republic of Hawai'i established with Sanford B. Dole as president.

1898 Congress passes the Newlands Resolution which annexes Hawai'i as a territory. Sanford B. Dole appointed first territorial governor.

1920 Hawai'i National Park on the island of Hawai'i (now Volcanoes National Park) and Maui (now Haleakala National Park) established by an act of congress.

1927 First nonstop flight to Hawai'i from the mainland.

1935 First 2,270-mile trans-Pacific flight from San Francisco to Hawai'i takes 21½ hours.

1941 Empire of Japan attacks Pearl Harbor on December 7; the United States declares war on Japan the following day.

1945 United Nations founded. Hawai'i listed as a non-self-governing territory.

1946 Great tsunami hits Hilo, killing over 100 people and causing $25 million in damage.

1959 Congress passes the Hawai'i Admission Act to admit Hawai'i as a state on March 18. Hawai'i becomes the 50th state on August 21.

1978 Hawai'i constitution establishes the Office of Hawaiian Affairs to administer funds and programs for Native Hawaiians.

1993 Congress passes the 'Apology Resolution' which "apologizes to Native Hawaiians on behalf of the people of the United States for the overthrow of the Kingdom of Hawai'i on January 17, 1893, with the participation of agents and citizens of the United States, and the deprivation of the rights of Native Hawaiians to self-determination."

Index

This 1916 Honaunau canoe displayed at Bailey House Museum in Wailuku, Maui, is part of an exhibit showcasing Hawaiian culture, artifacts, paintings, and furnishings from nineteenth-century Maui.

PHOTO BY JIM STEINHART / WWW.PLANETWARE.COM

Index

Index

Index

BEST OF THE BEST STATE COOKBOOK SERIES

Best of the Best from
ALABAMA
(original edition)*

Best of the Best from
ALABAMA
(new edition)

Best of the Best from
ALASKA

Best of the Best from
ARIZONA

Best of the Best from
ARKANSAS

Best of the Best from
BIG SKY
Montana and Wyoming

Best of the Best from
CALIFORNIA

Best of the Best from
COLORADO

Best of the Best from
FLORIDA
(original edition)*

Best of the Best from
FLORIDA
(new edition)

Best of the Best from
GEORGIA
(original edition)*

Best of the Best from
GEORGIA
(new edition)

Best of the Best from the
GREAT PLAINS
North and South Dakota,
Nebraska, and Kansas

Best of the Best from
HAWAI'I

Best of the Best from
IDAHO

Best of the Best from
ILLINOIS

Best of the Best from
INDIANA

Best of the Best from
IOWA

Best of the Best from
KENTUCKY
(original edition)*

Best of the Best from
KENTUCKY
(new edition)

Best of the Best from
LOUISIANA

Best of the Best from
LOUISIANA II

Best of the Best from
MICHIGAN

Best of the Best from the
MID-ATLANTIC
Maryland, Delaware, New
Jersey, and Washington, D.C.

Best of the Best from
MINNESOTA

Best of the Best from
MISSISSIPPI
(original edition)*

Best of the Best from
MISSISSIPPI
(new edition)

Best of the Best from
MISSOURI

Best of the Best from
NEVADA

Best of the Best from
NEW ENGLAND
Rhode Island, Connecticut,
Massachusetts, Vermont, New
Hampshire, and Maine

Best of the Best from
NEW MEXICO

Best of the Best from
NEW YORK

Best of the Best from
NO. CAROLINA
(original edition)*

Best of the Best from
NO. CAROLINA
(new edition)

Best of the Best from
OHIO

Best of the Best from
OKLAHOMA

Best of the Best from
OREGON

Best of the Best from
PENNSYLVANIA

Best of the Best from
SO. CAROLINA
(original edition)*

Best of the Best from
SO. CAROLINA
(new edition)

Best of the Best from
TENNESSEE
(original edition)*

Best of the Best from
TENNESSEE
(new edition)

Best of the Best from
TEXAS

Best of the Best from
TEXAS II

Best of the Best from
UTAH

Best of the Best from
VIRGINIA

Best of the Best from
WASHINGTON

Best of the Best from
WEST VIRGINIA

Best of the Best from
WISCONSIN

*Original editions available while supplies last.
All BEST OF THE BEST STATE COOKBOOKS are 6x9, comb-bound with illustrations, photographs, and an index.
They range in size from 288 to 352 pages and each contains over 300 recipes. **Retail price per copy is $16.95**

To order by credit card, call toll-free **1-800-343-1583**
or visit **www.quailridge.com.**

Q Order form

Use this form for sending check or money order to:
QUAIL RIDGE PRESS • P. O. Box 123 • Brandon, MS 39043

❏ Check enclosed

Charge to: ❏ Visa ❏ MC ❏ AmEx ❏ Disc

Card # _____

Expiration Date _____

Signature _____

Name _____

Address _____

City/State/Zip _____

Phone # _____

Email Address _____

Qty.	Title of Book (State) or Set	Total

Subtotal	_____
7% Tax for MS residents	_____
Postage ($4.00 any number of books)	+ 4.00
Total	_____